BRICK AND CLAY BUILDING IN BRITAIN

BRICK AND CLAY BUILDING IN BRITAIN

R. W. Brunskill

YALE UNIVERSITY PRESS
NEW HAVEN AND LONDON
in association with
PETER CRAWLEY

TO ROBIN, LESLEY, JOHN, LORNA, CAMERON AND RORY

Except where advertised as open to the public all the buildings mentioned or illustrated in this book are in private occupation and readers are asked to respect that privacy.

YALE UNIVERSITY PRESS
NEW HAVEN AND LONDON
302 Temple Street, New Haven CT 06511
47 Bedford Square, London WC1 3DP
www.yale.edu/yup
www.yaleup.co.uk

Published by Yale University Press
in association with Peter Crawley 2009
10 9 8 7 6 5 4 3 2 1

A catalogue record for this book is available from the British Library
ISBN 978 0 300 11687 8
Printed in China through World Print

Contents

List of illustrations 6
Preface and acknowledgements 11
Introduction 13

Part One   Clay, Brickmaking and the Use of Bricks 15
    1   The raw material, labour and transport 16
    2   Brickmaking 21
    3   The use of bricks 43
    4   Brick tiles and terracotta 64
    5   Brick chimneys 75
    6   Conclusion 78

Part Two   Glossary 85

Part Three   Chronological Survey 113
    1   Medieval to 1485 115
    2   Tudor and Elizabethan 130
    3   Jacobean, Stuart and Queen Anne 140
    4   Georgian 156
    5   Victorian and Edwardian 171
    6   Modern 182

Part Four   Building in Cob, Clay, Mud, Wychert, Turf, and Mud-and-Stud 193
    1   Introduction 194
    2   Variations in the use of the material 197
    3   Regional variations 210
    4   Earth building in Ireland 225
    5   The international context 231

Part Five   Special Topics 235
    1   The Brick Tax 236
    2   Cavity walling and damp-proof courses 237
    3   Header Bond brickwork 241
    4   Brickwork in Scotland and Ireland 245

Notes and references 248
Bibliography 252
Index 257

List of illustrations

1   Little Wenham Hall, Suffolk (RCHME)
2   Diagram: brickmaking by hand (RWB)
3   Diagram: clamp firing (RWB)
4   Diagram: Scotch kiln firing (RWB)
5   Exterior of downdraught kiln, Porth wen, Anglesey (RCAHMW)
6   Diagram: downdraught kiln firing (RWB)
7   Interior of downdraught kiln, Porth wen, Anglesey (RCAHMW)
8   Diagram: Hoffmann kiln firing (RWB)
9   Diagram: other continuous kilns (RWB)
10 Barn at Pentre bach, Llanfihangel Llanternum, Monmouthshire (RCAHMW)
11 St Nicholas, Chignal Smealy, Essex (PSC)
12 Manor House, North Wheatley, Nottinghamshire (PSC)
13 Brick wall at Orford, Suffolk (PSC)
14 Crinkle-crankle wall, Easton Park, Suffolk (PSC)
15 Diagram: bricklayers' tools (RWB)
16 St Nicholas, King's Lynn, Norfolk (PSC)
17 Window, Tyttenhanger, Hertfordshire (PSC)
18 Decorative panel, Bruton Place, London w1 (PSC)
19 Cottages at Cuttmill, Cuxham, Oxfordshire (RWB)
20 Bow windows at Burton Agnes Hall, Yorkshire, ER (PSC)
21 House at Shere, Surrey (PSC)
22 Wall at St Michael, Woodham Walter, Essex (PSC)
23 House at Brocklesby, Lincolnshire (PSC)
24 Brick and chalk walling, Stockton, Wiltshire (PSC)
25 Wall in Rat-Trap Bond, Alton, Hampshire (RWB)
26 Brick and flint walling, Chesham, Buckinghamshire (PSC)
27 Wall in Rat-Trap Bond, Farnham, Surrey (RWB)
28 Cottages at Bengeo, Hertfordshire (PSC)
29 Dated brick, Great Meeting House, Hinckley, Leicestershire (RCHME)
30 Arch at Gainsborough Old Hall, Lincolnshire (PSC)
31 Houses in Bedford Square, London, wc1 (PSC)
32 Dated mathematical tile, Westcott, Surrey (RWB)
33 Mathematical tiling, Bramhall, Cheshire (RWB)
34 Mathematical tiling, Tenterden, Kent (PSC)
35 Terracotta work, Sutton Place, Surrey (RCHME)
36 Refuge Assurance building, Oxford Road, Manchester (RWB)
37 Fireplace, Castle Acre Priory, Norfolk (PSC)
38 Chimney at Lemsford, Hertfordshire (PSC)
39 Pumping station, Ware, Hertfordshire (PSC)
40 Digswell Viaduct, Welwyn, Hertfordshire (PSC)
41 Chimney-stacks, Hodnet, Shropshire (PSC)

42 Georgian houses, Pershore, Worcestershire (PSC)
43 Chimney-stacks, Hafod-y-Bwlch, Denbighshire (RCAHMW)
44 Chimney-stacks, Tudor House, Newport, Essex (PSC)
45 Shire Hall, Woodbridge, Suffolk (PSC)
46 Moulded brickwork and terracotta, Holborn Union Offices, London EC1 (PSC)
47 Apron, High Street, Hemel Hempstead, Hertfordshire (PSC)
48 Segmental arch, Thornton Abbey, Lincolnshire (PSC)
49 Blind window, Heslington, Yorkshire, ER (RWB)
50 Dearne's Bond, Alton, Hampshire (RWB)
51 English Bond, Holy Trinity, Hull, Yorkshire, ER (PSC)
52 English Cross Bond, Smallhythe, Kent (PSC)
53 English Garden-Wall Bond, Blyth, Nottinghamshire (PSC)
54 Flemish Bond, Thame, Oxfordshire (PSC)
55 Sussex Bond, Barlwood, Surrey (RWB)
56 Flemish Stretcher Bond, North Wheatley, Nottinghamshire (PSC)
57 Header Bond, Westgate, Louth, Lincolnshire (PSC)
58 Monk Bond, Beccles, Suffolk (PSC)
59 Quarter Bonding, Madeley, Shropshire (RWB)
60 Raking Stretcher Bond, Plymouth Grove, Manchester (RWB)
61 Rat-Trap Bond, Colney Heath, Hertfordshire (PSC)
62 Stack Bond, Grosvenor Street, Chester (RWB)
63 Stretcher Bond, Wilmslow, Cheshire (RWB)
64 Bricknogging, Winchester, Hampshire (PSC)
65 Brick-on-edge coping, Heslington, Yorkshire, ER (RWB)
66 Stretcher brick tile (GW)
67 Header brick tile (GW)
68 Glazed header brick tile (GW)
69 Damaged corner brick tile (GW)
70 Brick tile elevation, house at Tenterden, Kent (PSC)
71 Twisted brick chimney, Ballingdon, Sudbury, Suffolk (PSC)
72 Corbelling, stable block, Tattershall Castle, Lincolnshire (PSC)
73 Crinkle-crankle wall, Easton Park, Suffolk (PSC)
74 Crow-stepped gable, Kinnersley Castle, Herefordshire (PSC)
75 Diaper brickwork, Copdock, Suffolk (PSC)
76 Dog-tooth brickwork, Orford, Suffolk (PSC)
77 Brick dressings to chalk, Burnham Overy, Norfolk (PSC)
78 Downdraught kiln, Porth wen, Anglesey (RCAHMW)
79 Dutch gable, Boston, Lincolnshire (PSC)
80 Galleting, Shere, Surrey (PSC)
81 Gauged brickwork, Chicheley, Buckinghamshire (PSC)
82 Gauged and moulded brickwork, West Malling, Kent (PSC)
83 Glazed bricks, All Saints, Manchester (RWB)
84 Great bricks, Waltham Abbey, Essex (PSC)
85 Herringbone bricknogging, Chiddingfold, Surrey (RWB)
86 Hitch bricks, Bengeo Hall, Hertfordshire (PSC)
87 Honeycomb brickwork, Seighford, Staffordshire (PSC)
88 Moulded brickwork, Willmer House, Farnham, Surrey (PSC)
89 Bricks used for paving, Ironbridge, Shropshire (RWB)
90 Peach wall, Farthinghoe, Northamptonshire (PSC)

91   Flush pointing, Balls Park, Hertfordshire (RWB)
92   Relieving arch, Balls Park, Hertfordshire (RWB)
93   Segmental arch, Chiddingfold, Surrey (RWB)
94   Rustication, Nun Monkton, Yorkshire, ER (PSC)
95   Terracotta, Sutton Place, Surrey (RCHME)
96   Door, terracotta work, Chester (RWB)
97   Tie plate, Welsh Row, Nantwich, Cheshire (PSC)
98   Tie plate, Beverley, Yorkshire, ER (RWB)
99   Tie plate, Shere, Surrey (RWB)
100   Tumbling-in, stable at North Wheatley, Nottinghamshire (PSC)
101   St Nicholas' Chapel, Little Coggeshall, Essex (PSC)
102   St Botolph's Priory, Colchester, Essex (PSC)
103   Thornton Abbey gatehouse, Lincolnshire (PSC)
104   North Bar, Beverley, Yorkshire, ER (RWB)
105   Rye House gatehouse, Hoddesdon, Hertfordshire (PSC)
106   Rye House gatehouse, handrail (PSC)
107   Tattershall Castle tower, Lincolnshire (PSC)
108   Tattershall Castle guardhouse, Lincolnshire (PSC)
109   Gainsborough Old Hall, Lincolnshire (PSC)
110   Pykenham's Gateway, Northgate Street, Ipswich, Suffolk (PSC)
111   Kirby Muxloe Castle, Leicestershire (PSC)
112   Tower wall, Kirby Muxloe Castle, Leicestershire (PSC)
113   Wainfleet School, Lincolnshire (PSC)
114   St Mary, Polstead, Suffolk (PSC)
115   Sutton Place, Surrey (RCHME)
116   Gatehouse to St John's College, Cambridge (PSC)
117   Layer Marney Tower, Essex (PSC)
118   St Andrew, Sandon, Essex (PSC)
119   Leez Priory, Essex (PSC)
120   Doorway at Roos Hall, Beccles, Suffolk (PSC)
121   Erwarton Hall, Suffolk (PSC)
122   Christchurch Mansion, Ipswich, Suffolk (PSC)
123   Entrance elevation, Burton Constable Hall, Yorkshire, ER (PSC)
124   Burton Constable Hall, Yorkshire, ER (PSC)
125   Burton Agnes Hall, Yorkshire, ER (PSC)
126   Sudbury Hall, Derbyshire (PSC)
127   Bramshill House, Hampshire (RCHME)
128   Carr House, Bretherton, Lancashire (SF)
129   Wilberforce House, Hull, Yorkshire, ER (PSC)
130   Balls Park, Hertford (RWB)
131   Corner detail, Balls Park, Hertford (RWB)
132   Market Hall, Winster, Derbyshire (PSC)
133   Spraysbridge Farmhouse, Westfield, Sussex (PSC)
134   The Old Hall, Aylsham, Norfolk (PSC)
135   Doorway detail, Old Hall, Aylsham, Norfolk (PSC)
136   Old Meeting House, Norwich, Norfolk (RCHME)
137   Detail from Old Meeting House, Norwich, Norfolk (RCHME)
138   Thornton Hall, Thornton Curtis, Lincolnshire (PSC)
139   House in Queen Anne's Gate, London, SW1 (PSC)
140   Pallant House, Chichester, Sussex (PSC)

141 Wickstreet Farmhouse, Hailsham, Sussex (PSC)
142 Chicheley Hall, Buckinghamshire (PSC)
143 Peckover House, Wisbech, Cambridgeshire (PSC)
144 Detail from house in South Street, Boston, Lincolnshire (PSC)
145 House in Castle Street, Farnham, Surrey (PSC)
146 Holkham Hall, Norfolk (RCHME)
147 Houses in Great Ormond Street, London WC1 (PSC)
148 Stables at Burton Constable Hall, Yorkshire, ER (PSC)
149 Window at Bailey Hall, Hertford (PSC)
150 Perrott House, Pershore, Worcestershire (PSC)
151 Sir John Leman's School, Beccles, Suffolk (PSC)
152 Cottages in Spain's Court, Boston, Lincolnshire (PSC)
153 House of Correction, Newport, Essex (PSC)
154 Farm building at Seighford, Staffordshire (PSC)
155 Union Place, Wisbech, Cambridgeshire (PSC)
156 Holy Trinity, Newcastle under Lyme, Staffordshire (PSC)
157 High Lighthouse, Harwich, Essex (PSC)
158 Detail from Holy Trinity, Newcastle under Lyme, Staffordshire (PSC)
159 Maltings, Heytesbury, Wiltshire (PSC)
160 All Saints, Margaret Street, London W1 (RCHME)
161 Digswell Viaduct, Welwyn, Hertfordshire (PSC)
162 Keble College, Oxford (PSC)
163 Granary, Welsh Back, Bristol (PSC)
164 Hotel at St Pancras Station, London NW1 (RCHME)
165 Royal Holloway College, Egham, Surrey (RCHME)
166 House near Seighford, Staffordshire (PSC)
167 Tower of Westminster Cathedral, Victoria, London, SW1 (PSC)
168 Detail of Westminster Cathedral, Victoria, London, SW1 (RWB)
169 Shakespeare Memorial Theatre, Stratford-upon-Avon, Warwickshire (RCHME)
170 St Martin, New Knebworth, Hertfordshire (PSC)
171 Porch, St Nicholas, Burnage, Manchester (RWB)
172 Sculpture, Mond Laboratory, Cambridge (PSC)
173 Guildford Cathedral, Surrey (RCHME)
174 Odeon Cinema, York (RWB)
175 Philharmonic Hall, Hope Street, Liverpool (RWB)
176 Bracken House, Cannon Street, London EC4 (RCHME)
177 Robinson College, Cambridge (PSC)
178 Office Building, Bow Street, Manchester (RWB)
179 Hillingdon Civic Centre, Uxbridge, Middlesex (PSC)
180 Detail of brickwork, Hillingdon Civic Centre (PSC)
181 Diagram: clay wall in relation to crucks (RWB)
182 Cob walling, Stoke St Gregory, Somerset (PSC)
183 Detail of cob wall, Brightley, Devon (PSC)
184 Clay daubing, Cumberland (RWB)
185 Clay lump, Oakley, Suffolk (PSC)
186 Wychert wall at Haddenham, Buckinghamshire (PSC)
187 Mud-and-stud, West Lancashire (RWB)
188 Diagram: earth building in England and Wales (RWB)

189   Cob cottages, East Budleigh, Devon (PSC)
190   Dwelling near Ormskirk, Lancashire (RWB)
191   Detail showing cruck truss, dwelling near Ormskirk, Lancashire (RWB)
192   Clay house at Great Orton, Cumberland (RWB)
193   Mud wall, Laughton, Leicestershire (PSC)
194   Wychert house, Haddenham, Buckinghamshire (PSC)
195   Diagram: the international context (RWB)
196   Header bond, Alderley Edge, Cheshire (RWB)
197   Header bond, Hughenden, Buckinghamshire (RWB)

Key to credits

RWB	R. W. Brunskill
PSC	Peter Crawley
RCHME	Royal Commission on the Historical Monuments of England (now English Heritage)
RCAHMW	Royal Commission on the Ancient and Historical Monuments of Wales
SF	Stephen Fish
GW	Geoffrey Wheeler

Preface and acknowledgments

The late Alec Clifton-Taylor and I published *English Brickwork* in 1977 and its success may be judged by it being reprinted within the year. In that book we attempted to provide for the reader an introduction to the delights of brickwork of all periods in all parts of England; something that would not be a textbook on brickmaking, bricklaying or building construction and that would not be simply an historical treatise, but would open the eyes of readers to the interest and delight to be enjoyed from this building material and its use. During the intervening years a great deal happened in the study, appreciation and renaissance of brickwork; it was felt that a new book was required and in 1990 *Brick Building in Britain* was published.

Sadly this had to be an individual effort rather than a continuation of the joint authorship as Alec Clifton-Taylor died in 1984, but only after completing three sequences of his very popular *Six English Towns* programmes on television. In these programmes and the accompanying books he was able to extend considerably the appreciation of brickwork in England for some of the towns were chosen largely because of their wealth of brickwork.

Between the publication of *English Brickwork* and *Brick Building in Britain* the academic study of bricks, brickmaking and brickwork developed apace. The new book benefited greatly from work published in the archaeological and architectural journals and in *Information*, the Bulletin of the British Brick Society. The names of T. P. Smith, M. Exwood, M. Hammond, D. H. Kennet, J. McCann and P. J. Drury come immediately to mind and the subject benefited considerably from the work of those named and many others. At the same time, technical study of historic brickwork was being developed. In addition to the publications of John and Nicola Ashurst for English Heritage and the books of Gerard Lynch, many interesting articles had been published.

The renaissance in the use of brickwork by architects of the period appreciably widened the range of products both for new construction and in building conservation. The Brick Development Association and large manufacturers, such as Ibstock, illustrated and detailed new building and conservation work in their bulletins and journals.

Official interest in historic structures generally, as exemplified by the 're-listing' process, accompanied by expanding interest in magazines and on television, showed a growing public interest in brickwork as well as in the use of other materials old and new.

It seemed appropriate for the surviving author of *English Brickwork* to prepare a new volume on the subject with chapters more detailed and wide-ranging. A mostly new set of photographs was produced—largely through the skill of Peter Crawley. The National Monuments Records of England and Wales were generous with their help. Material on brickwork in Wales and Scotland was added to extend the range from England to Britain.

Now, more than a decade later, a new edition seemed timely. However, this time the rapidly developing interest in the use of clay and other earthen materials suggested a new contribution to the book. Brick is about fired earth, clay is unfired earth (though in use had various additions), but both are essentially the same material and, of course, where clay could be found, brick could be manufactured.

In this age, so conscious of 'green' issues, the attractiveness of a material that remains in plentiful supply, requires only limited use of energy in extraction and preparation, and mostly human energy in erection, is bound to be substantial. Experiments in new use of unfired earth have been founded on considerable scholarly work and the names of Estyn Evans, Alan Gailey, Kevin Danaher and Philip Robinson in Ireland, Bruce Walker in Scotland, Eurwyn Wiliam and Gerallt Nash in Wales and John McCann, Ray Harrison, and Nina Jennings and the Plymouth University team stand out. Their work and that of many others has been summarised in the new Part Four added to *Brick Building in Britain*.

Finally, I have to thank my wife and daughters for their continued forbearance and I have to thank most especially Peter Crawley, Rosie Anderson and Yale University Press for their patience during the preparation of *Brick and Clay Building in Britain*.

R. W. Brunskill
Wilmslow, 2009

Introduction

For more than 80 years the indispensable book for the student of our native brickwork has been Nathaniel Lloyd's *History of English Brickwork*, which originally appeared in 1925 and was reissued in 1983. But Lloyd included very little about the period since 1800 and in the years following publication not only have countless scores of millions of bricks been laid, but also over two centuries of brickwork not covered by him have become worthy of study while, sadly, quite a few of the buildings he illustrated have been demolished or altered out of recognition and are no longer available for study. With a few important exceptions more recent books have dealt with brickwork as one of several building materials or have concentrated on technical items or matters of craftsmanship.

There seemed to be a continuing need for an up-to-date book which could illustrate by word, diagram and photograph how bricks have been used at different periods and in different parts of the country from the earliest times to the present day. In addition it seemed appropriate to extend the study by describing and illustrating the use of earth which had not been moulded or fired into bricks but which had been very widely used throughout the British Isles.

In Part One of the book the various clays and methods of moulding and firing bricks are described and illustrated, showing the slow transformation of a labour-intensive craft into a largely mechanised industry. The techniques used by craftsmen in Tudor, Georgian and Victorian periods are explained and illustrated, and these can be observed in humble buildings in scattered locations as well as in major buildings in the principal cities. The related use of tiles for cladding and terracotta for structure and decoration are considered.

Part Two is a glossary in which photographs and drawings elucidate terms used in brickwork; many are still in use, but some are obsolete or survive only in the regions. Terms applicable to building construction and materials in general, and not peculiar to brickwork, have generally been excluded, as have definitions that can be found in ordinary dictionaries. Brickwork erected under British influence in North America has been given some mention.

Part Three of the book is a chronological survey. Whereas Part One is arranged largely thematically and Part Two looks mostly at details of buildings, Part Three concentrates on complete buildings. Six periods have been chosen and for each a wide range of examples, taken from many parts of the country and from a variety of building sizes, has been illustrated. The introduction to this section as a whole and to each period attempts to relate the brickwork to architectural developments generally. Most of the examples are of buildings whose exteriors are readily visible, but many are in private ownership and one trusts that the privacy of the occupiers will be respected.

Part Four introduces the subject of building in clay and other earthen materials. After a short introduction the subject is covered technique by technique, from the use of solid clay as cob to the use of lightweight timber daubed with clay in the mud-and-stud technique. The distribution of examples of the techniques in various parts of the British Isles is then discussed. Finally, the techniques are put into their international context, ranging in date from mudbrick structures of distant millennia to the widespread use of clay for houses right up to the present day.

Finally, there are four special topics in Part Five: the Brick Taxes of 1784 to 1850 are studied and their inception, application, modification and removal are noted; the slow growth in popularity and the recent transformation of the cavity wall are detailed; the fascinating story of the adoption of extravagant Header Bond in the Georgian period, its decline and its rebirth in Victorian Manchester is told; and concluding this section, there is a note on brickwork in Scotland and Ireland.

Despite the enthusiasm of fashionable architects for glass and concrete, the general public remains attached to the use of brick. Old houses built of brick—or, increasingly of clay—are cherished; new houses of brick bring out the warmth and decorative possibilities of the material. No excuse therefore seems necessary for a new edition of a book on brickwork and its associated clay techniques.

The traditional county names and the Imperial Measure familiar to builders in clay have been used.

Part One
Clay, Brickmaking and the Use of Bricks

1. The raw material, labour and transport

The requirements for brick production

The production of bricks as we know them for use on the building site continues to depend on the traditional factors of availability of raw material, fuel, labour and transport. For raw material one has to look at the geology of the country and distinguish between superficial clay deposits, shales, deep clay deposits and other materials from which bricks may be made. For fuel one has to examine what was the availability and economy of using first wood, furze or peat and later coal, or nowadays gas and oil, as well as the benefits which come from mixing a fuel such as half-burnt coal ash with the raw material or the way of taking advantage of natural oils present in the clay. For labour the rare and expensive foreign craftsmen of the medieval period were succeeded by itinerant brickmakers working on contract, who were gradually transformed into master tradesmen or journeymen employees at the permanent brickyards, and finally immigrant workers once more played a role after the end of the Second World War. Ultimately, the production and use of bricks depends on transport: the carriage of raw materials and fuel to the brickyard and the transport of the finished product by water, rail or road from brickworks to building site.

Raw material

The raw material for brickmaking is traditionally called 'clay' or 'brick earth'. In fact it is not earth and need not be clay though for convenience it will be so called here. Clay used for brickmaking is a plastic mixture of sand and alumina and may contain varying quantities of chalk, lime, iron oxide, manganese dioxide or other chemicals. True clay, or aluminium silicate, would distort when fired but is needed to give plasticity, that is the ability to take a shape given by a mould; non-clay materials, such as sand, reduce the tendency to shrinkage of a plastic material on drying and help to prevent the cracking of bricks under heat. A mixture consisting mainly of clay and sand is sometimes called 'loam', while a mixture of clay and chalk is called 'malm'. Clay with a relatively large proportion of lime produces a whitish brick and Gault clay is most commonly associated with so-called white brick production. Clay which is relatively pure produces a bright red brick, though this is also dependent on the firing. Clay with a relatively high proportion of iron oxide produces a deep blue brick, again dependent on firing. All these clays are part of the superficial deposits which are found just under the topsoil in most parts of lowland Britain.

Shales are laminated deposits of clay-like rock which are capable of being made plastic when broken up and ground to a fine texture. They are most commonly associated with the Coal Measures and so were available in the coalfields, such as those in Northumberland and Durham, Lancashire and North Wales, Staffordshire and Leicestershire, to be used once the technology was available to grind the shale and press it into brick shape.

Deep clays were those which were found in very thick seams located perhaps under superficial clay deposits, and which were in quantities extensive enough to justify investment in quarrying machinery. The best-known examples are the clays found under the 'callow' or superficial deposits of Oxford Clay around Peterborough and in Bedfordshire. They formed the basis of the 'Fletton' brick industry which dominated brick manufacture in the early part of the twentieth century.

Thus from the *Holocene* period we have the alluvial clays of such districts as Humberside, East Anglia and the Thames and Medway valleys which gave birth to the medieval brick industry. From the *Pleistocene* period we have the clays of East Suffolk and the boulder clays of patches of Northern England and Eastern Wales. The *Eocene* period includes the clays which produce the mottled purple bricks which are found in the Reading area, but are best known for the London clays and their yellow-brown bricks. The *Cretaceous* period has given us the Wealden clays of Sussex stretching westwards to Dorset, and the Gault clays found in Kent but mainly centred on Cambridge. The Lias clays and Oxford clays of the *Jurassic* period with their high carbon content are an important deposit though of limited extent. From the *Triassic* period there comes the Keuper Marl which is a reddish-brown mudstone used especially in Nottinghamshire and Leicestershire. The *Carboniferous* period has given the Coal Measures shales, including the Etruria marl so important in the Staffordshire brick and tile industry. Finally hard shales of the *Devonian* period gave raw materials for the fireclay products of South Wales.

Brick clays from the superficial deposits were the sole source of raw material at least until Elizabethan times and were a major source until the middle of the nineteenth century—and continue to be a source for the few remaining brickyards of the southern countryside. The thin, patchily distributed small deposits were quite satisfactory for the temporary brickworks set up at the sites of early brick buildings.

The clay could be used with comparatively little preparation. By the middle of the sixteenth century boulder clay and river terrace deposits were sought for the red bricks which they produced. During the Tudor period sandy brick earths were preferred, but boulder clay and estuarine and river muds were still used. In the late seventeenth century attention was directed to the Keuper Marls, as around Nottingham, while fireclay for fire bricks and blue bricks was recorded in 1686 as coming presumably from Etruria marls. In Derbyshire, in the early nineteenth century, weathered and deeper beds of Keuper Marl were being exploited. During the nineteenth century the Keuper Marl, Lias Clay and Cretaceous clays, and the Carboniferous materials generally, were exploited. The oil-bearing deep-quarried clays of Bedfordshire were extracted from about 1880 onwards. At Fletton, near Peterborough, the deep stratum of a shale-like grey-green clay deposit 45 or 50 feet deep was discovered. The 'butts', as they were called, were found to have a constant moisture content, allowing them to be crushed into grains and then pressed by machinery into a brick shape which could be fired immediately, without drying. They were also found to have sufficient organic combustible material in their constitution to cut by two-thirds the fuel necessary for burning. They had a constant and correct amount of lime to prevent cracking during firing while the few impurities were easily removed at the crushing stage. Most clay bricks nowadays are made from these deep-quarried Oxford clays or from the Carboniferous shales.

Fuel

The original fuel used in brickmaking seems to have been wood: not timber such as was used for structural purposes in making houses or ships, but wood as used for fuel generally, either burnt directly or when turned into charcoal. It appears that wood of poor quality was adequate for brickmaking and insofar as most bricks were at one time made at or very near to the site of an intended building, one can assume that local supplies of wood were available. More permanent brickyards required more reliable supplies and presumably the brickmakers, like other tradesmen, arranged for regular supplies of wood from the coppices which were cultivated for just such a purpose. Where wood was scarce then furze gathered from the fields and peat collected from the mosses (peat-bogs) could be used.

Coal was burnt directly as a fuel or indirectly as ashes. Until the development first of the canal and then of the railway systems, brickmakers were dependent for coal on outcrop supplies, taken by horse and cart, or mined coal transported by sea and river vessels. Small outcrops were widespread and coastal and river transport was extensive so that coal was a feasible material for use as fuel, at least from the seventeenth century onwards. When Coal Measures shales were exploited as a raw material, then coal was at hand relatively cheaply. Some brickworks were established at collieries which required bricks for the lining of pit shafts. Sifted coal ash was an important fuel in London and the South-East. The inefficient grates of the myriad fireplaces of London produced vast quantities of the ashes of coal incompletely burnt. These ashes were coveted by the brickmakers who used the finer ash as an admixture to their raw material and the coarser breeze directly as fuel. Thus the waste products of one process helped to provide the fuel for another. During the nineteenth and the first half of the twentieth century the rail network made coal widely available. But more recently, as coal has become less competitive in fuel and transport costs, oil and gas have come into use although currently there are wide fluctuations in the relative costs of the various fuels.

Labour

Traditionally both skilled and unskilled labour was required in brick-making. In the early medieval period it seems that skilled brickmakers were attracted to England from Germany and the Low Countries so that early accounts record sums paid to '. . . the Flemynge' or '. . . the Docheman' for their skills. They understood the mysteries of selecting the clay, checking that it was ready for use, moulding the bricks, building the clamp, and above all knowing for how long to fire it. Local labourers could do the heavy work under their direction. In the earliest days the same workmen acted as brickmakers and bricklayers.

As the skills were learned by native Englishmen so a class of itinerant tradesman was created. The building owner would make a bargain with a brickmaker for the production of bricks for a specific building project, the building owner being responsible for getting the clay and providing the fuel, and the brickmaker being responsible for producing the brick with the aid of local labour belonging to his client or hired for the purpose.

More permanent brickyards established in the towns led to generations of permanently-based craftsmen, labourers, men, women and children gaining employment. But permanence was relative. Brick-making was a seasonal occupation, confined to the summer months. Building itself was a cyclical activity. At all times the survival of the brickyards depended on the continuing availability of clay immediately to hand; once supplies were exhausted or expensive transport became necessary, then the brickyard would be abandoned and another established elsewhere.

The great expansion of brick production in the period of the Industrial Revolution was accompanied by an expansion of population, which ensured that a correspondingly large labour force was available. Much of the work was arduous and unpleasant, but then so was much of any alternative employment whether on the land or in factory and workshop. Mechanisation of brick moulding and improved methods of firing reduced labour requirements, but at least until 1914, many bricks were still produced by the traditional processes developed by generations of brickmakers and their labourers. More recently mechanisation has continued apace and conditions for the few workers now employed in the industry are vastly improved.

1. Little Wenham Hall, Suffolk, c. 1275. East side.

Transport

For hundreds of years, until well into the nineteenth century, transport problems dominated the brickmaking industry. When bricks could only be carried from brickworks to building site by packhorse, or (where roads existed) by horse and cart, then transport costs made a very big difference between the cost of bricks at the yard and the cost of those same bricks at the site. Ideally, the bricks had to be made at the building site. Similarly, the cost of hauling heavy brick clay meant that, effectively, the brickyard had to be at the clayground. Even an extensive or deep claypit could cause problems. The association of brickworks and raw material is still maintained, albeit with the aid of modern methods of carrying the raw material, but transport improvements have widely extended the range of building sites to be served by one brickworks. A heavy, low-value material such as brick was suitable for canal transport, and as the canal network spread during the late eighteenth and early nineteenth centuries, so canal distribution was added to distribution by coastal or river shipping. Most large and expanding towns were served by canals and so bricks could be transported at a cost to match that expansion. The coming of the railways during the nineteenth century continued this expansion. The railways themselves were consumers of bricks on an enormous scale, especially for bridges and tunnels, and, while not always as cheap as water transport, railways offered speed. The provision of private sidings at the large, efficient mechanised brickworks of the late nineteenth and early twentieth centuries helped in the distribution, even if the full journey from brickworks to building site had to be completed by horse and cart. More recently road transport has supplemented and to a large extent superseded rail transport so that lorries carrying packaged bricks move directly from brickworks to building site, using their own cranes to lift the packages carefully to where they are required and with the minimum of waste. In spite of these improvements, though, the cost of movement of raw material and finished bricks still forms a significant component in the total cost of a load of bricks.

2. Brickmaking

In the manufacture of bricks there were traditionally five processes: getting and preparing the raw material, moulding the green bricks, drying them, firing them, and finally sorting them ready for dispatch to the building site. In modern brickwork the drying is not always necessary, while improvements in manufacturing and handling techniques mean that sorting is largely unnecessary.

The process of getting and preparing the raw material involved extracting the clay, cleaning it of imperfections, mixing it to the right consistency and making it available for moulding by the brickmaker.

First a site had to be selected from which the clay could be extracted. If the bricks were needed only for the construction of a single building then suitable clay might be found on or very close to the site; local knowledge, observation of the results of ploughing, experience of clay generally would lead the experienced brickmaker to find a spot for extraction. Often, preparing the site for the building revealed suitable clay and after the mid-seventeenth century, when subterranean cellars became popular in domestic design and construction, the very spoil from the site would help to provide clay for bricks. If the bricks were required in larger quantities for general sale and over a longer period, as in a town or on an estate, then larger and more reliable and long-term supplies were sought, but the location of the claypit still depended on observation and experience.

The next process was to strip off the 'callow' or 'encallow' from above the usable clay. The vegetable matter or upper levels of earth would be put on one side for use on the land or to help backfill the exhausted claygrounds. The usable clay could then be extracted. Superficial deposits varied considerably in depth and extent, but until mechanical excavation and haulage became possible the depth depended on what could reasonably be dug by hand, and the extent on what could reasonably be transported by cart or wheelbarrow. Only with the advent of steam shovels and dragline excavators in the late nineteenth and early twentieth centuries did it become feasible to tap the great depth of clay available, say, in Bedfordshire as part of the Fletton industry. At the same time it was only the use of tramways, aerial ropeways and conveyor belts that made it possible to bring the products of several shale deposits to a central brickworks. In exceptional circumstances, as where a supply of particularly valuable fireclay was to be tapped, then the material would, if necessary, be mined by adit or shaft and gallery as with coal and other minerals. Ideally a brickworks in the nineteenth or early twentieth centuries would be near the bottom of a slope, below the extractions, and next to a road, canal or railway on which the bricks could be taken away.

In general 3 cu. yds of clay was considered to be sufficient to make 1000 bricks while one acre of clay 2 ft thick could supply clay for 1,000,000 bricks.

Traditionally, clay was dug in the autumn, weathered in the winter, tempered in the early spring and made into bricks in the late spring, summer and early autumn to suit the building season of the Middle Ages and later.

The excavated clay was heaped up to a height of five or six feet on a specially levelled piece of ground and the stones were picked out. During the winter the wind, rain and, above all, the action of frost broke down the clods of clay which had been so laboriously dug from the pit. In the London area the pile was made of alternate layers of clay, breeze and chalk. In the spring the clay was turned over two or three times by the workmen who were also expected to beat the clods with spades and shovels and extract any pebbles or pieces of chalk which might affect the moulding or firing processes. To temper the clay further, it was trodden by men and horses and any remaining stones were taken out. The material was then passed, if necessary, through sets of crushing rollers and sieved before water was added to make the plastic paste. Where malm or malmed earth was to be used, as in the London area, the process was rather different in that the clay, here called brick earth, was washed with water and mixed with the accepted amount of chalk, then the slurry-like mixture was passed through a grid into a settling pit, excess water was drawn off, breeze, the eventual fuel, was spread on the top and the mass was left to digest during the winter months ready for use in the spring. The advantage of natural malm or chalky clay was that contraction was minimised during firing when the chalk acted as a flux; a good-quality brick was the result. Other brick earths could be 'malmed' with chalk, if available, for similar results.

From the eighteenth century onwards, but especially in the late eighteenth and nineteenth centuries, the introduction of the pug mill speeded up the tempering process. A pug mill consisted of an inverted metal cone with a set of knives projecting from a central vertical axle turned by one or two horses treading a circular path. The power from this simple horse-engine made it possible for the knives to slice and mix the clay and force it out of an orifice at the bottom of the inverted cone in a form suitable for use by the brick-moulder at his bench.

Another device similarly powered was the mixing pan. This consisted of a dish several feet in diameter with a perforated bottom. Clay placed in the pan was crushed under large rollers turned by a horse treading a path around the pan. Hard clays were crushed dry but most clay intended for hand moulding was rolled when wet.

The resulting raw material had the consistency of paste: enough water was needed for working the clay into the mould, but not so much that there was any danger of the unfired moulded brick losing its shape while being handled. Nor indeed, so much water that the time and cost involved in drying the green brick before it was fit for firing was out of proportion. For dry brickmaking processes, especially those involving machine pressing, only a minimum amount of moisture was needed and this had obvious advantages in assisting the speed and economy of manufacture.

The Oxford clays of Bedfordshire, and the Fletton bricks produced from them, have already been mentioned. They were especially suitable for brickmaking for four main reasons. The moisture content was consistent and limited, allowing the clay to be crushed, pressed and then fired immediately without the need for drying. The clay contained just the right amount of organic combustible material for the bricks to be fully burnt, but without the need for all but the minimum of added fuel. The lime content was just right for acting as a flux during firing. Finally the clay was clean, contained few impurities and required the minimum of preparation. The processes listed under traditional clay preparation did not apply to the clay for Flettons.

There are many variations in the moulding process, and technical terms associated with each, but after the introduction of moulding boxes and before the development of mechanised brickmaking, the processes were essentially simple and had some degree, at least, of similarity.

L. J. Harley has codified the processes. In his Method 1 the suitably tempered clay was moulded by hand into small blocks and then fired, but numbers were so few that they can be ignored in any study of bricks for building.

In his Method 2, the 'butter-pat' method, the tempered clay was divided into blocks of similar size and shaped into roughly rectangular blocks with the aid of flat wooden tools like butter-pats. Although these could have been used in building there is, in fact, little evidence of their use in this country.

For Method 3, the 'pastry method', a sheet of tempered clay was spread on a level bed of sand or grass and cut into slabs rather like squares of pastry. These, when fired, produced the tile-like slabs which were used in Roman and early medieval English building construction.

For Method 4 the bricks were moulded, as we would understand the term, into objects which we recognise as bricks. In one variation the tempered clay was thrown into a hollow box standing on a level surface. The clay was forced into the corners of the mould box and the surplus was struck off with a wooden bat or 'strike'. The filled box was then turned upside down onto a thin slab of wood called a 'pallet' to be taken away for drying. In another variation the tempered clay was thrown into a mould, pressed to fill the mould, the surplus struck off similarly, but after the mould box was taken away the green brick was left on the 'place' until dry enough to be taken safely away to the drying ground. The first variation developed into pallet moulding, the second into slop moulding.

In the diagram:
sand
water
spare pallets
clot of clay
green brick
on pallet
bench for
pallet moulding

mould

iron-lined mould

adjustment

stock

mould for brick with frog

barrow with green
bricks on pallets

2. Diagram. Brickmaking by
hand.

In pallet moulding, the brickmaker nailed onto his bench a piece of wood called a stock board, corresponding in size to the desired dimensions of the bed face of the brick. His mould box of wood (or later of wood reinforced or lined with brass or sheet iron) fitted closely, but not tightly, onto the stock board. Four metal pegs, driven into the flat surface of the bench, one at each corner of the stock board, regulated the thickness of the moulded brick. From the late eighteenth century onwards a raised block or 'lack' was fixed to the top of the stock board and this produced the 'frog' or recess in the brick. The idea of the frog had developed during the seventeenth century when the brickmaker would scrape a section of clay away after moulding to produce a recess. The frog is to be distinguished from the recess around the rim of the brick which indicated that a mould box had been repaired.

The pallet moulder sprinkled sand on the stock board, and on the inside faces of his mould box, to prevent adhesion of the clay and to ease removal of the mould. A clot of clay, sufficient to fill the mould with some to spare, was kneaded into the right size, shape and consistency. This was pressed by the moulder so as to fill the mould completely, especially at the corners. The excess was then taken off the top with the aid of a wire bow and a stick or strike, moistened with water, which also served to smooth the top of the moulded green brick. When turned onto the pallet a sand-faced green brick emerged.

In slop moulding, a process once popular in the Midlands and North of England, there was no stock board; the mould box was placed directly onto the bench top and mould and top were wetted rather than sanded. In this, as in all other processes, the dimensions of the mould box had to allow for shrinkage during drying and firing.

The rates of moulding achieved by moulders working to either process seem to us quite remarkable. Lloyd quotes figures to indicate that a brickmaker working alone in the late seventeenth century would be expected to mould 1000 green bricks during a fourteen-hour working day in the summer, although with a man to temper the clay and a boy to carry off the palleted bricks this figure could be increased to 2000 or even 3000. Dobson quotes figures to indicate that a moulder and clot moulder assisted by a man to feed the clay, a boy to take off the bricks and put them onto a wheelbarrow, and two men to barrow the bricks to the drying ground (in other words a team of five men and a boy), could mould 5000 bricks in a twelve-hour day. Even those figures could be exceeded on occasion and he quotes a Carlisle brickmaker as producing 1000 in an hour.

Although these experienced brickmakers could produce phenomenal numbers of bricks during the long working days of summer, the work was very hard and depended on efficient team work. As the demand for bricks increased, especially in the nineteenth century, and as improved methods of extracting and transporting clay made more or less permanent brickyards a possibility, so the thoughts of inventors turned to ways of increasing still further the speed of output and relieving the manual load by mechanising the process. The inventions developed in two directions, one leading to an extrusion process and the other to a system of pressing the clay into bricks.

From about the middle of the nineteenth century, extruded or 'wire-cut' bricks were made. In this process tempered clay was forced through a die until a green brick of the necessary dimensions could be cut off by means of a taut wire. In early examples of such machinery, clay from a hopper was forced into a chamber from which a piston pushed sufficient for a single brick through the die, to be cut off by the wire. These machines were called 'stupids'. In later examples a continuous supply of the clay was fed into the machine by an Archimedes screw, while the extruded clay was fed along a bed of rollers to a table on which a set of wires cut off a batch of bricks at a time. These were then automatically pushed to one side to free the table for the next extrusion. Wire-cut bricks may be perforated if an appropriate die is used. They cannot have a frog unless re-pressed, which was sometimes done if an especially dense brick was required. Wire-cut bricks are still produced in large quantities: they usually display some striations to betray their origin.

Shortly after the wire-cut process was invented and came into use, the more versatile pressing process was mechanised. In this the tempered clay was forced into a mould and then pressed to fit the whole mould exactly and uniformly. The clay could then be pressed and re-pressed until the desired density was obtained and until all the surfaces were perfectly formed. Usually the mould was designed so as to produce a frog on one or both sides of the brick and there was often provision for the moulder's name and trade mark to be impressed with the frog. With the dense bricks popular in the nineteenth and twentieth centuries the frog economised on material and kept down the weight of each brick. It also helped in bricklaying when very thin joints were desired.

Simple hand-operated presses were often used to finish off and make more uniform bricks which had been hand-moulded already. Such a press could be wheeled along the ranks of bricks in the early stages of drying. More complicated powered presses could mould many bricks at a time, coping with clay of a consistency unsuitable for hand moulding.

In the soft mud process, clay was forced directly from the orifice of the pug mill into multiple moulds which were automatically sanded for each cycle of the process; the green brick was then mechanically tipped onto a pallet ready for drying.

In the stiff plastic process, shales or hard clays were ground, screened and then dampened. A clot was initially pressed roughly into shape then transferred to dies and moulds whereby further pressings produced the green brick, which required little drying.

In the semi-dry process hard shale was ground to a powder, was screened to maintain consistency and then was lightly dampened. Hoppers filled with the powder served presses which produced, after several pressings, a thoroughly consolidated, but virtually dry, green brick which could be transferred directly into the kiln. Nowadays various surface finishes are sometimes desired in place of the smooth uniformity of pressed brick which was one of their main attractions to the Victorian architects. These can be given at various stages of pressing, and to a limited extent in the wire-cut process.

Early brickmaking processes depend on the moulder being able to use a clay sufficiently wet, and so sufficiently plastic, to be handled. Bricks made from such clay had to be dried before firing to allow both for handling and stacking and to allow for economical firing with limited cracking, shrinkage and waste. Hence the drying process was very important.

Slop-moulded bricks were so wet that it was necessary to allow them to dry, initially, right beside the moulding table. A flat piece of ground, therefore, was prepared and the bricks were laid on their beds on this flat ground, the bench being moved along if necessary as the ground was filled up. In a typical process, a boy took the raw bricks from the top of the bench and put them carefully onto a slightly curved, sand-covered floor to dry flat for a day. The bricks were then placed on their sides for another day, after which enough air had circulated round them to allow the bricks to be taken on a specially designed wheelbarrow to the hack or drying ground. Often the drying floor was open to the skies, but a covered floor obviously avoided waste from rain.

Pallet-moulded bricks were dry enough to be loaded on their pallets onto a long wheelbarrow specially designed for carrying the palleted bricks to the hacks (2).

To form a hack a long narrow bank was made, about six inches above the ground, of old bricks or drain tiles, so as to produce a flat, dry, well-drained surface. The green bricks were carefully placed on edge, about ⅜ inch apart and about seven courses high, across the length of the hack with ends exposed to the wind. After about ten days the bricks were 'skintled' at 45° and about two inches apart. Then after another three to six weeks the green bricks were sufficiently dry to be fired. To protect the bricks from the weather, a covering of straw matting, or later tarpaulins, was used. The use of hacks was very old-established.

Records from Hull show that grounds called 'rowmes' were cleared each season and covered with straw, hay or sand for the new season's bricks.

Later, bricks were dried in hovels or sheds with heated floors. Hot air was drawn along flues, made out of firebricks in the floor, with the aid of a chimney. A typical shed would be 30 or 40 ft in length and would have racks in which green bricks were placed. Chamber drying was a variation in which green bricks were placed on shelves on cars (trolleys) in separate chambers along a shed with a heated floor.

The idea of the tunnel drier was tried in Britain in 1845 and, with variations, in America in 1867 but an economical and workable system did not come into use until the very end of the nineteenth century. In the tunnel drier the green bricks were stacked on cars travelling on railway lines. A car would be added every hour to give a slow continuous process or the tunnel could be heated intermittently to dry a batch at a time. Hot gases introduced at the unloading end were drawn through to the opposite end of a tunnel about 100 ft long. Sometimes waste heat from a continuous kiln was employed; alternatively hot air was forced along underfloor ducts. Typically, three days were required for drying in a tunnel.

Green bricks were burnt or fired according to one of several processes. In the intermittent process a batch of bricks was heated, fired and cooled and then the process was repeated with another batch. In the continuous process there was a constant succession of bricks coming from a kiln which was continuously fired. Intermittent firing was by the updraught method in clamps or kilns or by the downdraught procedure in the appropriate kilns.

Firing bricks in a clamp is the oldest method and has been in use right from the Middle Ages to the present day. A clamp was a temporary construction made of the green bricks to be fired, and dismantled when firing had been completed. Clamps were fired in the brickyards but one of the main advantages of the clamp was that it could be assembled on the building site, burning bricks made of clay dug at the site. Traditionally a clamp was made by first preparing a level floor out of discarded bricks (if available); channels in the floor were filled with fuel, which was wood, charcoal, turf, coal or breeze. On the floor a couple of layers of green brick were placed on edge, diagonally and about 2 ins apart, with breeze in the gaps, then half a dozen layers of brick interspersed with layers of breeze or other fuel were placed in position, then green bricks were quite closely packed to a height of about 14 ft. The bricks were tilted inwards and the sides battered for stability. In effect an ordered pile of green bricks was assembled. There might commonly be about 30,000 to 45,000 bricks in a clamp but as many as 150,000 were not uncommon (3). In the London area the brick earth was 'soiled' with partly consumed ashes so that the green bricks provided some of their own fuel. A clamp would take two or three weeks to burn out though a big clamp might burn for as many as ten or twelve

old burnt
brick
capping

breeze

30 courses
of green
bricks

breeze

stretchers
breeze
headers
breeze

skintled bricks

firehole

a. clamp base

fire
channels

central
upright

necks

b. clamp under assembly

c. clamp while burning

d. detail of central upright

3. Diagram. Clamp firing.

weeks. After cooling the clamp was dismantled. The bricks at the bottom were often overburnt, fused together and would have to be discarded. The bricks around the edge of the clamp were usually underburnt, and as soft, pink or 'sammel' bricks, could be used only for hidden work not exposed to the weather. The remainder were properly burnt but had variations in colour and texture according to the vagaries of the burning process. All bricks were liable to distortion in clamp burning.

About as old as the clamp is the updraught kiln of the type usually known as the Scotch kiln (4). The base of the kiln consisted of firing chambers made in brick—firebrick if available. Firing was from the sides or from the end. There was a floor above the firing chambers reached by apertures in the ends of the battered brick walls of the kiln. Green bricks were carefully stacked within the kiln with gaps between to allow for circulation of the hot gases resulting from combustion of the fuel; 'kiss marks' on the edge of the kiln-burnt bricks indicate how they

b. Scotch kiln, firing.
(Sheds along side)

wicket   grates

a. Scotch kiln

c. Scotch kiln
cross-section

wicket

fireholes

d. Suffolk kiln

e. Newcastle kiln

4. Diagram. Scotch kiln firing.

5. Exterior of downdraught kiln, Porth wen, Anglesey.

were stacked. A typical Scotch kiln would contain between 20,000 and 50,000 bricks. The open top of the kiln was covered with old bricks and turf to help conserve heat, though flames could often be seen at night rising from the top of the kiln. The brickmaker determined the two-, three- or four-day period of firing. The kiln was then allowed to cool until it could be emptied of bricks. As with clamp burning the better quality bricks had to be sorted from those which were misshapen and overburnt and from those which were soft and underburnt.

Variations from the Scotch kiln included the Suffolk kiln with longitudinal fire tunnels below the floor and the Newcastle kiln, a horizontal-draught kiln with fireholes at one end and a chimney at the other. A double Newcastle kiln had fireholes at both ends and a central flue leading to a chimney.

The downdraught kiln (6) used fuel much more efficiently and in a manner more easily controlled than any of the updraught or horizontal kilns. The typical downdraught kiln was circular on plan with fireholes on the perimeter of the brick wall and a saucer-domed brick roof. Underneath a perforated tiled floor a flue led to a chimney-stack. There were baffles or 'bags' of firebricks inside the fireholes. The kiln was loaded with about 12,000 green bricks and the coal fires lit in their grates. Hot gases from the fires were directed upwards from the baffles then drawn downwards from the underside of the dome, through the

6. Diagram. Downdraught kiln firing.

a. cross-section

b. plan

7. Interior of downdraught kiln showing loading door and fire holes though the baffles have been demolished; Porth wen, Anglesey.

stacks of bricks, by the draught from the chimney. The cycle of burning took about fourteen days with two days for filling, three days for curing, two days for heating to full temperature, a day at the full heat and then three or four days to cool down and a day or two to empty. Many brickworks had several downdraught kilns operating simultaneously. They were reasonably economical in fuel and much easier to control than the updraught kilns. Some downdraught kilns were rectangular on plan with barrel-vaulted roofs and they had a much greater capacity than the circular or 'beehive' kilns; as many as 100,000 blue bricks were fired in Staffordshire downdraught rectangular kilns, for example (5,7).

The great disadvantage of the intermittent kilns was that they produced bricks infrequently but in large batches and this might not meet the demands of the customers. At the same time there was the waste of fuel and time in heating a kiln from cold to a high temperature only to have to return it to cold again. The advantages of intermittent kilns included their simplicity of operation and low cost of construction. When brickyards were small, dependent on uncertain supplies of superficial clay in immediately accessible clay grounds, and when the finished bricks could only be transported to distant building sites at disproportionate cost, the incentive to invest in a large-capacity kiln firing continuously was not great. However, when the demand for bricks increased tremendously in nineteenth-century towns and cities as a result of the Industrial Revolution in its various manifestations, the situation was transformed. Railway developments alone called for huge numbers of bricks for viaducts and tunnels while those same railway developments meant that finished bricks could be sold widely. The introduction of machinery and improved ways of preparing the clay gave a much longer life to many of the brickyards and further justified investment in improved kilns. Multi-chambered kilns had been patented in 1841 and 1843, but the invention which was called the greatest single development in brick manufacture was that of the circular continuous kiln, whose design was patented by Friedrich Hoffmann in Germany (and patented in this country by Humphrey Chamberlin) in 1859.

A typical Hoffmann kiln was circular on plan and had twelve annular chambers divided by brick partitions with small openings at the bottom and with barrel-vaulted roofs. Each chamber had an opening in the outer wall through which it could be charged with green bricks. A system of flues led from the chambers to a tall central chimney. Narrow apertures in the roofs of the chambers, thirty-two to a chamber, allowed the fuel of fine coal to be dropped into the chambers as required. By operating the dampers the draught was led in an anti-clockwise direction as successive chambers were warmed, heated to firing temperature and then cooled. A light-weight timber and corrugated iron roof protected the top of the kiln and the man attending to the firing. The brick walls of the kiln were battered and the openings in each chamber formed deep rather military-like embrasures (8).

In the normal firing cycle one chamber would be loaded with green

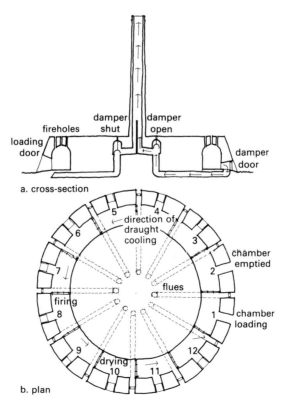

8. Diagram. Hoffmann kiln firing.

bricks, spaced apart to allow the flue gases to circulate, and the loading door would be bricked up. The next four chambers, running clockwise, would be full of bricks in various stages of drying and pre-heating, making use of warm flue gases coming from the cooling chambers. Then two chambers would be at the highest temperatures with bricks being burnt. A further four chambers would be cooling at various rates while the twelfth chamber was being unloaded; this chamber being next to the one which had just been loaded. The various openings in the partitions between the chambers were closed with sheets of paper to control the movement of the draught. The feed holes for fuel were attended to every few minutes and the firing process moved round in a counter-clockwise direction. It was essential for the efficient working of the Hoffmann kiln that firing was continuous, kilns being in operation for years until they had to be taken out of service for maintenance.

While very satisfactory in principle the Hoffmann kiln was rather less satisfactory in practice because of the limitations inherent in the circular shape. Hoffmann designed a rectangular version in 1870. The Belgian kiln was patented and the first one built in 1891. Others, such as the 'Warren's patent perfected kiln' applied the regenerative principle to the firing of bricks (9). All are rectangular on plan, though usually with rounded ends, and there are, as a rule, more chambers than the twelve

9. Diagram. Other continuous kilns.

a. cross-section (to larger scale)

b. elevation

c. plan

of the simple Hoffmann kiln. There was a thick spine wall between the two rows of chambers and the main flue ran under the spine wall to the chimney-stack, while a hot-air flue ran along the top of the spine wall. There were connections between the base of each chamber to the main flue and from the top of each chamber to the hot-air flue. Loading and firing were as with the original Hoffmann design.

The transverse arch, rectangular continuous kiln was invented around 1890, increasing the effective length—which is the distance the fire travels in one circuit of the kiln. In 1904 the Staffordshire transverse arch kiln was patented for the firing of blue engineering bricks. This operated on the same principle as the other rectangular continuous kilns, but as the barrel vaults ran from partition wall to partition wall at right angles to the spine wall, it was possible to have larger and more spacious chambers than where the barrel vault ran continuously around the rectangle.

The Hoffmann kiln and its variations dominated kiln design for nearly a hundred years and, until the 1950s, there were few towns in England which did not have one of these massive bunker-like constructions busily producing bricks from the local clays or shale.

The type of kiln now mostly used is the tunnel kiln. First built for the French Royal Porcelain Factory in 1751 the tunnel kiln, for all its potential virtues, was not generally used until 200 years later. The idea of the tunnel kiln is similar to that of the tunnel drier; cars of green bricks travel slowly along a long tunnel while they are heated, burnt and cooled.

Bricks, which nowadays are usually machine-pressed or wire-cut, are placed on small cars and taken through a tunnel drier for twenty-four hours. They are then stacked upon specially designed trolleys running along a tramway in a tunnel about 300 ft to 450 ft long, five to six feet wide and ten feet high. There are three zones:—pre-heating, firing and cooling—and the cars, each holding about 2,000 bricks, pass slowly from one zone to another. The whole sequence takes two or three days. Various fuels may be used, but in one version crushed coal is fed through small holes in the roof of the firing zone, but combustion is so complete and so well controlled that no chimney-stack is required.

As with drying tunnels a flow of hot air is maintained opposite to the movement of the loaded cars. Air is drawn from the cooling zone through the firing zone to pre-heat the green bricks as they enter the tunnel. It is important to reduce leakage of the hot combustion gases and to protect the car bogies and their rails from the great heat and so there is a close fit between loaded car and tunnel lining, and a seal of sand between the firebrick decks of the trolleys and the base of the tunnel wall.

Sand-lime bricks and concrete bricks

There are two types of brick in use in addition to clay bricks: sand-lime (calcium silicate) bricks and concrete bricks. Both are made to conventional brick sizes but with different processes, neither involving firing.

Sand-lime bricks are made by compressing a mixture of damp sand with thoroughly slaked lime and then curing the result by use of saturated steam. The mixture, typically 95% sand to 5% lime, is fed into moulds of brick shape, compressed at pressures of up to 200 tonnes and the resulting bricks may be brushed to provide a texture to the exposed surfaces. The bricks are placed on trolleys and covered for up to twelve hours in an autoclave of saturated steam. Any surface scum is removed by an application of weak acid, otherwise the bricks are ready for use.

The sand-lime process was developed in Germany in the 1880s and adopted on a fairly small scale in this country at the beginning of the twentieth century. Flint-lime bricks are made in the same way, but out of crushed flint rather than sand. Both sand-lime and flint-lime bricks have a bright, light-reflecting surface and quite a pleasant natural colour, though they can also be coloured with pigments added during the mixing process. Sand-lime bricks are of uniform colour, texture, size and shape with sharp, square arrises. Their fine texture makes them suitable for carving.

Concrete bricks are simply solid blocks made to brick sizes and should not be confused with hollow concrete blocks of larger sizes and different shape. The drab grey colour of concrete may be modified through the use of aggregates of crushed coloured stone in the mixture, and the cement-based texture may be improved by spraying the surface before curing to reveal the texture of the aggregate.

Both sand-lime and concrete bricks are used where clay for brickmaking is not available or where the cost of firing is regarded as prohibitive.

Transport

The relationship between the brickmaking site and the building site has already been mentioned. If clay was available on the building site, and bricks could be fired in a clamp, then transport problems were reduced to those of bringing the fuel to the clamp. Even then there might be locally available wood faggots, furze or peat. Where bricks were made in large numbers in a brickyard, as they were in such places as Hull, Beverley, Boston and Bury St Edmunds in the medieval period, then transport was involved either for the short distances to sites in the towns or the longer distances to rural building sites.

From medieval times carting for short distances and moving by water for longer distances was the practice. Carting for longer distances involved disproportionately high costs both for the transport itself and for mending roads damaged by laden carts. The widespread use of water transport up rivers far from the coast meant that many isolated building sites were, in fact, accessible for waterborne bricks. In the Thames and Medway areas water transport remained in use until the 1940s, and specially designed sailing vessels, called 'stumpies', brought bricks up creeks close to suburban building sites. According to

Woodforde the firm of Eastwoods developed a brickworks in North Kent taking advantage of canals and rivers opening off the Thames; they built their own sailing barges, having a fleet of seventy at one time. The return trips from London brought ashes, coke and cinders to be used in soiling the brick earth. The coming of the canals in the eighteenth and nineteenth centuries made available another means of water transport. Many bricks were made out of clay dug in canal excavations, fired and then used in canal bridges and aqueducts. In the industrial districts, especially, canal barges offered a cheap and adequate means of transporting a heavyweight, high-bulk, low-value, item.

The coming of the railways added to the benefits of the canals. Again, brick clay was excavated in cuttings and bricks were used in bridges and other engineering works (40). For railway buildings it was worth while to carry bricks for long distances; thus St Pancras Station and Hotel were built of bricks carried from the Midlands to London. For the ordinary builder, however, rail transport was expensive. From the early days of railways it was customary to build sidings into the brickworks both for the receipt of coal fuel and for the dispatch of bricks. The very big brickworks at Arlesey, Bedfordshire, owed their origin to the Great Northern Railway. It was estimated that 8 million bricks left the Arlesey brickworks sidings in 1858 alone. The Fletton brickworks at Stewartby in Bedfordshire were sited with transport on the adjacent main-line railway in mind from the beginning. Costs for the ordinary brickmaker are indicated by figures quoted by Dobson that rates current in 1850 would double the cost of common bricks at a sixty-mile radius from the brickworks, and this assumed a siding at the brickworks and ignored carting costs between railhead and building site. Cartage, indeed, remained expensive at any point. The Bedford Estate, for example, calculated that the carting of common bricks for only five miles meant a price of 48s. per 1000 as against 34s. per 1000 at the brickworks.

The advent of mechanical road haulage, first by steam lorry and then by motor wagon, introduced competition for the railways, but over short to medium distances rather than on the longer routes. After 1918 cheap trucks and cheap petrol extended the competition to the horse and cart over short distances. Whether carried by truck or cart there was great wastage, especially of common bricks, which were usually simply tipped at the site.

Nowadays nearly all bricks are moved by road. The large brickmakers have specially designed vehicles by which packaged sets of bricks, loaded on pallets by forklift trucks and unloaded by means of the vehicle's own hydraulic crane, can be transported relatively cheaply and with minimum waste. As common bricks have now virtually passed out of use the costly facing bricks justify careful treatment.

As long as delivery by horse and cart was involved, local brickworks could hold their own against those far distant, no matter how efficient. But once road transport became quick, cheap, efficient and universal, the proximity of brickworks to building site became less important and so we now have a regional or even a national pattern of brickworks rather than a local pattern.

Sorting the bricks

In the traditional brickworks it was often necessary to sort the bricks into various qualities before they could be transported to the building site. Some variations were intentional, others were a consequence of a particular method of manufacture.

One list of brick variations published by Dobson in 1850, and relating to bricks made of malm and burnt in clamps for the London market, will serve to illustrate the variations. Three groups were distinguished: those made wholly of malm, those made of clay with some malm added, and inferior bricks sorted out of the second group.

The best-quality bricks reserved for the best locations were the malms, and they cost 105s. per 1000. The same price was put on the cutters which were softer but of high quality and specially made for gauged brick arches and other rubbed work. Seconds at 63s. per 1000 were still expensive but considered of good enough quality for the front walls of superior buildings. Paviours, pickings and rough paviours ranged in price from 33s. to 50s. per 1000 and were of a soundness sufficient for paving, though they were not made as paving bricks. Washed stocks, at 35s. per 1000, were adequate for all ordinary brickwork.

The three grades of common bricks ranged in price from 29s. to 33s. per 1000. Grey stocks were sound but irregular in colour and not considered suitable for facings. Rough stocks were irregular in shape as well as inconsistent in colour. Grizzles were soft and 'tender', unsuitable for outside work, not being water-resistant.

Discarded from among the common bricks were place bricks, under-burnt and not suitable for permanent building work, shuffs which were unsound as they were full of fissures, and burrs or clinkers, the fused and misshapen bricks from near the fireholes, which were unsuitable for any structural walling, though they could presumably be used for hardcore. Such bricks may often be seen in rockeries and garden walls.

Size and shape

We are so accustomed to the nominal dimensions of 9 ins by 4½ ins by 2½ ins or 3 ins for normal bricks that we tend to ignore the variations in size and shape which are to be seen in brick buildings of many periods. Compared to some other brick-using countries, the Netherlands and the United States, for instance, our bricks are rather large. Within Great Britain there was a tendency for bricks to increase in size from the medieval period to the Victorian, and then to diminish somewhat during the twentieth century until metric bricks increased again in size.

10. Brickwork of several periods (indication of various alterations), Pentre bach, Llanfihangel, Llanternum, Monmouthshire.

At all times there was a temptation for brickmakers to supply smaller bricks and builders to demand larger bricks as long as they were sold by number and not by size or weight.

Roman bricks, reused in some medieval buildings, were tile- or slab-like and sizes of 9 by 9 by 1 ins up to 18 by 12 by 1½ ins are to be expected. The early medieval bricks at Little Wenham Hall, of 1270–90 (1), are about 8¼ by 4 by 2 ins in dimension; those made in Hull (51) were 10 by 5 by 2 ins, but a size of 9½ by 4½ by 2 ins was common in the late fifteenth century. Medieval Great Bricks (84), mostly from mid-twelfth to mid-thirteenth century, were about 11 to 14 ins long by 6 to 7 ins by 1½ to 2 ins thick. From about the mid-thirteenth century bricks settled into the familiar size and proportions, possibly under influence from continental Europe, and probably through the development of regular bonding, which required the length of a brick to be twice the breadth plus the thickness of a joint. Medieval bricks tended to be thin, those dated 1340 in Norwich city wall being 2⅛ ins thick and some from a bridge of about 1400 at Pleshey, Essex, being between 1⅞ and 2 ins thick. Other bricks of the fifteenth century are between 1⅞ and 2¼ ins thick. At York, in 1505, a standard size was established of 10 by 5 by 2½ ins. The Brickmaker's Charter of 1571 established what was called the Statute Brick of 9 by 4½ by 2¼ ins. It has been suggested that brick dimensions in the medieval period were determined by the poor quality and excessive water content of the clay; long drying periods were needed, so bricks had to be small enough to stack properly and thin enough to dry evenly. Clamp firing also has been held to set dimensions for close fitting so that the thickness ought to be one tenth of three times the length so that a brick 9 ins long and 4½ ins wide should be 2⁷⁄₁₀ ins thick.

The great spread in the use of bricks in the seventeenth century, and especially after the Restoration of 1660, was marked by the use of thicker bricks and a range between 2⅜ ins and 2⅝ ins thickness was customary. The fine-jointed gauged bricks tended to be thinner, having been rubbed down from a rough 2½ ins to a fine and smooth 2⅛ ins thickness. Improved methods of preparing the clay for moulding may have allowed the use of somewhat thicker bricks. An Act of 1769 specified a *minimum* size for bricks in the London area of 8¼ ins by 4 ins by 2½ ins, but this rather protected builders from brickmakers than established a standard size for strict adherence.

The next change came in the late eighteenth and nineteenth centuries when bricks, especially in the North and Midlands, South Wales and Scotland, came to hover around the 3-in mark in thickness. No doubt this was affected by the Brick Tax of 1784 which was levied per 1000 bricks irrespective of size. The change in 1803 when double duty was charged on bricks more than 150 cu. ins in volume curbed any excesses, though the limitations imposed by the size of the bricklayer's hand must have been equally effective. Nevertheless, the architectural fashion in the nineteenth century was in favour of large and thick bricks and many buildings can be seen in our towns and cities in which all the bricks are about 3 ins deep. Those used by Jesse Hartley in the warehouses at Albert Dock, Liverpool, for instance, in 1841–5, are 3⅛ ins thick.

In the early twentieth century there was a return to thin bricks as part of the Vernacular Revival Movement. Sir Edwin Lutyens was especially fond of small, or at least thin, bricks and he encouraged their manufacture especially in Sussex. He specified 2-in thick bricks for the red brick details to the local blue-grey bricks in Folly Farm, Sulhamstead, Berkshire in 1906 and 1912. He recommended using 2-in thick bricks of lengths between 12 ins and 36 ins for his work at New Delhi. He was quite happy to use tiles in among his bricks; at The Deanery at Sonning in Berkshire, for instance, he used sets of tiles radiating at intervals among the brick arches.

Under Dutch influence there was a further period of popularity of thin bricks among some architects in the inter-war period. Dudok, the great Dutch architect who designed the Hilversum Town Hall, and other influential buildings in that locality, used thin bricks, and English architects, such as the firm of Burnet, Tait and Lorne, responsible for a large number of public buildings, and Harry Weedon, the architect for many Odeon cinemas during those years, used thin bricks. At the same time the neo-Georgian movement in architecture encouraged the production of facing bricks of rather smaller size and definitely thinner proportions than had become customary in the Victorian and Edwardian periods. For facing bricks, at least, the designers of banks, post offices, town halls and theatres encouraged the production of 2½-in-thick bricks from the remaining traditional kilns in the southern and eastern counties of England.

The advent of the British Standards Institution and its specifications did at last provide the machinery for standardised dimensions for the architects who wanted them and the brickmakers who were willing to supply them; for more efficient methods of brickmaking ensured that standards once set could be maintained. British Standard 657 of 1936 specified 8¾ by 4³⁄₁₆ by 2 or 2⅝ ins but allowed 2⅞ ins to meet the conventions of the North of England. British Standard 3921 of 1965 specified 8⅝ by 4⅛ by 2⅝ ins. The metric version, British Standard 3921 of 1969, gave dimensions of 215 by 102.5 by 65 mm, but there have been experiments recently with bricks of other metric dimensions.

The range of sizes quoted here gives only the broad tendency for bricks to grow in size from the medieval period to the late nineteenth century. There were many variations within this tendency and size alone can never be regarded as a reliable dating criterion.

Moulded bricks

Recent research has shown that from the medieval period to the present day specially shaped bricks have formed an important adjunct to conventional bricks. Bricks may be of a special shape to meet particular constructional needs, as in turning a corner or thickening a wall, or they may be of special shape to facilitate decoration, as in providing Gothic or classical mouldings.

At the present day 'specials' include so-called 'standard specials' and specially manufactured specials. By standard specials are meant those bricks which are shaped on plan, such as squinted or angled bricks for turning corners, or curved bricks for making bow windows or curved garden walls, or those which are shaped in cross-section, such as chamfered bricks to be used in plinths. Specially manufactured bricks

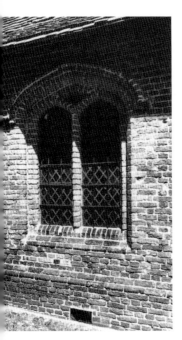

11. Moulded brickwork, St Nicholas, Chignal Smealy, Essex.

12. Moulded brickwork in Artisan Mannerist style. Manor House, North Wheatley, Nottinghamshire.

include those which are needed for particular jobs and are made to special order, rather than being manufactured for stock like standard specials.

In fact moulded bricks were used to make up architectural details from the earliest days of medieval brickwork. Bricks moulded to follow conventional architectural details around doors and windows seem to have been made at the same time and at the same location as the bricks for general walling. Sometimes they were left bare with the rest of the bricks, though in other instances it was expected that they would be rendered in imitation of masonry dressings. (11,12,30)

The great period of moulded brickwork was the Victorian. Both classically based and Gothic Revival details were devised by the architects and reproduced in moulded brickwork, in addition to the great use of terracotta work so characteristic of the period.

Colour

The colour of *brickwork* comes from a combination of the colours of bricks and mortar. The colour of each *brick* (and bricks may be uniform in colour or mottled or irregularly shaded) comes from the chemical composition of the brick clay, the amount of iron oxide present, the nature of any sand used in the moulding process, and the intentional or accidental variations in firing. The range of colours available from the one basic raw material contributes to the popularity of brickwork, while the regional variations still to be observed in historic buildings in different parts of the country contribute to the sense of place which many people find desirable or comforting.

Although the main elements of clay suitable for brickmaking are alumina and silica, other elements are usually present in small but significant quantities. The main element affecting colour is iron oxide. The greater the amount of iron oxide the redder the brick, and the deeper the red; a clay with 7% iron oxide can produce a colour so deep that in firing it converts to what is usually termed a 'blue' brick. The presence of magnesium oxide will help to produce a yellow brick. Limestone and chalk, if finely ground, will change the iron oxide to produce a buff or yellowish colour. If there is little or no iron oxide present then the limestone or chalk in the clay will produce a whitish brick. Gault clays are heavy and bluish in colour before firing but afterwards they produce a pale grey or so-called 'white' brick (149). Coal Measures shales are fired to emerge as mainly red bricks. As polychromatic brickwork was very popular in the Victorian period, the industrialised brickworks of the day adjusted the chemical composition of the clays and shales they used so as to make available the reds, yellows and blues wanted by the builders and their architects (163).

The nature of the sand used in the moulding process could affect the surface colour of the brick (though not necessarily the body colour) after it had been fired. The nature of the sand could be changed by 'staining' with metallic oxides; thus manganese oxide added to the sand could produce a brown-surfaced brick after firing.

The firing process affected the finished colour even if its basis had been set by the chemical composition of the clay or shale. The varieties associated with clamp and updraught kiln burning were largely accidental, but in downdraught kilns the skilful brickmaker could command some versatility.

In the wood-fired kilns popular for so long in central southern England fly ash reacted at high temperature to produce the silver-grey bricks so often to be seen in the Thames Valley, for instance (19). Generally, too low a temperature or too short a firing period produced light-coloured bricks—hence the sammels or underburnt bricks from the outer surfaces of the clamp—whereas too high a temperature and too long a firing period produced vitrified bricks, or vitrification of the most exposed surfaces of bricks, hence the pronounced blue-black of headers characteristic especially of Tudor buildings in the South-East (118). Dark brown and purple bricks could be produced by a smoky atmosphere during firing; this could be created in a downdraught kiln by adjusting the dampers on the chimney flue.

Of the shale bricks probably the most notorious colour is the bright red, reviled by architectural critics of the Modern Movement, but now back in fashion, while the colour most appreciated is probably that of the Staffordshire Blue brick (156). To some extent the blue/purple/deep grey colour was induced by the shale but the natural red was converted by longer firing and greater heat—up to 1200°C rather than the 900°C normal in the continuous kiln.

Multicoloured bricks, popular once more, were originally produced in downdraught kilns. Stacked on bed so that one end and one side at least were exposed, the bricks, after initial burning, were exposed to a reducing atmosphere; by restricting the admission of air and creating a lot of smoke, then repeating the process several times, this reducing atmosphere coloured the bricks in a range of effects.

Sand-lime and concrete bricks have their own colour characteristics and both could benefit from pigments introduced during the mixing process, though concrete bricks never entirely lose the drab greyness of cement.

Special-purpose bricks

The best-known of the special-purpose bricks are firebricks, but in this category also come light-weight insulating bricks and glazed bricks.

Firebricks were needed where great heat had to be resisted, as in furnaces, factory chimneys and kilns. The brickyards themselves were quite big consumers of firebricks as high temperatures were reached in downdraught and continuous kilns. Good quality firebricks were expensive but much sought after, and throughout the nineteenth century there was a significant export trade in firebricks from Britain to places where ingredients for their manufacture were not available.

Fireclay, or refractory clay, has a high proportion of alumina in its composition and is free of lime, magnesia or metallic oxides. There might be 22% to 35% alumina to 55% to 75% silica. Fireclays were found in the Coal Measures, just below the coal seams, and so were usually mined rather than quarried like most brick clays. The raw fireclay was crushed and finely ground, then often mixed with a proportion of 'grog' (which here meant pulverised burnt fireclay) both for economy and to reduce shrinkage and cracking in the kiln. The mixture was then 'soured', or left in storage, for a few weeks. It was then passed for hand moulding or machine pressing, dried, and then fired in the kiln at a temperature of 1500°C or more for seven days. Fireclay was available in most coalfields but that from Stourbridge in the West Midlands was highly regarded in the nineteenth century, while the firebricks from Glenboig in Strathcyde had a good reputation and added to the export trade from the Clyde ports.

Firebricks were hard and dense. In complete contrast were the 'fossil' bricks which were soft and light-weight, and in fact could float on water. Fossil bricks were the invention of an Italian brickmaker, Fabbroni, who discovered, towards the end of the eighteenth century, that an Italian infusible earth called fossil meal could make a brick only one-sixth of the weight of an ordinary brick. Light-weight bricks were in demand for vaulting, as in Gothic Revival buildings, and they were also used for their heat-insulating properties.

Glazed bricks were popular in the nineteenth and early twentieth centuries for situations where cleanliness or light-reflecting properties were needed. For cleanliness alone the salt-glazed brick was adequate; where light-reflection or an alternative colour was needed then twice-fired enamelled bricks (also called glazed bricks) were employed.

Simple glazed bricks were made out of carefully pressed fireclay or shale material, re-pressed and trimmed if necessary to give precise surfaces and sharp arrises. The bricks were fired in a downdraught kiln, or sometimes a tunnel kiln, and after a temperature of 1200°C was reached, common salt was thrown into the kiln; this was repeated once or twice and the bricks then allowed to cool. The salt gave a glassy finish to the exposed surfaces of the bricks. The brown colour which resulted was similar to the salt-glazed stoneware used for sanitary goods.

The more fully glazed enamelled process resembled pottery manufacture in that ordinary pressed bricks of a dense clay were heated in a kiln to a temperature of 1200°C, cooled, and extracted from the kiln. In an adjacent workshop two faces of each brick were washed in water then dipped first in a bath of slip, then in a bath of colouring solution and finally into a glaze. The treated bricks were returned to a kiln for the second firing. Such glazed bricks were used externally, as, for instance, to reflect light in an area or light well, or internally, as in a dairy or butcher's shop. However, the surface does tend to craze with small cracks.

3. The use of bricks

Structural matters

A brick-walled building had to sustain the live loads of the people and objects housed in the building, the dead loads of the structure including the brick walls themselves, and the side or wind loads coming, for instance, from the direct pressure of a high wind on one part of a building and the suction induced by such a wind passing over and around the building. A brick-walled building had to rely on stable foundations. The brick walls could be expected to act in conjunction with other parts of the structure such as the intermediate floor and roof construction.

Potential collapse in a brick-walled building came from defective foundations, crushing of any overloaded parts, sliding (or shear) of one section of wall over another, buckling or sideways collapse of part or the whole of a wall in the horizontal or vertical planes, or the inward or outward collapse of an inadequately stabilised section of a brick wall.

In theory excessive live or dead loads on an inadequate foundation would result in the collapse of the wall at the over-stressed part of the foundation. In practice the loading from relatively low buildings would require no special preparation other than removal of the topsoil, and the limited foundations in old brick buildings may be a source of amazement and even alarm when exposed. Where walls were taller, as in multi-storey factory buildings of the nineteenth century, or where loads were concentrated, as from tall factory chimneys, then the brick walls were thickened out, course by course, as footings and bedded on concrete. Where the ground itself had an exceptionally low bearing capacity then special foundations such as elm piling would be needed, and where kept wet, the elm piles could last for centuries.

Similarly, in theory, excessive live and dead loads on an inadequate brick wall could result in collapse through crushing of the bricks. In practice, again, this rarely occurred; even the less than adequately burned bricks from primitive clamps were structurally adequate provided that heavy point loads, as from floor beams or roof members, were spread by way of stone or timber pads. Conditions which might, on the face of it, lead to failure through crushing were more likely to lead to an earlier collapse through vertical or horizontal buckling; a collapse which would be hastened by the effects of wind pressure and suction. Nevertheless crushing strength was a matter which concerned the engineers who were trying to work out a structural theory for the use of brickwork, and nineteenth-century textbooks and technical publications were full of tables of crushing strengths for bricks made according to several processes and originating in different parts of the country. It was not until close control of the manufacturing process became possible at the end of the nineteenth century that the crushing strength of bricks in use became a matter capable of realistic calculation and of great significance.

Collapse of a brick wall through shear alone was unlikely though shear, or the sliding of one course of bricks on top of another, might well be the indication of danger from some other factor. While structural designers and bricklayers took care to tie bricks together through bonding there was very rarely any attempt to break the horizontal joints which ran through a brick wall at every course. It was always assumed that the bedding mortar could not be expected to act as a glue sticking bricks to each other, though in practice the mortar might contribute a great deal to the stability of a wall. Exceptionally, vertical or horizontal reinforcement of a wall with steel bars or wrought-iron hoops was provided, but even then the reinforcement was not primarily intended to prevent sliding. In practice, collapse through shear action would accompany some other failure rather than be a cause on its own.

Buckling or sideways collapse in either the vertical or horizontal plane might come from excessive live or dead loading or from wind pressure and suction. In either case the tendency to collapse could best

below left
13. Part of Georgian brick wall at Orford, Suffolk. Showing Flemish Bond with closers and double headers, Header Bond in the blind windows, gauged brick flat arch, simple projecting plat band, S-shaped tie plate.

below right
14. Crinkle-crankle wall, half a brick thick, at Easton Park, Suffolk.

be countered by providing adequate buttressing. In the horizontal plane there might be external buttresses dividing the wall into short stretches, or internal partitions, tied into an external wall and acting with flanking walls to divide up a long wall into short sections. In the vertical plane the live loads and dead loads on floor beams, or on the beams which were part of roof trusses, would ensure that each vertical stretch of wall was divided into sections, each tied into the depth of the building. A tall building might also be designed so that extra stability came from thickening the sections of walls which might become overloaded. Where such thickening or buttressing or tying was difficult to achieve, as for instance in the triangular gable at the head of a brick wall, then extra precautions had to be taken: the purlins of heavy roof construction would be built into the gable walls, tying them back to the trusses and the whole frame of the roof; or a system of tie plates linked tightly together by means of wrought-iron rods tightened by a turn-buckle would be threaded through the floors or the attics (13). The tie plates were often quite decorative and used to build up a pattern or spell out the initials of the owner or date of construction. The crinkle-crankle wall was an unorthodox but effective way of giving stability to brick boundary walls. Instead of breaking up the length of the wall into sections regularly buttressed, the wall was built so as to snake gently but adequately on plan. The wall thus buttressed itself, and brick walls only 4½ ins thick have been built on this principle to great lengths (14).

All these structural precautions against collapse assumed that the bricks of the wall acted properly together, that the wall acted as brickwork rather than as a collection of individual bricks. Cohesion depended on proper bonding, adequate bedding on mortar, and, sometimes, on the use of bonding timbers to help provide horizontal reinforcement. In many ways a brick wall acts like a stone wall, and in some parts of the country a bricklayer is still called a brick mason just as brickwork was often linked with masonry in the chapter headings of old textbooks. But brick walls are generally much lighter than stone walls, gaining stability from the more efficient interlocking of small components through proper bonding of adequately fired bricks. Brick walling was probably at its most vulnerable during the changeover period when brickwork was superseding timber-framing with its own interlocking of members effective both in compression and tension through triangulation and scientific jointing. It was during this period that brick walls were sometimes left to stand alone without being tied into the rest of the structure. The effectiveness of structural brickwork may be seen in pictures of wartime bombing when tall walls or piers of brickwork remained upright even when timber floors and roof beams had been burnt away. Or in pictures of road accidents, where a runaway lorry might demolish part of the wall of a corner shop but the rest stood apparently undisturbed.

Over the past twenty or thirty years scientific brickwork design has led to three types of structural brickwork being added to the traditional variety. One is reinforced brickwork, used from time to time in the late nineteenth and early twentieth centuries, but now benefiting from more realistic calculations on the interaction between bricks and reinforcement. Another is calculated brickwork, whereby tall buildings may be constructed of brickwork to constant dimensions, but with scientifically calculated strengths of bricks and mortar. The third is diaphragm walling which develops buttressing to give long lengths of thick but hollow walls of thin brick diaphragms. Whether in traditional mode, as part of scientific brick design or used in combination with frames of other materials, brickwork has great structural versatility.

Bricklaying

Assuming that the structural design of the brick building is adequate, that foundations are good, that bricks of sound quality are used and that

15. Diagram. Bricklayers' tools.

above left
16. St Nicholas, King's Lynn, Norfolk: rebuilt as a 'hall church' about 1419 with much of the walling in 'structural brickwork' of bricks rendered and lined to imitate masonry.

above right
17. Window surround in part cut and rubbed and part moulded brickwork; fine joints contrast with regular brickwork. Tyttenhanger, Hertfordshire.

due precautions have been taken against vertical or horizontal collapse, the effectiveness of the structural design nevertheless depends on the craftsmanship of the bricklayer and his team.

Conventionally the bricklayer had to select the bricks, allowing for variations in colour, size and shape, lay them vertically and to a level horizontally, neatly finish them at all corners, projections, junctions and apertures and ensure in the use of his mortar that every brick was satisfactorily bedded down with all the other bricks. His practical skills had to be matched with aesthetic sensitivity so as to ensure, for instance, that all vertical joints were ranged with all other vertical joints and that all joint widths related to the demands of the design and the dimensions of the bricks. Apart from using his trowel to drop and trim the mortar the bricklayer had to be able to use his level and plumb rule for horizontal bedding and vertical alignment, his axe for cutting bricks to fit and his Frenchman and other tools for pleasingly finished mortar joints. Brickwork of special complication or special quality might require other tools and greater skill as, for instance, in producing a gauged-brick flat arch out of soft rubber bricks finely brought to shape with the aid of axe and rubbing brick (15). Fine brickwork required fine jointing with special mortars and this more accurate work had to be merged with ordinary brickwork to produce the convincing pieces of brick wall which can so delight our eyes (17,18).

Bricklayers were not necessarily operating at the same levels of skill all the time. In a Georgian town house, for instance, the below-ground work, partition and party walls were often left to the least skilled bricklayers using the poorest quality bricks and mortar on work not

18. Decorative panel of brick relief sculpture, Bruton Place, London W1.

meant to be seen, while the most skilled bricklayers concentrated on producing the finest effects on the visible outer face of the front wall. In such circumstances the more careful and more expensive bricklayer would be laying selected bricks of the best quality and most consistent dimensions as an outer skin against a wall of ordinary bricks, perhaps of irregular shape, and laid on thick mortar joints. In such cases it was impossible to line up all the horizontal joints through the thickness of the wall and so the outer skin was only tied back occasionally as a header was built into the outer skin, the remaining headers being bats or half bricks cut as snapped headers by the bricklayer on the site. This technique meant that the outer skin contributed little or nothing to the stability of the whole wall and could itself collapse through buckling outwards. The practice was roundly condemned but still widely used and the fine frontages of our Georgian terraces in London and provincial towns often prove to survive through the undeserved success of such botched construction.

The rate at which the bricklayer and his labourer were expected to lay bricks depended on the complexity of the work as well as the skill and dedication of the team. Batty Langley, writing in 1749, expected that a bricklayer and his mate would lay 1000 bricks in ordinary walling in the standard summer working day of twelve hours from 6 a.m. to 6 p.m. In concealed brickwork, as in foundations and party walls, the two should be able to lay 1500 bricks 'and not overheat themselves'. For front walls in which four courses rise eleven inches 'a tolerable good bricklayer without hurry or driving would lay 500 bricks in a day—which is about one brick per minute—with great neatness'. Even that rate would be reduced if jointing and pointing of special quality was required. As the proportion of common brickwork hidden by plaster declined and that of facing brickwork increased so the expected rate of bricklaying diminished. Nowadays, of course, the twelve-hour working day is no longer normal though it might well be worked in special circumstances.

Bonding

Bonding consists of the arrangement of bricks in a pattern for constructional and aesthetic purposes. In early brickwork bricks were laid in rather a haphazard manner and seem to have depended more on the benefits of mortar than we would nowadays accept as wise. It is really essential for the stability of the wall that its bricks are properly bonded. If a wall were built of two adjacent skins of bricks making a width of nine inches, it would tend to collapse as the inner and outer skins moved away, under load, from the continuous vertical joint between them. A 9-in wall with header bricks crossing from skin to skin, bonding them together, would be correspondingly stable. In a way the greater the proportion of headers the more stable the wall; certainly the longer the continuous vertical joints in the wall are, the weaker it is assumed to be. At the same time a wall with vertical joints running right through the brickwork, like a series of piers butted against each other, would be weak since no pier would be giving support to any other pier. Thus bricks have to have staggered vertical joints in one plane as well as being crossed in the other plane; bonding achieves this and gives stability. As bonding developed from its inadequate medieval beginnings, so the aesthetic as well as the practical benefits became clearer.

One early bond was English Bond with its alternate courses of header

19. English Bond with flared headers; rough brick segmental arches, dentilation under the eaves. Cuttmill, Cuxham, Oxfordshire.

20. English Bond, Burton
Agnes Hall, Yorkshire, ER.

and stretcher bricks (19, 20). This was a very strong bond, lacking any continuous vertical joint in any part of the brickwork. The main variation of English Bond was English Cross Bond where each alternate stretcher course was moved over half a brick. The staggered, network effect was much favoured on the Continent, and in Belgium, Holland and northern France it was very popular and remains so. In this country English Cross Bond (52) is not often found except in sixteenth-century buildings erected under continental influence, such as Bachegraig in Clwyd. The main development was, in fact, English Garden-Wall Bond with several courses of stretchers between the header courses. This would in theory weaken the wall but the commonly found three or five stretcher courses do not seem to have made any obvious difference. There is no doubt that true English Bond was considered the strongest and most decorative and so would be used, say, in a railway viaduct as well as in the exposed walls of a railway station, but side and rear walls of the station buildings as well as non-structural boundary walls might well be built in the cheaper Garden-Wall Bond.

After its flourish in the medieval period and up to the early seventeenth century English Bond passed out of general use until revived in the nineteenth century for structural purposes and because its appearance matched the Gothic Revival buildings on which it was used.

English Bond was succeeded in the early seventeenth century by Flemish Bond (21) which has alternate header and stretcher bricks in each course. A tendency towards Flemish Bond may be seen in some sixteenth-century brickwork, such as the brick towers and porches which were being added to older churches in Essex (22). Every now and

21. Flemish Bond, house at Shere, Surrey.

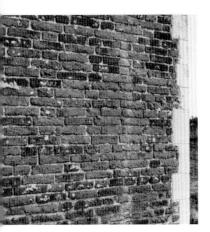

22. Flemish Stretcher Bond with one stretcher course between the alternate header and stretcher courses. St Michael, Woodham Walter, Essex.

then a course of alternating headers and stretchers is apparent. The regular use of this pattern in every course, however, is assumed to have been seen first in the Dutch House (Kew Palace) in Kew Gardens, built in 1631.

The origin of Flemish Bond and its name is unclear. It is not a bond characteristic of Flanders or adjacent parts of France or Holland, though it was known in medieval buildings in the Low Countries. A likely source is Poland, where Flemish Bond has a very long history. In fact what we call Flemish Bond the Germans call 'Pölnischer Verband', i.e., Polish Bond. Presumably the use of this bond in Poland spread to Baltic ports and so by way of trade routes to England. Just why it suddenly appeared in regular form and swept across the country with the spread of brickwork generally, and Dutch-type detailing in particular, during the later seventeenth century is not yet clear.

Flemish Bond became the fashionable bond for all decorative brickwork from end to end of the country from the middle of the seventeenth century until challenged, but not overwhelmed, by the return of English Bond nearly two centuries later. Flemish Bond is not quite as strong as English Bond as there are some joints in the middle of the wall which run uninterruptedly from top to bottom; on the other hand it is strong enough for most purposes and was regarded as more easy on the eye than the more boldly-layered English Bond. There are acres of Flemish Bond brickwork in the terraced houses of London, for instance, even if some of it is a false facing to the structural wall.

Cheaper versions of Flemish Bond introduced either more stretchers between the headers or more courses of stretchers between the true Flemish courses of alternating headers and stretchers. The former version included Monk Bond, with two stretchers between each pair of headers, and Sussex Bond, with three stretchers between each pair. The latter version, usually known as Flemish Stretcher Bond, might have as few as one stretcher course, but two, three or four courses were more common between the Flemish courses; it was cheaper to lay than Flemish, Monk or Sussex Bond. All these variations were used in boundary walls as well as for buildings while the variations were used on side and rear walls when true Flemish Bond was used on the fronts of buildings (22).

A third member of the family of brickwork bonds was Header Bond (13). This consisted of headers only and was used for decorative purposes even though the bond was structurally very strong. It was employed mainly for domestic buildings and is found most commonly in the South of England, especially in such counties as Berkshire and Hampshire. It was, of course, slower, more difficult and more expensive to lay bricks in Header Bond than in any other and the bond was correspondingly ostentatious. Sometimes the bond was confined to a panel or to a curved wall (where it made some constructional sense) but usually the bond was used in the front wall to a house when the remainder was in some other bond. After almost entirely passing out of use in the early nineteenth century Header Bond was resurrected fifty or

23. Stretcher Bond,
Brocklesby, Lincolnshire.

so years later in conjunction with cavity walling, when the Header Bond leaf was made out of snapped headers. The effect was relieved, from a decorative point of view, by the use of stretcher courses in some instances, at about every fourth course.

The fourth bond, which came into use in the later nineteenth century and which has now become the almost invariable choice, at least for cavity walling, is Stretcher Bond (23). In fact some utilitarian walling was done in the medieval period in Stretcher Bond with the occasional header here and there. Walls faced entirely with Stretcher Bond have to be tied back in some way to a backing wall or the inner leaf of a cavity wall. Stretcher Bond is by far the most monotonous bond ever used, and one regrets that considerations of architectural morality prevent the architects of the present day from introducing the snap headers which their predecessors used unhesitatingly to relieve the monotony.

There are also certain non-structural bonds used in bricknogging where the brick panels fill in spaces between structural members of some other material, usually timber in the past and concrete at the present day. Thus bricks may be laid diagonally, in herringbone fashion, in vertical lines as Stack Bond, or in alternate blocks of horizontal and vertical work as in basket-weave brickwork. Bricks were also bonded with other materials to help provide stability or to help with

24. Brick and chalk chequerboard work, Stockton, Wiltshire.

25. Rat-Trap Bond, Alton, Hampshire.

corners and openings. Brick lacing courses to flint work are often to be seen providing horizontal reinforcement while bricks block-bonded to the flints give neat surrounds to door and window openings. Bricks may also be introduced to flint walls to give a decorative chequerboard effect (24,26).

A further variation lay where some orthodox bond was used with some or all of the bricks laid on edge rather than on bed. The most popular version was Rat-Trap Bond (also called Silverlock's or Chinese Bond) which arranged the bricks as in Flemish Bond but on edge (25). Rather less popular were versions of Monk Bond and Sussex Bond, again with bricks on edge rather than on bed (27). In Dearne's Bond there was a simulation of English Bond, but with a course of headers laid on bed alternating with a course of stretchers laid on edge. All these bonds saved on bricks, mortar and bricklayer's time and also provided some degree of heat insulation, though this was at the expense of some loss of stability. Throughout their period of use in the late eighteenth and early nineteenth centuries they were regarded as inferior to regular brickwork and their use was confined to cottages, outbuildings and boundary walls (28), as noted in Special Topic 2.

26. Brick lacing courses and dressings to flint wall, Chesham, Buckinghamshire.

27. Rat-Trap Bond, Sussex Bond version, Farnham, Surrey.

Hidden within the thick walls of tall buildings and some engineering works are further complications of bonding. Conventional bonding of walls two bricks or more thick could lead to an inadequate tie between inner and outer faces, especially if unsupervised bricklayers skimped on the hidden work. One improvement was to have the interior of the very thick wall filled with bricks laid diagonally but in different directions in each alternate course. This, combined properly with outer and inner facings, could produce a very strong wall. It is always interesting to look (from a safe position) at exposed brickwork when buildings are under demolition or alteration.

Bonding was inevitably modified as corners, projections, recesses and openings interrupted the run of any particular bond. Closers were used at such breaks to bring the bond to a neat termination. The bonding of Georgian buildings had to take account of the change of dimension, colour and jointing of rubbed bricks or superior facing bricks used around openings or as decorative elements such as pilasters. A change of bond was sometimes unavoidable, especially in a wall of Flemish Bond, and a couple of headers or a couple of stretchers would be introduced to make up the dimensions required. Some bricklayers

28. Rat-Trap Bond used on two-storey cottages at Bengeo, Hertfordshire.

were able to make patterns from these corrections, giving a vertical relief to the horizontal emphasis which is one of the characteristics of all brickwork.

Openings

Openings in brickwork affected the bonding but introduced a different technique in the assembly of brickwork. In early walling a window or door-head would normally be of stone or in voussoirs of cut brick. In the later medieval period moulded brick sections came into use and the head of a door or window would have an approximation in brick (or occasionally in terracotta) of the conventional masonry details. From the early seventeenth century onwards brick versions of classical details done in moulded or gauged brickwork were fashionable. Segmental, half-oval, cambered and 'flat' arches were used for the visible brick opening though there was usually a timber lintel behind to carry most of the load (12).

During the Georgian and early Victorian periods the most common door and window heads consisted of flat arches which were, in fact, slightly cambered on the underside. Rubber bricks were specially made up to voussoir shape, but finished on site so as to fit snugly together. The joints needed the minimum of mortar and that might simply be a lime putty; nicks in the length of the rubbers indicated the position to be expected for joints across the length and they, too, were filled with lime putty in imitation of mortar joints (13, 31).

Throughout these periods rough arches were also made out of ordinary bricks, roughly cut to shape or relying on tapered mortar joints to achieve the required shape. Stone remained in use. Terracotta

29. Date of 1722 scratched on brick, Great Meeting House, Hinckley, Leicestershire.

returned for use in decorative heads to openings. For cheap and utilitarian work, as in cottages and farm buildings, courses of bricks were supported on thin timber lintels or directly on stout door and window frames.

Polychrome

Colour in brickwork derives from the colours of the bricks themselves, the colour of the mortar and any applied colour. The appreciation of the colour of brickwork by the observer often changes from the distant view, when all items merge in one colour, to the close-up view when colours of individual bricks separate themselves from the colour of the mortar and from each other. Colour also changes over time with the weathering of bricks and the growth of lichens on the surface.

30. Brick arch, probably using special bricks to arch, jambs and sill, Gainsborough Old Hall, Lincolnshire.

The earliest use of coloured pattern in brickwork in Britain probably lies in the diapering which was popular from the early medieval period until the seventeenth century and was restored to fashion as part of the Gothic Revival in architecture during the nineteenth century. Diaper patterns usually took the diamond shape after which they were named but hearts, saltire crosses, zigzags and many other patterns were sometimes used. The patterns were formed as the bricklayer incorporated flared or vitrified headers into his bonding pattern. Firing in clamp and kiln produced a proportion of bricks whose ends were overburnt to a deep blue colour, or which had a grey-blue finish through exposure to wood smoke, or which were vitrified through excessive heat. Sometimes glazed headers were produced through introducing salt during firing. The bricks were sorted at the clamp on the site or from the kiln in the brickyard so that the bricklayer would always be able to begin a diaper pattern for decorative purposes or simply to use up the headers. However, the proportion of headers flared or vitrified would vary from firing to firing. Some buildings show that diaper patterns once begun could not always be sustained. Evidence is beginning to accumulate suggesting that ordinary headers were painted to complete a diaper pattern and that sometimes whole brick walls were painted to look like patterned brick walls! During the nineteenth century, of course, as blue bricks became available, so consistent and geometrically perfect diaper patterns could be contrived by the architect and specified for creation by the bricklayer.

As diaper patterns died out they were succeeded by the plainer, less inventive, and generally less decorative patterns christened by Alec Clifton-Taylor the 'Georgian Diaper'. The simplest and most common used flared headers and ordinary red bricks together in Flemish Bond. This gave a simple, steady pattern to a whole elevation. These patterns might also be used in conjunction with the colour contrast which came from the use of red or orange rubbed bricks to make quoins, window-heads, plat bands and other brick versions of dressings or architectural ornaments.

However, the great age of polychromatic brickwork was the Victorian. Polychrome resulted from the combination of two movements: one was the restoration to favour of exposed brickwork after the Regency period, when stucco was popular and the alternative to masonry was utilitarian brickwork (sometimes of poor quality) stuccoed and lined-out in imitation of masonry; the other was the desire to follow Italian Gothic precedent in polychromatic work whatever the building material.

Ruskin gave his approval to the use of exposed brickwork as an alternative to stone, referring to the Lamp of Truth in *The Seven Lamps of Architecture* and accepting that brick was a moulded material; it did not pretend to be other than a moulded material. It could be used with stone or in its own variations to reproduce the effects of the Italian Gothic including the polychromatic. *The Ecclesiologist*, having condemned brick as a material for church building, realised, after noting the wonderful brick Gothic churches such as Albi Cathedral in France, built between 1282 and 1480, that brick self-coloured or polychrome was appropriate enough.

William Butterfield combined polychromy and brickwork in his influential church of All Saints, Margaret Street, London (160). Even through the grime accumulated since work began in 1849 the visitor cannot fail to be overwhelmed by the vigour, thoughtfulness and originality of the colour inside and out. Butterfield's lead in the combination of red brick, yellow brick, blue brick and yellow stone at All Saints, Margaret Street, was followed by G. E. Street in such brick churches as St James the Less, Pimlico, by Waterhouse in his King's Weigh House Congregational Chapel of 1889 and by Pearson in the huge St Augustine, Kilburn. Their example in these London churches was followed from end to end of Britain.

Few brick buildings of the Gothic Revival were without an alternation of blue and red, or yellow and red, bricks in window arches. Many used blue, red and yellow or white bricks in stripes, chequerboard and diaper patterns inside and out. During this period of the second half of the nineteenth century brickworks could produce bricks of different colours but consistent quality almost at will, and quantities small or large could be transported by rail; thus Staffordshire Blues could appear as part of polychromatic work in East Anglia or Yorkshire as well as in London and in Staffordshire itself. The design was that of the architect but the execution depended on the skill of the bricklayer in interpretation.

Polychromatic work spread from top to bottom of the architectural range. Warehouses, railway stations, churches, mansions, law courts, office buildings, hotels showed the full range of polychromy. But terraces of workers' houses, pubs and shops, farm buildings and workshops also showed how simple devices, using the structural material to emphasise the architectural design, could create brickwork at its most vital if not necessarily at its most agreeable.

Mortar, jointing and pointing

Like stones, bricks had to be bedded properly if they were to make a stable wall. Early bricks were like most stones in that they were rather irregular in shape: twisted, bowed, marred by cracks and deeper fissures; they had to be bedded in deep joints of mortar not so much that they might be stuck together as if by adhesive, but more that one might bear adequately on another.

Simple masonry has traditionally been bedded in clay. This material is of course susceptible to leaching away at the surface under the attack of rainwater. A thick stone wall could survive the loss of some bedding material at the surface but a relatively thin brick wall had not that flexibility. It was important therefore that the bedding material should come to the surface of the brickwork and resist the rain. At the same time the jointing material played some part in the decorative appearance of the brickwork; its outer surface was therefore sometimes given a 'pointing' to improve appearance or was 'repointed' to replace what had weathered away. We have thus to consider the jointing material, its constituents, preparation and use, the pointing in bedding or additional mortar, and the repointing where necessary.

Traditionally, mortar was made of a mixture of lime and sand with water. The lime used in the mortar was prepared through slaking in water the quicklime which resulted from burning limestone or chalk in a kiln. Ordinary lime mortar sets relatively slowly and so helps in gradually consolidating a brick wall. Later, cement was included as an addition to or substitute for the lime. Hydraulic lime, made from special limestone, sets more quickly and is more resistant to water. Sand should be clean, sharp and well graded from fine to coarse, should come from a pit rather than the sea-shore, and should not contain dirt or silt or any vegetable matter. Early brick mortars had a high proportion of lime: one part of lime to one and a half of sand; but later a proportion of one part of lime to three of sand became more common.

During the eighteenth century various attempts were made to produce a cementing material more satisfactory than lime. Parker's Cement, of 1796, also called Roman Cement, was made by burning lumps of natural septaria at a temperature of 1100°C and grinding the result into powder. Portland Cement was invented in 1824 and is stronger than lime when used in mortar. The usual mixture is one part cement to three of sand. However, pure cement mortar is usually considered too strong for all but the densest bricks and other mixes were used: 'compo', for instance, consisted of one part cement to two or three parts lime and nine to twelve parts sand; it is stronger than lime mortar but sets more quickly; it is more open-textured than cement mortar.

During the nineteenth century various attempts were made to match the strength and colour of mortar to the hard, dense, red or blue bricks which were so popular. One form of black mortar consisted of one part lime to three parts of ground ashes or ground clinker. Another consisted of a mixture of lime with black moulding sand from the foundry or blacksmith's shop. Iron filings and scale from the foundry were also added in the belief that greater strength would result.

The purest mortar, used for instance with gauged brickwork, was called lime putty. It consisted of slaked lime to which a little extra water had been added. After the evaporation of this extra water lime putty remained, brilliant white in colour.

There are various ways in which the mortar was traditionally finished on the surface. This applies to the bedding mortar or to any pointing mortar extending the bedding mortar to the surface. The earliest technique and one still used was to finish the mortar flush with the surface of the bricks. With very uneven bricks, this can make the joint seem too wide, as the mortar slobbers onto the surface, so a flush joint was often wiped down with a piece of rag (29). Another technique was to consolidate the flush surface by pushing a bucket handle into the joint to give a neat concave effect. Nowadays bricklayers like to consolidate the surface by pushing in the trowel to give a weathered effect or, if working overhand from scaffolding inside a building, to give a struck effect, pushing in the bottom of the mortar. A beaked finish set the mortar slightly back from the brickwork arrises and gave a neat appearance from highlight and shadow. The penny-struck joint had a line scored into the mortar with a coin or similar object. Recessed joints have been popular from time to time recently, but are not traditional, and may give problems with frost action or water penetration. Another variation in pointing, found sometimes in parts of the South of England, such as Surrey, is 'galleting' in which chips of flint or small pebbles were pushed into the damp mortar; the finished result can be rather bizarre.

Probably the most interesting of the pointing techniques is tuck pointing (originally called tuck and pat work). This was intended to give the appearance of fine-jointed gauged brickwork to ordinary bricks

31. Flemish Bond brickwork, tuck pointing, Coade stone dressings to doorway, Bedford Square, London WC1.

(31). The procedure was to lay the bricks in a bedding mortar and rake out the surface as if for a recessed joint. A special pointing mortar was made up of brick dust, as well as lime and sand, so as to give a colour as close as possible to the brick colour. This was finished to give a flush joint. While the pointing mortar was still damp a groove was put in to make a pattern of horizontal and vertical joints. This was then filled with lime putty which was pressed against a rule to give a sharp line. The wall then had the appearance of uniform brickwork with a thin, precise network of joints. Vertical joints were usually slightly thinner than horizontal joints. Since the pattern was all-important the lime-putty lines did not always coincide with the vertical joints in the actual brickwork. In London, where blackened brick surfaces had a phase of popularity (as in parts of Bloomsbury), the lines were in blackened mortar. Tuck pointing seems to have come into use in the early eighteenth century and remained popular until the early twentieth century. It is a technique well represented in London and generally is confined to towns. It was taken by British bricklayers to the colonies and was widely used in brick buildings in Australian towns, for instance.

Bastard tuck pointing is the name given to the formation of a projecting joint cut against a straight edge from an ordinary pointing mortar coloured to resemble the brickwork.

Most lime mortar is very weather-resistant but some was found liable to decay. Ideally the mortar should weather at the same rate as the brickwork. If deterioration has been serious and water is passing through the joints then repointing would be necessary: this job is easy to do badly but difficult to do well. The jointing mortar should be raked out by hand to a depth equal to the width of the joint; the pointing mortar should then be applied to give a finish similar to what appears to have been intended. This is difficult to achieve and all too often a crude weather finish is given to an excessive amount of cement mortar, the bricks to be saved being lost in it.

Bricknogging

Although we are mainly concerned with solid load-bearing brickwork there are other related techniques which are of interest such as brick-nogging.

Bricknogging is the term given to the use of brickwork in panels of frame construction, usually timber-frame construction. Bricknogging may be found in the outer walls of a building or in partition walls. Bricknogging may be an original feature or a replacement for an earlier infill material. The use of 'wall-tyle', a ceramic slab-like material, as an infill to timber-frame panels, especially tall narrow panels, is long-standing; early medieval examples have been found in York, for instance. Bricknogging, however, is rather different as it implies the use of ordinary bricks within the framing members.

J. McCann has shown that bricknogging is in fact an old-established practice and he has quoted a number of instances, mostly from Essex, from the late fifteenth and sixteenth centuries. Examples from the seventeenth century onwards are more numerous. The normal infill was wattle and daub and this had the advantage of flexibility, but gave poor heat insulation and was vulnerable to the weather and to attack by rodents. The colour contrast between the panel and frame, whether black and white or not, was decorative. The use of brick rather than wattle and daub gave the choice of exposed decorative pattern or plastering; gave potentially greater weather-resistance, less need for regular maintenance or replacement, and more security against burglary or infestation. McCann considers that the technique was part of the enthusiasm of the fifteenth century for patterning and declined at the higher social levels as this fashion changed in the late sixteenth century, the technique, nevertheless, moving with popular taste to vernacular buildings in the late sixteenth and seventeenth centuries.

Where bricknogging was intended it was essential to have studs deep enough to receive the bricks so that they were flush or very slightly set back from the surface of the timber. It was then necessary to provide recesses in the studs to receive the mortar. Bricknogging is found most commonly in Essex and East Anglia where narrow panels were traditional. Common brick patterns included diagonal bedding in alternate panels or in the same rather wider panel, or in a herringbone pattern, or in a sort of basket-weave of alternate horizontal and vertical coursing. Another popular pattern was the use of opposed triangles of brickwork.

4. Brick tiles and terracotta

Brick tiles (Mathematical tiles)

Brick tiles, also known as mathematical tiles, are clay tiles specially shaped so that they can be hung vertically on new or existing walls of various materials, but give the appearance of brickwork. They were introduced early in the eighteenth century, their use flourished for the rest of that century and much of the nineteenth but they were then abandoned, except for a brief reintroduction for special purposes in the mid-twentieth century. They were used mostly on small domestic buildings in the towns of south-eastern England, but they have also been used on large country houses and in other parts of lowland England. At one time thought to be a cheap substitute for bricks during the period of the Brick Tax, they are now recognised as a sophisticated and quite expensive way of meeting the demands of fashion when exposed high-quality brickwork was favoured. They were also regarded as unusually weatherproof. Their twin virtues were well summarised by Loudon: 'The walls of cottages may be protected and ornamented by mathematical tiling.'

The standard brick tile has a tapered cross-section, with the lower part moulded to resemble the header or stretcher face of a brick and the upper part resembling a roofing tile. Courses of brick tiles fitted into each other and the joints were pointed to resemble brickwork. There were subtle variations in cross-section and the brick-like exposure varied somewhat in dimensions, but the same general form was followed. Sometimes brick tiles were scored or grooved during moulding so that they could be cut on site to make headers or closers, but generally the header tiles were specially made. Corner tiles were available to help maintain the appearance of a solid wall at the corners or at window reveals, but they were not used very often.

Most brick tiles were burnt to produce a red colour matching the colour of bricks in the locality, but white and pale yellow brick tiles were made and used at quoins and as window dressings, matching the corresponding details in brickwork. Glazed black or deep blue tiles were also made and were especially popular in Lewes and Brighton.

Generally the brick tiles were bedded in mortar which had been applied to butt-edged boarding used as a sheathing to timber-frame construction. Often, and especially in later examples, holes were provided in the upper parts of the tiles, corresponding to peg-holes in roofing tiles, so that individual tiles or rows of tiles could be nailed to the boarding. On occasion tiles were nailed to battens, and modern tiles for new or replacement work sometimes have nibs so that they can be hung

32. Mathematical tile (brick tile) dated 1724 (discovered by Miss Joan Harding FSA). The Malthouse, Westcott, Surrey.

33. Mathematical tiling (brick tiling) used as cladding in a prefabricated school construction, Bramhall, Cheshire.

on the battens. Tiles were even applied by one or other of these techniques to solid walls of brick, flint or stone which it was desired to protect or modernise. Usually only the front wall of a building was finished in brick tiles, the sides and rear being clad in hung roofing tiles or left with structural walls exposed. In these circumstances the brick tiles would be stopped against a wooden fillet. The same device was usually employed at the door and window openings. Window frames were usually close to the wall surface, at least in the timber-framed buildings, and shallow reveals were finished in wood. Brick tiles were often run over the window head, but sometimes specially shaped tiles were arranged to imitate gauged brick voussoirs at the window and door heads. Usually the tiles were placed uniformly over the main façade of a building, but sometimes they were mixed with other materials: cladding the storeys above a brick ground floor wall, for instance, or the projecting surface of a bay or oriel window when the main wall surface was of brick. Very occasionally English Bond was simulated, sometimes Stretcher Bond, but Flemish Bond was most commonly to be seen, though in Lewes and Brighton, in Sussex, Header Bond was more popular.

Brick tiles have been found on several building types, but generally they were employed on small and medium-sized domestic buildings in the towns. However, they were used in the countryside and the earliest dated tile was found in a house called The Malthouse in Westcott, a Surrey village. They were also utilised on some large country houses, either as the main visible cladding material as at Althorp in Northamptonshire, or hidden in a light-well as at Penrhyn Castle in North Wales. Many towns of Kent (34) and Sussex are almost crowded with buildings faced in brick tiles: use in Lewes was especially prolific. In that town also may be found the Jireh Chapel of 1805, a plain but carefully designed timber-framed box entirely clad in red brick tiles. At a recent count there were over 900 examples known to have existed, about 400 each in the two counties of Kent and Sussex with barely a tenth of these figures in each of Surrey, Hampshire and Wiltshire and a handful in such counties as Essex, Suffolk, Norfolk and Cambridgeshire. Other parts of the country where timber-framed buildings were common, such as the West Midlands, have produced hardly a single example in spite of careful investigation. Some cities such as York, full of timber-framed buildings, have yet to reveal any brick tiles in spite of the intensive work of the Royal Commission on Historical Monuments.

As already mentioned, the earliest known instance of the use of brick tiles is at The Malthouse, Westcott, Surrey where a medieval timber-framed house was clad in brick tiles one of which had the initials M F and the date 1724 scratched in its surface (32). A date of 1725 has been given for the introduction of brick tiles in Kent, though not linked to a surviving example. The first known use of the term 'mathematical tile' was by Sir John Soane on 23rd March 1799 in reference to prices of such tiles. They had been used by Henry Holland at a house in Sloane Place,

34. Mathematical tiling (brick tiling) in Flemish Bond, Tenterden, Kent.

Chelsea (now demolished) in 1777–8 under the name 'weather tyle'. The tiles said to have been used in the porch at St Leonard, Deal, Kent, are not now accepted as brick tiles, though some cladding material formerly existing at St Peter, Bekesbourne, Kent, may have been early brick tiles. Among the large country houses may be mentioned Chevening Park in Kent, clad in brick tiles as part of building operations between 1786–1796 by James Wyatt, but the tiles were removed in 1970, reputedly much to the improvement of the appearance of this red brick house. At Althorp Park the house was clad in brick tiles in Header Bond by Henry Holland in building campaigns of 1786–1790; Belmont, near Faversham in Kent, was built in 1792 to the designs of Samuel Wyatt and clad in pale yellow brick tiles. The buildings making up the Royal Crescent in Brighton in 1799–1807 were built of brick, but covered in black glazed brick tiles in Header Bond. A red brick house in Winchester of 1673 was clad on the front elevation (but not on the equally prominent side elevation) about 1783 in English Bond brick tiles; it has recently been restored. Among smaller buildings, Lamb House in Rye dates from 1755, a cottage in Farnham, Surrey, bears a date of 1757, two more houses in Rye have been quoted as of 1817 and 1819, while houses infilling a site in Lewes date from 1825 and have black glazed brick tiles. The technique seems to have died out in the second half of the nineteenth century. It was briefly resurrected in the 1950s when brick tiles were manufactured as a cladding material for the light-weight framed-construction schools of the CLASP system (33).

Brick tiles gave the appearance of brickwork but their use raises the two questions of why brickwork should be simulated rather than other building materials and why bricks themselves could not be used and had to be imitated. There is no doubt that during the Georgian period brickwork was fashionable throughout lowland Britain and especially in the towns. Timber-frame and all but the best-quality masonry was out of fashion and so it is hardly surprising that in south-eastern England, distant from good building stones and with a long tradition of wattle and daub infill to timber-frame construction, brickwork, real and imitation, should have been popular. Among the reasons for using brick tile rather than brick may be mentioned the convenience of using the material on jettied upper floors of older buildings which had been underbuilt on the ground floor with brick. In towns the use of tiles rather than bricks in providing a new face would minimise encroachment on the public street or market-place. On existing buildings of light or suspect structure, cladding in light-weight tiles rather than heavy brickwork was prudent. It has also been suggested that the proportions of carefully designed elevations would be better maintained with a cladding of thin tile than with a facing of heavier brickwork. Given the difficulty of attaching a thin skin of brickwork to an existing framed building, it has been calculated that it might even have been cheaper to clad in tiles rather than bricks. The use of tile cladding was in any case widespread in the South-East and brick tiles were really a special variation on the commonly used plain roofing tiles.

It seems that brick tiles were subject to the Brick Tax from its introduction in 1784 until all tiles were freed from tax in 1833. Although not mentioned by name, it is now accepted that brick tiles were covered by the general reference to tiles 'by whatever name or names such tiles now or hereafter may be called or known'. The rate of tax was rather higher than on most bricks, but as tiles were so much more expensive than even the best-quality bricks, the tax as a proportion of their cost was not high. Allowing for the tax the cost of cladding a façade in brick tile rather than 9-in brickwork might be rather less.

Brick tiles, or mathematical tiles, then, were used for fashion and utility. They had all the advantages of hung plain tiles in being weather-resistant and light-weight. They had all the advantages of brick in precision of line and surface and consistency of colour. Except when deliberately revealed on the sides of buildings they made an entirely convincing deception: only slipped tiles or sagging courses gave the technique away. The real mystery is not that they were used at all but rather that they were not used more often.

Terracotta

According to Nathaniel Lloyd, 'The line of demarcation between moulded brick and terracotta is an extremely fine one, so fine as often not to be discernible.' Certainly terracotta is moulded but its resemblance to brickwork is really rather less than Lloyd implied, since raw material, method of moulding, firing and incorporation in buildings are different from brickwork. Terracotta, or 'burnt pot earth', is made from extremely fine clay from which all impurities have been sieved out. This material of tile or even pottery quality is poured into a mould, made into a hollow block, then fired in a kiln to a very high temperature, at least 1000°C and normally rather more, before being considered for use in building.

The colour of terracotta varies with the raw material as well as through the method of manufacture, though most terracotta falls into a range between buff and red. The texture is usually smooth and tile-like though glazed terracotta has also been produced and has had its periods of popularity. In spite of the doubts expressed by a correspondent to *The Builder* in 1846, terracotta blocks have proved very durable as long as the baked surface has been maintained intact.

Terracotta has been used in this country in two main phases. The first was for a period of about fifty years from 1520 or rather earlier, the second for about seventy years from about 1844. There was an interlude of about seventy-five years in the late eighteenth and early nineteenth centuries when Coade stone, a variety of terracotta, was in use. There has also been an epilogue during the period between the two World Wars when glazed terracotta had many advocates.

In the first phase it is believed that Italian craftsmen were brought to this country to help introduce the 'antique' style of decoration to buildings. Shrubland Old Hall, near Coddenham, Suffolk, of about 1524 is an early example as is Great Cressingham Priory in Norfolk. It is believed that terracotta ornament was used in the English Pavilion at the Field of the Cloth of Gold at Calais in 1520. Terracotta was used to make mullions, transoms, and window surrounds in the main elevation as well as shell-like decorative battlements to the turrets at Layer Marney Towers about 1521. Glazed roundels of very high-quality

35. Terracotta work, Sutton Place, Surrey

terracotta work can be seen at Hampton Court Palace of the same date. The most extensive and elaborate terracotta work of this period is at Sutton Place in Surrey. Current research is suggesting that this might have been the work of native rather than immigrant craftsmen. Terracotta fragments have also been found in the remains of Nonsuch Palace, also built in Surrey and begun in 1538. In all these examples the terracotta work helped to introduce the 'antique' style of decoration to England; the architecture was still Gothic and the material was used in mullions and transoms, tracery and ornament, but the detail was of classical inspiration.

The building now called Old Hall Farm at Kneesall in Nottinghamshire is different. Located at a distance from the East Anglian and the Thames Valley groups of terracotta instances, here the work is strictly structural, undecorated and has no obvious relation to the work of these craftsmen. However, like the others, it is a piece of fashionable architecture, having been built as a hunting lodge for Sir John Hussey at some time between 1522 and 1536.

The use of terracotta, then, was short-lived, was related to the introduction of classical decoration rather than full Renaissance architecture into this country, and was associated with projects for rich and fashionable members of society in England.

The reintroduction of terracotta some 300 years later was heralded by the invention of Coade stone and its use during the Georgian period. The so-called 'Coade's Material' was first produced in Lyme Regis, but in 1768 Miss Coade established at Lambeth, in London, a factory 'for statues and every piece of architectural ornament'. The formula and method of manufacture was never made public and when production ended in the 1830s the secret went too. It is known that a sort of china clay was one constituent and that feldspar and quartz were involved while H. N. Blanchard, a former apprentice to the Coade family, worked for other firms later in the nineteenth century, but Coade stone as such was never reproduced.

Coade stone was never used as a complete structural material but as one from which architectural details could be reproduced; some of these were purely decorative roundels and panels, others were in imitation of masonry dressings for doors and windows. The process was very successful in reproducing sharp-edged ornament of classical inspiration, and so hard and weather-resistant is the material that nearly 200 years after its use the Coade stone panels at Heaton House, Manchester, by James Wyatt, 1772, were still thought to be painted cast iron. Coade stone dressings abound in Georgian London and may be seen, for instance, in the surrounds of the doorways in Bedford Square (31).

For the reintroduction of terracotta proper into architecture in England much of the credit should go to the Manchester architect Edmund Sharpe and his patron John Fletcher. Being accustomed to the manufacture of firebricks from the clay which was a by-product of his coal mining at Hollins Colliery near Bolton, Fletcher commissioned Sharpe in 1842 to build a church essentially out of the same durable material. The church of St Stephen and All Martyrs at Lever Bridge, near Bolton in Lancashire, was the result. It was of thorough-going Gothic design, full of terracotta imitations of Gothic masonry detailing, and exterior and interior down to font, organ case and bench-ends were of terracotta. The technique of terracotta manufacture had to be virtually reinvented and experiments in mixing, modelling, moulding, firing and fixing conducted until the procedure for making what were now hollow blocks had been perfected. So impressive was the work that Sharpe was invited by Thomas Worsley of Platt Hall, Manchester, to design another of his 'pot churches'. Holy Trinity, Platt Lane, Manchester was built in 1845–6 as a version of a Lincolnshire church of the fourteenth century, complete with a tall tower and spire. Again everything possible was made of terracotta, and the imitation tooling on the blocks together with the ostensibly carved ornament produces a most convincing result. After over 150 years of the Manchester atmosphere All Saints appears to be in remarkably good condition. However, Sharpe was diverted to other things and left the task of developing his work to others.

Terracotta seems to have been revived during the period from about 1870 to about 1914 partly as a substitute for building stone, which was becoming relatively scarce and expensive as many of the better beds in the quarries were worked out, and as the cost of labour for stone carving increased. The material was believed to be resistant to the air pollution which had been seen to attack masonry, for it was hoped that the smooth, impervious facing of terracotta blocks would be self-cleaning in the rain. Victorian economy saw in terracotta a cheap way of providing the architectural detail which enormous public buildings required inside and out. It was also regarded as a 'new' material, one which was in the spirit of the age and one which could combine in polychromy with brickwork itself.

During the Victorian period the manufacture of terracotta was perfected. The raw material was a carefully selected mixture of marl, ball clay, fireclay and 'grog' (that is, ground-up residue from previously fired terracotta mixes) and was allowed to weather for one or two seasons before use. The ingredients were then ground and sieved and mixed with water to improve plasticity and ensure that chemical action among the constituents had been completed. Sometimes the water treatment lasted months or years to make perfection of the material absolutely certain. Moulding took place in plaster of Paris moulds which had been made oversize to allow for a shrinkage of one inch in every twelve during firing. The moulds themselves were made according to special drawings carefully prepared to the architect's design details. Within the mould the hollow body, about 1–2 ins thick, was strengthened by clay fins creating compartments within the block. After shrinkage had begun the blocks were taken from the moulds; they were hand-finished and then allowed to dry at a constant temperature, being turned occasionally. Any glazing desired was then applied. The terracotta blocks were then fired in a downdraught intermittent kiln over a period from seven to fourteen days. Temperature was gradually raised to about 1200°C, when vitrification took place. Usually three versions of each block were made and fired to allow for failures.

One of the earliest major buildings in London to use terracotta was Dulwich College, designed by Charles Barry, the son of the famous designer of the Houses of Parliament. It was built between 1866 and 1870 and made use of terracotta blocks from the Blashfield firm. One of the best-known buildings employing terracotta is the Royal Albert Hall in London, designed by Captain Fowke and others, and built between 1867 and 1871. Here the material was supplied by one firm on one contract and the 80,000 blocks were transported from the Gibson Canning works at Tamworth.

The architect most closely associated with terracotta in the Victorian period was Alfred Waterhouse. He subscribed to the use of architectural polychromy advocated by Ruskin and developed by Street, as in the Law Courts in the Strand, and Butterfield, as in his church of All Saints in Margaret Street, London. He was a mature designer in brickwork of several colours and extravagant patterns. However, Waterhouse had a special reason for considering terracotta in his designs. His earliest major building was the Assize Courts in Manchester, begun in 1859, and its gritstone surface quickly suffered in the sooty Manchester atmosphere. Another of his gritstone buildings is Owens College (now the University of Manchester) begun in 1870, but when he was called to design the buildings for Liverpool University in 1877 he chose brick and terracotta. In a lecture in 1883 he advocated terracotta rather than stone because it was resistant to pollution and 'made from a clay found in the same pit as the coal which did the mischief it seems the only building material which can successfully withstand its corroding influence. In terracotta the fire will at once give us those beautiful accidental tints of which we might avail ourselves if we chose boldly to use them.'

Waterhouse had put the theory to the test in the Natural History Museum in London, of 1879–80, and continued with the Birmingham Victoria Law Courts, of 1887–91, and Girton College, Cambridge, of various dates from 1873. His most triumphant use of terracotta was in the series of buildings he designed for the Prudential Assurance Company, including its headquarters in Holborn, London, built in 1899–1906; all of them are very assertive now that they have been cleaned and stand as Waterhouse built them. Although the material was not quite as perfect as Waterhouse had hoped, the many buildings displaying terracotta inside and outside have dismissed the doubts expressed by the correspondent to *The Builder*, who in 1846 wrote, 'We are concerned that terracotta will not bear exposure and that use should therefore be confined to internal decoration.' (36)

Moulded brick and terracotta work were by no means confined to large and prestigious buildings. Just as coloured brickwork was a relatively cheap way of relieving the monotony of terraces of workers' housing, so terracotta was an equally economical way of giving accent to the door and window details of such houses. Whether plain or decorated, the terracotta blocks were a substitute for and acknowledgement of the stone details of traditional houses in the countryside. Firms like Edwards of Ruabon had provided the spiky chimney-pots; now they provided the robust detailing.

As the Edwardian period was drawing to a close architectural terracotta began to lose favour among the more fashionable architects. The emphasis had already moved from Gothic Revival detailing, for which the material was well suited, and through the Art Nouveau phase, for which it was also quite appropriate, into the Vernacular Revival development of the Queen Anne style. The natural materials and traditional detailing of Voysey were no more appropriate to terracotta than the grander but still countrified designs of Lutyens. At the same

opposite
36. Terracotta work, Refuge Assurance Building, Manchester

time some of the drawbacks of the material were becoming apparent. The very popularity of terracotta put too much pressure on the manufacturers, and skimpy preparation of the materials, over-elaborate moulding and inadequate firing told their tale. There was too much twisting of the blocks in the kiln, resulting in the use of excessively wide joints on the building. Because of wastage in the kiln and breakage on site, it was necessary to make duplicates and to fill the hollow blocks with concrete as they were assembled, and with the expense of the raw material itself, terracotta was by no means as cheap as had been expected. But it was also not self-cleaning. The sooty rain deposited its sticky blackness ever thicker over brick and terracotta alike, contrary to what had been expected.

There was a period when glazed terracotta was tried and the bronzed elevations of the Midland Hotel in Manchester, of 1898, provided a brave and once-unpopular monument to this technique. Fashion then turned to faience. The term has been loosely used but here is intended to mean glazed terracotta slabs. Each slab was solid, about one inch thick, and had a key pattern on the back; they were extruded or moulded. Faience slabs were twice fired; first the body was fired at a high temperature and then the body and glaze were fired together at a lower temperature. During the past twenty years or so it has proved possible to anneal and burn the clay and glaze in one firing at a high temperature, ensuring complete vitrification and a non-crazing finish. Faience slabs are not structural; they provide a facing to concrete, brickwork or breeze blocks. They have been popular during the period of the Modern Movement in architecture, giving a smooth, regular plane and, to some degree, a self-cleaning surface to the blank expanses for which the movement called.

After sharing the unpopularity of all things Victorian for so long, terracotta has returned to appreciation if not perhaps to favour, along with the reaction which has fostered the study of Victorian architecture. The qualities of the material, especially when used with the marvellous brickwork of the Victorian period, certainly justify that appreciation.

5. Brick chimneys

A great deal of the interest of brickwork stems from the use of the material to make ornamental what would otherwise be simply utilitarian. This is seen very often in the design of chimneys from hearth to chimney-pot, where the fireback and chimney-breast, the flues and chimney-stack demonstrate the craft of brickmaker and bricklayer meeting the task of conducting smoke from the fire to the atmosphere.

Open hearths and wall fireplaces seem to have developed side by side during the Middle Ages. Many of the great castles of the twelfth and thirteenth centuries retain fireplaces and chimney-stacks as well as providing evidence of former central hearths pouring smoke into the upper reaches of open halls. The surviving examples are of stone, but the reintroduction of brickwork on a substantial scale during the fifteenth century brought examples in that material.

For the hearth itself clay tiles were sometimes used, though the distinction between small tiles laid on edge and contemporary brickwork of the Flemish pattern is not great (Salzman, p. 98, is not sure whether the 'flaunderstile' at Eltham in 1400 is tile or brick). For the fireback the fire-resistant properties of brickwork meant that herringbone pattern panels in stone chimney-breasts as well as brick fireplaces came to be seen (37). For the fireplace the versatility of brickwork meant that shallow arches could be contrived over the fireplace openings. Fireplace and chimney-breast could be incorporated in brick walls, stand safely proud of timber-frame walls or be inserted into the heart of timber-frame buildings, making permanent and fireproof what had previously been vulnerable and insubstantial inglenooks and smokebays of timber and daub. Many farmhouses of the sixteenth and seventeenth centuries, especially in the eastern and south-eastern counties of England, demonstrate this use of brickwork in the core of a timber-frame dwelling.

At first the design of stone and brick fireplaces seems to have followed that of their timber counterparts whereby the smoke was encouraged upwards to gather in a deep pyramidal hood and so emerge by way of a narrow flue. Later, experience pointed to the need to limit the size of the gathering and smooth its surface, to raise the height of the chimney so as to increase the draw of the flue, and to improve the detailed design of the stack to discourage downdraughts within the chimney and encourage swift evacuation of the smoke away from the vulnerable junction between stack and roof, especially where the roof was thatched. Thus tall, straight and fairly narrow brick chimneys proved to be efficient and they are characteristic of early Tudor, Elizabethan and Jacobean buildings.

37. Herringbone brickwork in fireplace, Castle Acre Priory, Norfolk.

38. Crooked chimney, Lemsford, Hertfordshire.

These very characteristics provided an opportunity for the use of decorative brickwork. The flues in the stack might be square-set, diamond-set, octagonal or circular on plan; they might be raised singly or in groups of two, three or more; a sturdy base made an appropriate penetration of the roof covering. The tall shafts lent themselves to spiral, lozenge, scalloped and other decorative finishes. At the top of the stack, oversailing courses of brickwork helped prevent smoke falling down the outside and gave further opportunities for decoration. It seems that chimney-pots were not used at that time (41, 43, 44).

During the late seventeenth and eighteenth centuries chimney-stacks were designed to be in character with the classically inspired architecture of the buildings they served. As slate and tile came into general use, especially in the towns, chimney-stacks had less need to be tall, nor was it so necessary for social reasons to advertise that a building had lots of fireplaces. So chimney-stacks of this period were of classical proportions and generally less decorative. The universal use of coal as a fuel and the problems which sometimes arose with wind eddies in crowded roofs meant that the bricklayers had to introduce a bend in the stack to reduce downdraught—sometimes with bizarre results (38). The Gothic Revival of the nineteenth century brought a return to the form of earlier chimney designs, though with exaggerated dimensions.

The nineteenth and early twentieth centuries saw the greatest use of brickwork for industrial chimney-stacks. The earliest use of very tall stacks was probably in connection with lead mining in the late eighteenth century, but these were always of stone. Shortly afterwards tall stacks were introduced to serve the early steam-engines working mines or providing motive power to mills. Again, these were of stone though the basis of tall chimney design was being established. From the early nineteenth century onwards numbers multiplied and brick came extensively into use, especially in Lancashire and the Midlands. At first the stacks were often incorporated in the fabric of the mills they served but later the free-standing chimney became universal. The need for a substantial draught to serve several boilers, the need to take smoke away from the vicinity of the mill, and the desire for advertisement and prestige all led to the construction of chimney-stacks 150 ft and more in height (39).

Early free-standing mill, pithead and brickworks chimneys were often square on plan and made use of iron straps to maintain the integrity of the fabric. For the tall chimneys of the late nineteenth and early twentieth centuries a circular plan was used. Experience showed that a minimum one-brick thickness was required for the top 20 ft of a chimney, with a half-brick thickness added in every 25 ft or so, giving a base of nearly 4 ft in thickness at the bottom of a chimney 200 ft high. The steps were incorporated in the flue to give the outside surface of the chimney a taper whose graceful effect was testimony to the skill of the bricklayers. The later chimneys, with flue gases of high temperature, had a firebrick lining, often with a cavity between the firebrick and the structural brickwork. The detailed design of the chimney related to that of the mill it served and so there were many Italianate and some Gothic campanile-style chimneys. Polychromatic effects included architectural pattern-making, but equally popular was the device of picking out the name of the mill or its owner in white, glazed bricks.

There has been large-scale destruction of brick industrial chimneys during the past fifty years as the number of textile mills has declined and as the remaining mills have been converted from steam operation to the use of individual electric motors serving each piece of machinery. Unfortunately, there has also been some vindictive destruction on the part of those who see the tall, graceful chimneys as symbols of capitalist exploitation of the workers, rather than as the epitome of the bricklayer's craft.

39. Tall chimney serving pumping station, Ware, Hertfordshire.

6. Conclusion

Characteristics of bricks and brickwork

Taking raw material, fuel, labour and transport into consideration we have a building material which is versatile, often economical and sometimes fashionable.

Bricks are versatile because their size, shape and weight make them suitable for one-handed operations of the bricklayer, his other hand being available for the jointing by mortar. The arrangement of joints and the ease with which bricks may be cut mean that the small units can be used for a great range of building applications. Bricks are both structural and decorative; the bricks themselves provide the structural strength and the ornamental appearance in a long-lasting, hard-wearing, weather-resistant and pollution-resistant building material. Bricks are fire-resistant: they do not burn themselves and can protect other materials from fire. Bricks are durable: if properly burnt they have a virtually indefinite life. Bricks require no maintenance and brickwork properly employed and erected in a craftsmanlike manner requires little maintenance. So bricks and brickwork are versatile and economical.

The extent of the economy in using bricks has, of course, varied with time and with the availability of alternative building materials. As long as timber was widely and freely available from the wild or from conserved timber woodlands one would expect it to be cheaper than a manufactured material. Similarly, whenever and wherever stone was available from ground surfaces and open quarries it was likely to be cheaper than a manufactured material and no more expensive to transport. Where cob, and unbaked clay generally, were considered suitable for particular purposes they were likely to be cheaper than brick, because the unfired material was made on site and required neither fuel nor transport. However, when timber became scarce and expensive, when good-quality building stone came from more and more remote quarries, when the costs of masons' labour became more and more severe, or when the vulnerability of cob to weather and damage became a factor, then the balance of advantage began to change. Above all, when building materials were required in huge quantities for speedy erection the claims of bricks and brickwork for economical construction became considerable.

Whatever the reasons, brick has experienced several changes of fashion in the past 100 years. It has become abundantly clear that medieval brickwork was used because it was fashionable, and this distinction continued through the early Tudor and into the Elizabethan

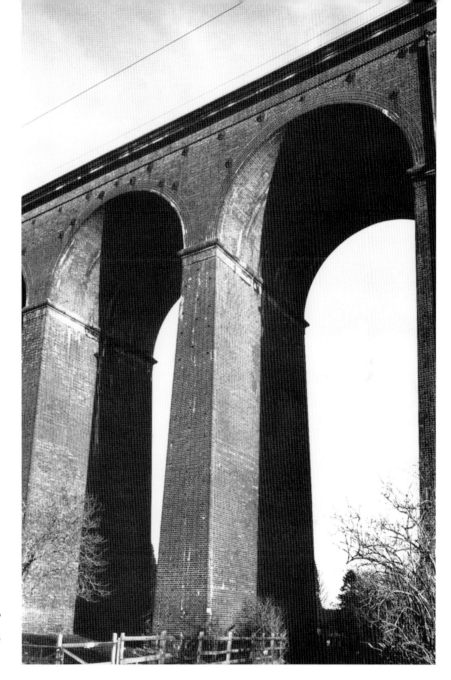

40. Digswell Railway Viaduct, Welwyn, Hertfordshire, 1850. Sir William and Joseph Cubitt; reputedly 13 million bricks were used.

period. Nearly all brickwork was confined to the construction and decoration of the buildings of the wealthiest in the land and found in the richest parts of the country. Brick must have been chosen over timber or stone because of its prestigious associations (1). At the same time, and at a lower social level, the bricks needed for fireplaces and chimney-stacks were of the most expensive variety, but were only required in relatively small numbers. Excessively tall, unnecessarily decorative, chimney-stacks were part of a fashion which swept right across lowland Britain in the late sixteenth century (44). A period of popularity for brickwork accompanied the fashion for all things Dutch in the late seventeenth century (45). In the Georgian period brick remained fashionable for middling buildings (31) and Kent was not

41. Diagonally set chimney-stacks on boldly projecting chimney-breast, Hodnet, Shropshire.

beyond selecting bricks for the large Norfolk country house, Holkham Hall (146), though he chose a colour which could masquerade as stone from a distance. In the Regency period brick was used but concealed by stucco. In the early Victorian period the churches and major public buildings had to be of stone, but midway through the queen's reign brick received the accolade of respectability and it was used for numerous large and important buildings (including Sandringham) as well as innumerable houses, mills, factories and warehouses (36,39) (46). A return of rendering as part of the Vernacular Revival style in the early twentieth century merged with the neo-Georgian period between the World Wars when whole cliffs of brickwork dominated fashionable West London. A post-war dalliance with concrete, steel, glass and aluminium simply demanded the return of brickwork to fashion and favour (179).

above right
42. Georgian houses, Pershore, Worcestershire.

right
43. Chimney-stacks with sunken decoration, Hafod-y-Bwlch, Denbighshire.

Overleaf left
44. Elaborately moulded chimney-stacks, Newport, Essex.

Overleaf right
45. Shire Hall, Woodbridge, Suffolk.

46. A superb example of Victorian brickwork of the finest craftsmanship. Holborn Union Offices, London EC1.

Thus the story of the use of bricks has been taken from a consideration in general of the structural properties of brickwork to a consideration in particular of these most prominent monuments to its strength and versatility. The current revival of interest in brickwork as building material for the present day must surely lead to further interest in its historic use and to a determination that the best and the most representative examples of all phases and uses of brickwork should be conserved.

Part Two:
Glossary

ACCRINGTON BRICKS: hard, smooth, deep-red pressed bricks made of shale from the Coal Measures near Accrington in East Lancashire; widely used for engineering and industrial purposes and also for other building types in the late nineteenth and early twentieth centuries. One of the trade names, 'Nori', is 'iron' spelled backwards and indicates the character of the brick.

AIR BRICK: a brick perforated to provide ventilation.

AMERICAN BOND: a term used in the United States for ENGLISH GARDEN-WALL BOND (*see* under BONDING).

APRON: a projecting panel below a window sill, sometimes ornamented; a popular embellishment in the eighteenth century.

47. Apron, High Street, Hemel Hempstead, Hertfordshire

ARCH BRICKS (TAPERED HEADERS, TAPERED STRETCHERS): special bricks tapered in length or width to serve as voussoirs in arches.

ARRIS: the sharp edge between two adjacent surfaces of a brick.

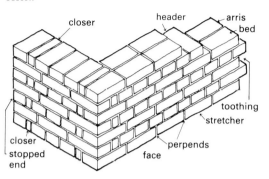

BAT (BRICK BAT): a broken section of brick, larger than a quarter brick, used sometimes as an alternative to a closer (q.v.) in bonding and generally to make up dimensions in a wall.
    HALF BAT: a bat which has been cut or manufactured to be half the length of bricks used in a wall.
    THREE-QUARTER BAT: a bat which has been cut or manufactured to be exactly three-quarters of the length of a full brick.

BED JOINT: the horizontal joint between two courses of brickwork. A brick is bedded on mortar spread over the bricks below; the bottom horizontal surface of a brick is its bed (*see* diagram under ARRIS).

BEEHIVE KILN: a brick kiln cylindrical in shape and with a brick cupola top; an intermittent kiln operating on the downdraught principle whereby hot flue gases directed upwards to the underside of the cupola are then drawn down, with the aid of a draught induced by a tall chimney, through the bricks which are to be fired.

BELGIAN KILN: a continuous kiln based on the principle of the Hoffmann kiln (q.v.) but rectangular on plan and making use of a system of grates set in the chamber floors to achieve high temperatures. The design was patented in Belgium, but was employed in Britain for firing facing bricks or firebricks.

BLACK MORTAR: mortar containing crushed ashes in place of much of the sand normally used in the mix and giving a dark grey appearance; popular in the industrial North and Midlands for its cheapness, its assumed weather-resistance, and especially for use in thin joints between machine-made pressed bricks.

48. *left* Segmental arch in rough brick, Thornton Abbey, Lincolnshire

BLIND WINDOW: a recess in a wall having jambs, head and sill formed in the brickwork but without a window frame or glazing. Some such windows were blocked as a result of the Window Tax, but many (probably most) were deliberately included as architectural details, especially by builders following copy-book designs.

Dearne's bond

49. Blind window, Heslington, Yorkshire, ER

BLOCK BONDING: the use of several courses of brickwork at a time in joining one wall or part of a wall to another. Block bonding may also be used in the thickness of a wall, as where facing bricks are bonded to common bricks of different dimensions.

50. Dearne's Bond, Alton, Hampshire

DUTCH BOND: a rare variation of Flemish bond (q.v.) in which alternate courses are moved half a brick to left or right; also called STAGGERED FLEMISH in the United States.

Block bonding

BLUE BRICKS: *see* STAFFORDSHIRE BLUE BRICKS

BONDING: the regular arrangement of bricks in a pattern for strength or decoration.
AMERICAN BOND: *see* ENGLISH GARDEN-WALL BOND
CHINESE BOND: *see* RAT-TRAP BOND
DEARNE'S BOND (DEARNE'S HOLLOW WALL): the use of alternate courses of headers and bricks laid on edge in a 9-in thick wall. The headers act as ties, the bricks laid on edge have a 3-in cavity between. There is some saving of bricks over a solid wall and this bond was sometimes used for humble buildings and garden or boundary walls.

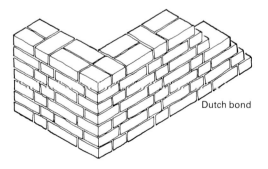
Dutch bond

ENGLISH BOND: a bond created from alternate courses of headers and stretchers. English bond is considered to be very strong because of the complete absence of straight joints running vertically in the wall, but it is more difficult to lay and more expensive than many other bonds.

English bond

51. English Bond, Holy Trinity, Hull, Yorkshire, ER

ENGLISH CROSS BOND (ST ANDREW'S BOND): like English bond, but each alternate course of stretchers is moved over half a brick to give a stepped effect to the joints. The term DUTCH BOND is sometimes used, presumably because of the prevalence of the bond in Holland, Belgium and northern France.

English cross bond

52. English Cross Bond, Smallhythe, Kent

ENGLISH GARDEN-WALL BOND: the use of more than one course of stretchers between two courses of headers gives a bond which has many of the advantages of English bond, but is much cheaper. Usually there are either three or five courses of stretchers, but other combinations may be seen. It is one of the most popular of all brickwork bonds, especially in the North of England. It is sometimes called AMERICAN BOND, COMMON BOND, or LIVERPOOL BOND in the United States.

English garden wall bond

53. English Garden-Wall Bond (above English Bond), Blyth, Nottinghamshire

FLEMISH BOND: alternate headers and stretchers used in each course; considered to be more decorative, but less strong, than English bond; rarely to be seen in Flanders.

Flemish bond

FLEMISH CROSS BOND: similar to Flemish bond but with additional headers at intervals in place of stretchers.

54. Flemish Bond with chequer effect, Thame, Oxfordshire

FLEMISH GARDEN-WALL BOND (SUSSEX BOND): the use of three stretchers between each pair of headers in place of the single stretcher of Flemish bond.

Flemish stretcher bond

56. Flemish Stretcher Bond with four stretcher courses between the Flemish Bond courses, North Wheatley, Nottinghamshire

HEADER BOND (HEADING BOND): the use of nothing but headers in each course of brickwork. Header bond was mainly employed for decorative effect, but has also been in demand for engineering work because of its great strength. This bond is useful for curved walls.

IRREGULAR BONDING: the use of headers to establish a bond, but with no consistent pattern.

Flemish garden-wall (Sussex) bond

55. Sussex Bond, Barlwood, Surrey

FLEMISH STRETCHER BOND: a bond in which courses of alternate headers and stretchers are separated by several courses of stretchers. Usually there are three courses of stretchers, but there may be any number from one to six; sometimes called AMERICAN WITH FLEMISH BOND in the United States.

Header bond

57. Header Bond, Westgate, Louth, Lincolnshire

MIXED GARDEN BOND: a variation of Flemish Stretcher bond in which headers do not lie above each other in any regular pattern.

Mixed garden bond

MONK BOND (YORKSHIRE BOND, FLYING BOND): a variation of Flemish bond with two stretchers in place of one between each pair of headers.

Monk bond

58. Monk Bond, Beccles, Suffolk

QUARTER BONDING (RAKING STRETCHER BOND): a variation of stretcher bond with each brick overlapping the one below by a quarter brick rather than the usual half brick.

Raking stretcher

59. Quarter bonding, Madeley, Shropshire

60. Raking Stretcher Bond, Plymouth Grove, Manchester

QUETTA BOND: a variation of Flemish bond in which continuous vertical voids are left in the interior of the wall; vertical reinforcement is placed in the voids which are then filled with mortar.

RAKING STRETCHER BOND: *see* QUARTER BONDING

RAT-TRAP BOND (CHINESE BOND, ROWLOCK BOND, SILVERLOCK'S BOND): a variation of Flemish bond (or Sussex bond) having alternate headers and stretchers in each course, but with the bricks laid on edge instead of on bed. The resultant wall has a cavity between each pair of stretchers. Using fewer bricks to reach a given height, a wall in Rat-Trap bond is cheaper than one in other bonds. It may be no less weather-resistant, but could be less stable.

Single Flemish bond

Double Flemish bond

Rat-Trap bond

STACK BOND: consists of bricks on end with continuous vertical joints. It cannot be used in load-bearing walls.

62. Stack Bond, Grosvenor Street, Chester, Cheshire

61. Rat-Trap Bond, Colney Heath, Hertfordshire

SINGLE FLEMISH BOND: gives the appearance of Flemish bond on the outside face only of a wall more than 9 ins thick. The same appearance on both inner and outer faces is given by DOUBLE FLEMISH BOND

Stack bond

STRETCHER BOND: a bond consisting of bricks laid so that every course consists of stretchers only. It is the usual bond for cavity walls, but is rarely used for solid walls because of the lack of bonding bricks running across the wall.

racking back

Stretcher bond

63. Stretcher Bond, Wilmslow, Cheshire

SUSSEX BOND: *see* FLEMISH GARDEN-WALL BOND
YORKSHIRE BOND: *see* MONK BOND

BONDING BRICKS: bricks which are smaller than normal bricks (e.g. bats or closers) and are used to make up a pattern or bond in brickwork.

BOND TIMBERS: pieces of timber built into the inner face of a wall to provide horizontal reinforcement. They may be visible in agricultural or industrial buildings, but in houses they are generally concealed by plaster.

BREAKING JOINT: the avoidance of continuous vertical joints by laying the bricks in one course across the joints in the course below.

BREEZE: cinders or coarse ashes remaining after the finer ash has been sieved out of domestic refuse collected by scavengers. As breeze resulted from incomplete combustion in domestic fires it was sufficiently combustible to act as a fuel for burning bricks in clamp or kiln.

BRICK ASHLAR: walls with a stone ashlar facing to a backing of brickwork.

BRICK BAT: *see* BAT

BRICK EARTH (BRICK CLAY): strictly the term applies to the superficial deposits of the silty clays of the Pleistocene period such as may be found in parts of the Thames and Kennet valleys, Middlesex, East Anglia, the northern part of Kent, West Sussex, and the southern part of Hampshire, but in practice the term is generally applied to all clays from which bricks are made.

BRICKMAKER'S TABLE: the bench used for moulding bricks by hand.

BRICKNOGGING: the use of bricks as an infilling between the members of a timber frame either as the original infill or as replacement of some other material; the bricknogging may be visible in external walls, but may be concealed in internal partitions.

bricknogging

64. Bricknogging in herringbone brickwork, St Cross, Winchester, Hampshire

BRICK ON EDGE: the use of bricks laid on edge rather than on bed and displaying upright headers; commonly employed as a coping to a 9-in brick wall, as a sill, or for a flat arch.

Brick on edge

slips

BRICK TAX: the tax or duty levied on bricks in 1784, increased from time to time and finally repealed in 1850.

BRICK TILES (MATHEMATICAL TILES, WALL TILES): tiles with part of one face moulded like the face or end of a brick. They were laid in mortar or nailed to battens on a wall of timber-frame or, sometimes, onto a solid wall, and then pointed to look like bricks.

brick tile (mathematical tiles)

65. Brick-on-edge coping, Heslington, Yorkshire, ER

BRICK ON END: the use of bricks on end rather than on bed and so displaying upright stretchers; commonly used for a flat arch, as a soldier course (q.v.), or generally for decorative purposes.

BRICK SLIPS (BRICK FACE SLIPS): thin pieces of brick which have been specially made to match the headers or stretchers of ordinary brickwork. They are used, for example, to cover concrete beams or stanchions in order to give the illusion of a continuous brick wall.

66. Stretcher brick tile (mathematical tile)
67. Header brick tile (mathematical tile)
68. Glazed header brick tile (mathematical tile)
69. Damaged corner brick tile (mathematical tile)

70. Brick tile elevation, Tenterden, Kent

BULLNOSE BRICKS: bricks with one arris, or occasionally two, rounded; used where a sharp arris would be inconvenient or liable to damage.

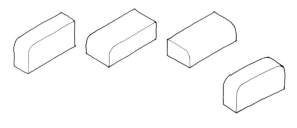

BULL'S-EYE: a small circular or oval window opening or blind window; a popular device of the late seventeenth and early eighteenth centuries.

BURRS: bricks which have been fused together in lumps, usually through excessive heat in the kiln.

CALCIUM SILICATE BRICKS: bricks made not from clay, but from sand or crushed flint mixed with hydrated lime, compressed and then allowed to harden. FLINT-LIME and SAND-LIME BRICKS are alternative terms.

CALLOW: a. the topsoil which has to be removed from a clayground before the clay can be extracted for brick-making.

b. the top layer of inferior clay removed from above the clay deposits used for making the 'Flettons' of Bedfordshire.

CAMBERED ARCH: an 'arch' whose upper edge (extrados) is horizontal, but whose lower edge (intrados) is slightly curved or cambered in order to avoid the illusion of sagging.

CANT BRICK: a special brick moulded so that one corner (SINGLE CANT) or two corners (DOUBLE CANT) are cut off diagonally.

CAPPING BRICK: a special brick shaped so as to be laid on edge to finish the top of a wall but without projecting beyond the face of that wall (cf. COPING BRICK). A HALF-ROUND CAPPING BRICK has a semicircular contour whereas a SADDLEBACK CAPPING BRICK has a pointed shape.

CARVED BRICKWORK: decoration created by carving solid brickwork rather than by making use of moulded bricks. Usually bricks similar to those employed for gauged brickwork were used, but they were of larger dimensions, laid with fine joints, carved with hammer, bolster etc., and then brought to the desired finish through use of a rubbing brick.

CASINGS: the bricks used as cladding to the pile of unfired bricks which forms a clamp.

CAVITY WALL (HOLLOW WALL): a wall built of two vertical leaves of bricks or blocks separated by an air space, but linked by special header bricks, patent glazed ties, or ties of wrought iron, cast iron or galvanised steel wire. Traditionally the air space was kept quite free of any material lest a bridge for moisture penetration might be provided, but it is now quite common to fill the cavity with a material which improves insulation while still acting as a moisture barrier.

cavity ties

cavity wall

CEMENT MORTAR: mortar using Portland cement with sand as a partial or complete substitute for lime. It is stronger and more weather-resistant than lime mortar, but suffers from shrinkage whereby cracks may be formed while setting. This mortar was often called 'compo' and this term is still current in the North of England.

CHEQUERED BRICKWORK: a regular pattern on the surface of a brick wall created, for example, through the use of flared or vitrified headers in Flemish bond. The term is also used of alternate squares or rectangles of brickwork and other materials, including flint, which may be mixed to give a kind of chessboard pattern.

chequered brickwork

CHIMNEY: the structure containing a flue which serves a fireplace. The *chimney-breast* contains the fireplace and may project into a room or out beyond an external wall; the *chimney-stack* takes one or more flues in a structure above roof level and may consist of a number of *shafts* or *stalks*, one to each flue.

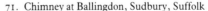

71. Chimney at Ballingdon, Sudbury, Suffolk

CHIMNEY-POT: a terracotta funnel terminating a flue and designed to improve the draught. There were very few in use before the reign of George III and the large majority are Victorian or later.

CHINESE BOND: *see* RAT-TRAP BOND under BONDING

CHUFFS (SHUFFS): bricks which are very soft or full of cracks and which tend to disintegrate when drawn from the clamp or kiln. The condition may be caused when inadequately dried green bricks are set in the clamp or kiln or when rain has fallen on hot bricks.

CLAMP: a stack of unburnt bricks made ready for firing.

CLAY: a plastic earth which is made of sand and alumina, but may contain varying quantities of chalk, iron oxide, manganese dioxide etc.

CLINKER: *see* DUTCH CLINKER

CLOSER: a brick cut or moulded so as to expose a half-header and used to complete the bonding pattern especially at the return of a wall or round a window or door opening (*see* diagram under ARRIS; *see also* KING CLOSER and QUEEN CLOSER).

CLOSURE: a brick slip, usually 2 ins thick, acting with a header to provide the bond in early types of cavity wall.

COMMON BOND: *see* ENGLISH GARDEN-WALL BOND under BONDING

COMMON BRICKS: ordinary cheap bricks not usually used where appearance or great structural strength are important. They often have surface imperfections such as 'kiss marks' (q.v.).

COMPASS BRICKS (RADIAL or RADIATING BRICKS): tapered bricks specially made for creating circular shapes, such as bull's-eye windows.

COMPO: *see* CEMENT MORTAR

CONCRETE BRICKS: bricks moulded from cement, sand and some aggregate such as crushed stone. Unlike clay bricks they are not burnt in a kiln. They were used as common bricks in districts which lack clay or cheap fuel, but are rough to handle and are easily chipped.

CONTINUOUS KILN: a kiln in which the sequence of operations is uninterrupted since many chambers are combined in the one kiln. The Hoffmann kiln is the best-known type of continuous kiln.

COPING BRICK: like a CAPPING BRICK (q.v.); a brick shaped so as to be laid on edge to finish and protect a brick wall, but made so that the ends project and help to throw rain clear of the wall. There are HALF-ROUND and SADDLEBACK COPING BRICKS.

CORBELLING: the use of projecting headers or courses for structural or decorative purposes.

72. Corbelling, stable block, Tattershall Castle, Lincolnshire

CORBIE STEP: *see* CROW STEP

COSSEY WHITES: bricks, light yellow in colour, which were popular in and around Norwich about 1830.

COURSE: a horizontal layer of bricks.

COWNOSE BRICK: a special brick with a semicircular end.

73. Crinkle-crankle wall, Easton Park, Suffolk

CRINKLE-CRANKLE WALL: a garden or park wall which was usually only half a brick in thickness, but which gained stability from serpentine curves on plan. Such walls are found mainly in East Anglia.

CROW STEP (CORBIE STEP): the finish of a gable parapet in a series of horizontal platforms like large steps. This detail was popular in seventeenth-century brickwork, especially in East Anglia. It was also used in other materials and other areas, for example Scotland, where the platforms were known as corbie steps.

74. Crow-stepped gable with tile copings, Kinnersley Castle, Herefordshire

CURF: square heaps of clay loosely thrown up to benefit from weathering and frost action after excavation.

CUT AND RUBBED BRICKS: bricks cut to shape with an axe or bolster and then rubbed to a precise finish with a rubber brick.

CUTTERS: bricks made from natural or mixed sandy loams of uniform texture which, when burnt, are capable of being cut and rubbed to the required shape.

DAMP-PROOF COURSE: a horizontal layer of impervious material included in a brick wall to stop rising damp. Slate, asphalt, lead and bituminous felt have been commonly used; also, less commonly, two courses of blue bricks, or, rather rarely, patent glazed stoneware tiles.

DEARNE'S BOND: *see* BONDING

DENTILATION (DENTILATED BRICKWORK): a tooth-like effect produced by the projection of alternate headers or smaller blocks. The detail is usually seen under a cornice, at eaves level, or at a string course (*see* illustration 46).

DIAPER: a pattern made by using bricks of a different colour along with the general walling bricks. Diamond, square, lozenge and heart shapes are commonly contrived by means of blue-flared or vitrified headers.

diaper brickwork

76. *above* Dog-tooth brickwork, Orford, Suffolk

77. *below* Brick dressings used with chalk, Burnham Overy, Norfolk

75. Diaper brickwork (with tumbled-in brick buttresses), Copdock, Suffolk

DOG-LEG BRICKS: bricks specially made for use where two walls join at an obtuse angle so as to avoid the use of cut bricks with straight joints and an uneven arris.

dog-leg bricks

DOG-TOOTH BRICKWORK: a term sometimes given to the use of bricks laid diagonally to expose one corner as an alternative to the use of dentilation; also called HOUND'S-TOOTH or (in the United States) MOUSE-TOOTH.

DOWNDRAUGHT KILN: an intermittent kiln, circular or rectangular on plan, in which the hot gases from the burning fuel are drawn upwards to be deflected downwards from a brick vault or dome, with the aid of a draught induced by a tall chimney, and so fire the green bricks.

DRESSINGS: those parts of the walls of a building (such as at door and window openings) which are carried out in a

78. *above* Downdraught kiln with aperture for access and with fireholes, Porth wen, Anglesey.

material superior to that used for the main walling. Dressings may be in a different substance, such as the Portland stone used with brickwork in many classically inspired buildings, or they may be in a superior version of the general walling material, as gauged brickwork is used with ordinary brickwork. Sometimes brick dressings are employed with poor-quality stone, flint, cobble or pebble walls.

DRYING HACK: *see* HACK

DUTCH BOND: *see* BONDING

DUTCH CLINKERS: small hard bricks, usually rather yellow in colour, reputedly brought in ships coming from the Netherlands during the second half of the seventeenth century and incorporated in brick walls near the ports of East Anglia and Kent, or used as paving bricks. This type of brick is also called klinkart.

DUTCH GABLE: a gable whose outline is composed of convex and concave curves, sometimes crowned by a pediment.

EFFLORESCENCE: the powdery white deposit on the surface of new brickwork which comes from the drying out of salts in the bricks or mortar.

ENGINEERING BRICKS: dense bricks of uniform size and high crushing strength coupled with low porosity. As the name suggests, they have been employed mostly for structures such as railway viaducts, but because of their strength or uniformity they have also been used in buildings.

ENGLISH BOND, ENGLISH CROSS BOND, ENGLISH GARDEN-

WALL BOND: *see* BONDING

FACE: the exposed side of a brick (*see* diagram under ARRIS).

FACING BRICKS: bricks selected for use on the exposed surface of a wall because of their superior appearance to common bricks.

FAIENCE: a type of glazed terracotta slab in which the body has first been fired at high temperature and then the body and glaze fired at a lower temperature. However, the term is rather loosely used in relation to terracotta, and has other meanings.

FIREBRICKS: bricks capable of resisting high temperatures and used for lining fireplaces, chimneys, kilns, etc. They are made from fireclay (q.v.) and burnt at a high temperature.

FIRECLAY: a type of clay usually obtained by mining in the Coal Measures and containing a high proportion of silica. It is primarily used for making firebricks.

FIREHOLES: chambers in the walls of kilns containing the fire (usually of wood or coal).

FLARED BRICKS (FLARED HEADERS): bricks laid as headers which are dark at one end through being placed close to the source of heat in a clamp or kiln, and which are used to form patterns in diaper or chequerwork.

FLAT ARCH (STRAIGHT ARCH, FRENCH ARCH, JACK ARCH, SOLDIER ARCH): the use of a soldier course (q.v.) of bricks

79. Dutch gable, Boston, Lincolnshire

on edge or on end to make the head of an opening. The head is not arched in the true sense of the word but the friction from the vertical joints gives something of the structural effect of an arch.

FLEMISH BOND, FLEMISH GARDEN-WALL BOND, FLEMISH STRETCHER BOND: *see* BONDING

FLEMISH BRICKS: thin bricks imported from the Low Countries or made locally in imitation of them.

FLETTONS: common bricks made from the Oxford clays of the Peterborough area and widely used in the London area.

FLINT-LIME BRICKS: *see* CALCIUM SILICATE BRICKS

FLUSH JOINT: *see* JOINTING

FLUSH POINTING: *see* POINTING

FLYING BOND: *see* MONK BOND under BONDING

FOSSIL BRICKS: lightweight insulating bricks made from infusible earths from Italy known as 'fossil meal'; such bricks are only about one-sixth the weight of ordinary bricks.

FRENCH ARCH: *see* FLAT ARCH

FROG: an indentation in the surface of a brick which reduces its weight, makes it easier to handle and minimises the clay used in its manufacture. When laid 'frog up' the indentation is filled with mortar by the bricklayer. Sometimes there are two frogs, one to each surface.

frogs

GALLETING: the use of pebbles or chips of stone or flint pushed into mortar joints, probably for decoration, but possibly for assumed strengthening.

GAUGED (GUAGED (*sic*), GAGED) BRICKWORK: the use of rather soft bricks sawn to shape then rubbed to a smooth surface and precise dimensions by use of a stone or another, harder, brick. Brighter brick colours and very fine joints are characteristic of gauged brickwork which is

80. Galleting, Shere, Surrey

81. Gauged brickwork, Chicheley, Buckinghamshire

82. Gauged and moulded brickwork, West Malling, Kent

most frequently to be seen in arches to door and window openings.

GAULT BRICKS: bricks made from Gault Clay which is associated with the chalk belt of eastern England. They are normally yellowish in colour but may emerge as pink or red according to their position in the kiln.

GLAZED BRICKS: bricks with shiny surfaces resulting from a secondary firing when salt was applied in the kiln to give a salt-glazed finish. Usually only one end and one face are glazed. Such bricks were much used in the nineteenth and early twentieth centuries for situations where easy cleaning or light-reflecting qualities were important, or in the hope that a glazed brick wall would be self-cleaning in the rain.

83. Glazed bricks, All Saints, Manchester

GREAT BRICKS: a term sometimes used in documents to indicate large thin bricks (e.g. 11 × 12 × 2 ins) used, infrequently, in medieval England.

84. Great bricks used as voussoirs, Waltham Abbey, Essex

GREEN BRICKS: those which have been moulded but not yet fired.

GRIZZLES: grey bricks either made of special clay and used as facings, or underburnt bricks intended to be hidden or used in an unobtrusive location.

HACK: a long double row of green bricks in course of drying. The bricks are placed on edge, seven or eight courses high, on prepared platforms and usually protected by movable lightweight timber roofs, or by permanent open-sided sheds known as HACK HOUSES.

HACK BARROW: a lightweight barrow with a long grilled top on which rows of bricks, usually thirteen to a row, are placed. Such barrows are used to take green bricks from the moulding bench to the hacks.

HACK HOUSE: *see* under HACK

HAND-MADE BRICKS: bricks moulded by hand with the aid of a wooden mould and stock board. Because they are less uniform than machine-made bricks they are sometimes preferred for facings.

HEADER: a brick laid to expose one end (or in a 9-in wall, both ends) for purposes of bonding or pattern-making (*see* diagram under ARRIS).

HEADER BOND, HEADING BOND: *see* BONDING

HERRINGBONE BRICKWORK: bricks laid not horizontally but diagonally, and sloping in opposite directions. Herringbone brickwork is used in bricknogging where the timber frame is carrying the loads.

85. Herringbone bricknogging, Chiddingfold, Surrey

86. Hitch bricks, Bengeo Hall, Hertfordshire

HITCH BRICKS: interlocking hollow bricks invented by Caleb Hitch in 1828 and made at his brickworks at Ware in Hertfordshire.

HOFFMANN KILN: a type of kiln circular on plan and designed for the continuous production of bricks. The kiln was divided into many chambers, usually about a dozen, and each chamber in turn was loaded with 'green' bricks which were dried, burnt, cooled and removed chamber by chamber so that a batch of new brick was produced every day. By means of a system of ducts and flues the heat from the continuously burning furnace was directed to pre-heating and firing, while the waste heat from a chamber which was cooling was used to help in drying the green bricks which had just been loaded into another chamber.

HOLLOW BRICKS: those with holes or cavities occupying more than 25% of the volume. They have been developed for uses in which light weight or good insulation properties are required.

HOLLOW WALL: an obsolete term for a cavity wall.

HONEYCOMB BRICKWORK: the omission of certain headers or stretchers in a brick wall for purposes of ventilation or decoration; found for instance in brick hay-barns and in the sleeper walls which carry the ground-floor joists in modern houses.

87. Honeycomb brickwork, Seighford, Staffordshire

honeycomb

HOOP-IRON BOND: a type of reinforced brickwork in which flat bars of wrought iron, having been dipped in tar and sanded, are laid in every sixth course of a brick wall.

HOT WALL: *see* PEACH WALL

HOUND'S-TOOTH: *see* DOG-TOOTH BRICKWORK

INTERMITTENT KILN: one which has to be filled, heated to firing temperature, cooled and emptied at each firing.

IRREGULAR BONDING: brickwork given stability through the use of headers and broken vertical joints, but without a regular bonding pattern.

irregular bond

JACK ARCH: *see* FLAT ARCH

JOINTING: the use of mortar between adjacent bricks, horizontally and vertically, as a spacing and bedding material.

FLUSH JOINT: a mortar joint which has been finished flush with the surface of the brickwork.

KEYED JOINT: a term used to describe both a joint left recessed or raked out to receive plaster or stucco, and a joint pointed and finished to a concave section.

RAKED-OUT JOINT: a joint which has been cleared of mortar to a depth of ½ or ¾ in from the face of the brickwork. This may be done for decorative reasons or to form a key for subsequent rendering.

RUBBED JOINT: a flush joint which the bricklayer has made by rubbing excess mortar off the surface of the brickwork with a piece of rag, rubber or some comparable material.

SCORED JOINT (RULED JOINT): a joint in which grooves have been impressed by running the point of the trowel against a straight-edge (i.e. a piece of wood about 3 ft long with smooth, straight, parallel edges) so as to give the appearance of very precise brickwork.

STRUCK JOINT: a joint with mortar pressed in at the bottom (like a weathered joint upside down), characteristic of bricks laid overhand from within a building rather than in the normal way from outside.

WEATHERED JOINT: a joint in which the mortar (or the pointing mortar if used) has been pressed in at the top by the bricklayer's trowel.

KEYED BRICK: a brick with one stretcher surface indented to act as a key for external rendering or internal plastering.

KICK: a term formerly used for the projection sometimes rising from the moulder's bench which forms a shallow frog in the moulded brick.

KILN: a furnace in which bricks are burnt. Although the terms kiln and clamp were originally interchangeable, a kiln has come to mean a permanent structure in contrast to a clamp, which was dismantled after every firing. (*see also* BEEHIVE, BELGIAN, CONTINUOUS, DOWNDRAUGHT, HOFFMANN, INTERMITTENT, NEWCASTLE, SCOTCH, SUFFOLK, TUNNEL and UPDRAUGHT KILNS.)

KING CLOSER: a three-quarter bat with half a header exposed as a closer. The brick is often given a diagonal cut-back from the exposed half-header, but this is hidden within the thickness of the wall.

king closer

KISS MARKS: discolorations of the surface of bricks resulting from the method of stacking unfired bricks on top of each other in the kiln.

KLINKART: *see* DUTCH CLINKERS

LACING COURSES: one or more courses of bricks serving as horizontal reinforcement to walls of flint, cobble, pebble, or some other awkwardly shaped material.

lacing course

LAP: in bonding, the projection of one brick over the one below.

LARRYING: the use of a wet fluid mortar allowing the bricks to be slid into position, with further mortar poured to fill vertical joints.

LEAF: the thin brick wall which forms an element of a cavity wall; there are an inner leaf and an outer leaf as well as the cavity between.

LIME MORTAR: a mixture which usually consisted of about one part slaked lime to six parts sand, though sometimes with the addition of a little cement when that became available. Proportions of lime and sand have, however, varied quite considerably in the past.

LIME PUTTY: quicklime slaked and sieved and mixed with water and possibly a very little sand to form a white mortar.

LIVERPOOL BOND: *see* ENGLISH GARDEN-WALL BOND, under BONDING

LOUDON'S HOLLOW WALL: an 11-in wall in Flemish bond with a 2-in cavity between stretchers and a 2-in closure (q.v.) behind each header.

Loudon's hollow wall

MALMS: bricks made out of a naturally occurring or artificial mixture of fine yellow alluvial clay and about one-sixteenth proportion of chalk. Such a clay is found in the London area.

MATHEMATICAL TILES: *see* BRICK TILES

METRIC BRICKS: bricks made to metric dimensions, e.g. $215 \times 107.5 \times 65$ mm.

MIXED GARDEN BOND: *see* BONDING

MODILLIONS: small projecting brackets, usually in a series below a cornice.

MONK BOND: *see* BONDING

MORTAR: the material used in bedding one brick upon others and in jointing and pointing generally (cf. BLACK MORTAR, CEMENT MORTAR, LIME MORTAR).

MOULD: a wooden box without top or bottom and with inner sides usually lined with brass or thin sheet-iron. In brickmaking the mould is placed over a wooden stock to

form the complete mould into which the clay is thrown. The dimensions of the mould allow for the shrinkage of green bricks in drying and firing.

MOULDED BRICKWORK: the use of bricks moulded to a selected shape before firing and built up to make ornamental architectural details.

88. Moulded brickwork, Willmer House, Farnham, Surrey

MOUSE-TOOTH: *see* DOG-TOOTH BRICKWORK

NEWCASTLE KILN: a type of rectangular horizontal-draught intermittent kiln used especially in the North-East of England during the nineteenth century. Usually there were two fireholes at one end and a chimney at the other, but such kilns could be placed back-to-back with a chimney in the middle.

NOGGIN: *see* BRICKNOGGING

PALLET BOARDS: thin boards on which newly-moulded bricks are placed before they are taken to the hacks.

PALLET MOULDING: a process in which the moulds are sanded rather than wetted to minimise adherence of the clay. The stock board having been attached to the bench, the mould is dusted with sand then placed in position; the clay is rolled in sand on the bench and thrown into the mould, the surplus is cut off and the mould then lifted off so that the green brick may be turned onto the pallet board.

PAMMENTS: thin paving bricks between about 9 ins and 12 ins square.

PAVING BRICKS (PAVIOUR BRICKS): bricks of special composition and dimensions to serve as paving; designed for hard wear, low porosity and for resistance to frost. Nowadays many paviours are produced in interlocking shapes.

PEACH WALL (HOT WALL): a sort of hollow wall with a cavity or horizontal flues formed in the brickwork so that hot air may be drawn from a furnace at one end in order to help protect shrubs and fruit from the cold.

PERFORATED BRICKS: vertical perforations are introduced into bricks, usually when the latter are wire-cut, so as to save material and weight without materially reducing strength.

perforated bricks

PLACE BRICKS: cheap, underburnt red bricks used as commons rather than as facings.

PLAT BAND: a rectangular moulding of shallow projection usually denoting externally the horizontal division between the storeys. On a brick building it may be of brick, stone or stucco (cf. STRING COURSE).

PLINTH BRICK: a brick chamfered on end or face to provide for a reduction in thickness between the plinth and the main part of the wall.

plinth bricks

POINTING: the application of a superior mortar to the raked-out joints of ordinary mortar.
    FLUSH POINTING: pointing the joints of a brick wall but scraping the mortar smooth with a trowel, a rag, a piece

89. Bricks used for paving, Ironbridge, Shropshire

90. Peach wall: flues made of two courses of brick-on-edge between courses of headers, Farthinghoe, Northamptonshire

of a rubber, etc., to obtain a uniform wall surface.

TUCK POINTING: a method of pointing in which lime putty is inserted into a pointing mortar which matches the colour of the walling brickwork, and is cut into precise lines so as to give the illusion of thin joints in fine-quality brickwork. In the best-quality work the vertical joints are slightly thinner than the horizontal.

91. Flush-pointed brickwork with penny-joint in gauged brickwork

POLYCHROME BRICKWORK: the use of several colours for decorative effect. The term is usually applied to nineteenth-century work with, for example, arch voussoirs of several colours following Italian Gothic precedent.

PRESSED BRICKS: bricks moulded under pressure before firing so as to give smooth surfaces and sharp arrises.

PROJECTING HEADERS: patterning like diaper work (q.v.) but made by projecting headers in ordinary brickwork.

PUG MILL: a device for mixing and refining clay for brickmaking. The pug mill consists of a tub of iron placed vertically (and usually tapering downwards) in which there is a shaft from which projects a set of knives arranged in spiral fashion. The shaft was usually turned by a horse treading a circular path around the mill. Clay was inserted at the top, mixed by the knives and forced out through an orifice at the bottom to be taken away to be moulded into bricks.

PURPOSE-MADE BRICKS: bricks which have been moulded to a special shape, usually to deal with a specific building problem. Where, for instance, a wall was to be built to an irregular plan then purpose-made bricks would be required to give a neat finish at the corners.

PUTLOG HOLES (PUTLOCK HOLES): the recesses left in a brick wall to receive the horizontal bearers of scaffolding. These holes should be filled as the scaffolding is taken down, but sometimes this was not done or the brickbats used as fill dropped out revealing the holes.

putlog holes

QUARTER BONDING: see BONDING

QUEEN CLOSER: a half bat or two quarter bats cut to show a half-header width.

queen closer

QUETTA BOND: see BONDING

QUOINS: groups of bricks projecting from the general surface of a building at its corners in imitation of the corner stones of a masonry building (see illustration 131).

RACKING (RACKING BACK): reducing the height of a brick wall in steps from a corner or termination. The corners of brick walls are usually raised first to ensure perfectly vertical lines and horizontal courses; the walls are racked back from the corners for subsequent completion (see STRETCHER BOND).

RADIAL BRICKS: special bricks intended for walls curved on plan. Radial headers are used in walls one brick or more thick; radial stretchers are used in walls half a brick thick, such as the leaves of a cavity wall.

RAKED-OUT: see JOINTING

RAKING STRETCHER BOND: see BONDING

RAT-TRAP BOND: see BONDING

RECESSED JOINT: see JOINTING

RELIEVING ARCH: an arch built within a wall above an opening and transmitting loads to both sides of the opening in order to relieve the lintel or flat arch at its head.

RENDERED BRICKWORK: brickwork covered externally by some variation of plaster. The finish may be stucco, i.e. lime/sand or lime/cement/sand brought to a very smooth finish, or it may be rough-cast, i.e. coarse sand or washed gravel mixed with slaked lime and thrown on, or it may be pebble-dash, i.e. small washed pebbles thrown onto wet cement.

92. Relieving arch in rough brickwork, Balls Park, Hertfordshire

ROMAN BRICKS: thin tile-like bricks used by the Romans and reused in later buildings on Roman sites, as at Colchester.

ROUGH BRICK ARCH: an arch made up of bricks which have not been moulded or cut to voussoir shape. The necessary taper is provided in the mortar joints. Such bricks are usually made of one or two rings of brick-on-edge.

93. Rough brick segmental arch, Chiddingfold, Surrey

ROWLOCK: an American term for laying bricks on edge rather than on bed; thus Rowlock bond is the same as Rat-Trap bond.

RUBBED BRICKWORK: *see* GAUGED BRICKWORK

RUBBED JOINT: *see* JOINTING

RUBBER: a rather soft brick made of specially well-mixed and carefully fired clay, capable of being rubbed with a harder piece of stone or brick to the desired shape.

RULED JOINT: *see* SCORED JOINT under JOINTING

RUSTIC BRICK: a facing brick with surfaces (often only one end and one face) which have been improved by a sand covering or a scratched pattern before firing. They are often given variegated colours at the same time.

RUSTICATION: in stonework, a method of emphasising each block by surrounding it with deeply recessed joints to yield shadows; sometimes imitated in brickwork by sinking every fourth or fifth mortar course and chamfering the edges of adjacent bricks.

94. Rustication in brickwork, Nun Monkton, Yorkshire, ER

SADDLEBACK COPING BRICK: a purpose-made brick with its top bed sloping in two directions (*see* CAPPING BRICK and COPING BRICK).

SAMMEL BRICKS (SANDEL BRICKS): rough-textured underfired bricks, pinkish in colour.

SAND-FACED BRICKS: bricks with one face and one end sanded before firing to give a rough-textured finish.

SAND-LIME BRICKS: *see* CALCIUM SILICATE BRICKS

SCORED JOINT: *see* JOINTING

SCOTCH KILN: a type of updraught intermittent kiln of rectangular plan and battered sides but with an open top. There are openings at the ends for filling and emptying the kiln and fireholes at low level at each of the long sides of the kiln.

SEGMENTAL ARCH: an arch in which the underside (intrados) and the upper edge (extrados) of the bricks form segments struck from the same centre. It may be a rough arch or one formed out of moulded or gauged-brick voussoirs (*see* illustration 48).

SHALES: hard laminated rocks which may be crushed or broken down through weathering and mixed with water so as to form a plastic mass from which bricks may be moulded and fired. Suitable shales are found in the coalfields, especially those of Durham, Yorkshire, Lancashire and Staffordshire.

SHIPPERS: bricks imperfect in form but sound and hard-burnt, used as ballast for ships.

SHUFFS: *see* CHUFFS

SILVERLOCK'S BOND: *see* RAT-TRAP BOND under BONDING

SINGLE FLEMISH BOND: *see* BONDING

SKEWBACK: the backward-sloping voussoirs at the springing of a flat arch.

SKINTLE (SKINTLING): diagonal placing of green bricks in the hack; this is done after the drying process has progressed sufficiently for the bricks to be moved.

SLOP MOULDING: a type of brick moulding in which the mould is wetted rather than sanded; there may be no stock on the moulder's table. The moulded green brick is laid on a sanded flat surface before being taken to the hacks to dry.

SNAP HEADERS: half bats, with one end exposed, used to provide a bonding pattern, as in the outer leaf of a cavity wall.

SOFT-MUD PROCESS: a mechanised version of the traditional pallet-moulding process of brickmaking.

SOIL (SPANISH): finely sieved ashes mixed with clay, so helping to provide an integral fuel for burning the green bricks.

SOLDIER ARCH: *see* FLAT ARCH

SOLDIER COURSE: a course of bricks laid on end, standing upright like soldiers.

soldier course

SPANISH: *see* SOIL

SPECIALS: purpose-made bricks of non-standard shape, e.g. bullnose bricks.

SPRINGER: the first brick on each side of an arch; in a flat arch it may incline backwards as a skewback.

SQUARE STOP END: a special brick with header and stretcher faces of equal dimensions, used for instance at the end of the brick-on-edge coping to a wall.

SQUINT BRICK: a special brick with one corner cut diagonally at an angle of 30°, 45° or 60°.

STACK BOND: *see* BONDING

STAFFORDSHIRE BLUE BRICKS: hard, dense bricks varying in colour from slate-grey through all the darker blues to deep purple, made out of Staffordshire shales. They were intended for engineering or industrial purposes and much employed in damp-proof courses. They were used, especially in the 1960s and 1970s, as facing bricks in many building types.

STAFFORDSHIRE KILN: a rectangular kiln operating on the principles of the Hoffmann kiln and of a design patented in 1904. The arches and vaults over the chambers were placed transversely. Such kilns were used especially for burning Staffordshire blue bricks.

STIFF PLASTIC PROCESS: a brickmaking process in which ground, screened and dampened shale is pressed to make a roughly rectangular clot, and then pressed again to make a smooth-sided brick ready for firing.

STOCK, STOCK BOARD: in pallet moulding the stock is an iron-faced block of wood fixed to the surface of the moulder's bench. The mould fits over the stock. The thickness of the brick is regulated with the aid of stock pins which limit the drop of the mould onto the stock.

STOCK BRICK: this term has three main meanings, one being the name given to any brick made with the aid of a stock board, another being the ordinary brick of any particular locality, and the third being more specifically the yellowish common bricks of the London area.

STOPPED END: a free-standing wall brought to a neat termination with the aid of closers (*see* ARRIS).

STRAIGHT ARCH: *see* FLAT ARCH

STRAIGHT JOINTS: vertical joints which are directly above other vertical joints; since this situation is avoided in proper bonding a straight joint usually indicates an alteration, or an expansion joint.

STRETCHER: a brick placed on bed to expose one long face (*see* diagram under ARRIS).

STRETCHER BOND: *see* BONDING

STRIKE: a piece of thin wood about 1 ft long and 3 ins wide used to smooth the surface of the moulded brick after excess clay has been struck off.

STRING COURSE: a horizontal projecting band, sometimes of dentilated or dog-tooth brickwork, usually at an intermediate floor level (*see* PLAT BAND and illustration 76).

STRUCK JOINT: *see* JOINTING

STUPIDS: the name given to early wire-cut brickmaking machines in which clay was inserted into a hopper and then pushed by a piston through a die before being cut by wire into brick shapes.

SUFFOLK KILN: a simple rectangular, open-topped, up-draught intermittent kiln with firing-holes at the ends.

SUSSEX BOND: *see* FLEMISH GARDEN-WALL BOND under BONDING

TAX BRICKS: bricks of larger than normal dimensions made to evade the early brick tax which was levied simply on the number of bricks made. Subsequent legislation eliminated the advantage of using very large bricks, but bricks thicker than normal remained in use especially in the North and Midlands.

TEMPERING: the action of bringing brick clay into a state ready for use by the brickmaker. Weathered clay is turned over, mixed with the right amount of water, chopped and then wheeled either directly to the moulder's bench or, later, to the pug-mill.

TERRACOTTA: a block of uniform and fine-textured clay which has been moulded to the required shape and then fired at a high temperature in a kiln. Terracotta blocks are usually hollow. They may be moulded to provide architectural details. Terracotta is normally unglazed, but glazing may be arranged with a second firing.

THREE-QUARTER BAT: *see* BAT

95. Terracotta, Sutton Place, Surrey
96. Nineteenth-century terracotta, Chester

TIE RODS and TIE PLATES: wrought-iron tie rods were threaded through buildings terminating in tie plates at each end. When tightened they prevented walls from bellying out. Sometimes, as for example to protect gable walls, they were included as part of the building design; but often they were the result of repair work.

TILE-CREASING: the use of one or two courses of tiles in a wall, for example under a coping or a sill, for decorative or damp-proofing purposes.

TOOTHING: bricks projecting like teeth in alternate courses in order to bond with other brickwork (*see* diagram under ARRIS), cf. BLOCK BONDING.

TUCK POINTING: *see* POINTING

tuck pointing

97. *above* Tie plate, Welsh Row, Nantwich, Cheshire

98. *top right* Tie plate, Beverley, Yorkshire, ER

99. *above right* Tie plate, Shere, Surrey

TILE: a square or rectangular piece of burnt clay thinner than a brick.

TUMBLING-IN: the term used to describe the courses of brickwork laid at right angles to the slope of a gable or chimney-breast and tapering into the horizontal courses.

TUNNEL KILN: a continuous kiln in which cars loaded with green bricks pass slowly along a tunnel in which they are pre-heated, fired and then allowed to cool before being unloaded.

UPDRAUGHT KILN: an intermittent kiln in which the hot gases rise up through the bricks to an open top. Newcastle, Suffolk and Scotch kilns are updraught kilns.

VITRIFIED HEADERS: bricks which have been given a dark glaze at one end by being placed in the hottest part of the kiln, or through the addition of salt during the firing process.

VOUSSOIRS: wedge-shaped bricks used in the construction of arches, including flat or cambered arches.

WALL-TILES: *see* BRICK TILES

WARP: a term sometimes used for the clot of clay thrown into the mould.

WASHBACK: a slurry of clay and chalk contained in a pond and allowed to settle before being made into London stock bricks.

WEATHERED JOINT: *see* JOINTING

WEEP HOLE: a vertical joint left free of mortar to allow water to drain away from a cavity wall above a damp-proof course.

WHITE BRICKS: *see* COSSEY WHITES

WICKET: the aperture through which bricks are loaded and unloaded in a kiln, such as a Scotch kiln.

WIRE-CUT BRICKS: brick clay extruded through an aperture and cut (like cheese) into brick shapes by wires and

100. Tumbling-in of brickwork in the gable; stable at North Wheatley, Nottinghamshire

then burnt in the kiln. Wire-cut bricks are less dense than pressed bricks, they may be perforated but do not have a frog, and they often show on the surface the parallel scratch lines resulting from the extrusion process.

YORKSHIRE BOND: *see* MONK BOND under BONDING

Part Three:
Chronological Survey

In this section the use of brickwork is illustrated, period by period, from the Middle Ages to the present day. The examples have been chosen to illustrate the use of brickwork in buildings as a whole as well as to show the development of details in brickwork.

Building types of a wide range have been illustrated but with an emphasis on those which are characteristic of their particular period: parish churches and gatehouses show medieval and Tudor brickwork, country houses and county towns demonstrate the skills of the Georgian bricklayers, while the nineteenth and twentieth centuries are represented largely by public, commercial and industrial buildings. At the same time, examples have been chosen from the regions and counties particularly notable for the different sorts of brickwork—the eastern and south-eastern counties of England, for earlier brickwork, London and the great industrial cities for later brickwork.

By following the sequence of illustrations one may appreciate the changing use of brickwork from its early days as a rough alternative to stone, through its development as a building material in its own right, to its emergence as a decorative material with which brickmakers, architects, bricklayers and sculptors have exercised skills of the highest order.

Period I   Medieval to 1485

In this section we look at brickwork during the long medieval period until the eve of the royal acceptance of the material under Henry VII.

Bricks of this period vary appreciably in size, ranging from small, thin bricks to the Great Bricks of a size not repeated until the early years of the Brick Tax. Generally bricks were thin, around 2 to 2¼ ins in thickness: those at Kirby Muxloe, for instance, were 9½ ins long and 2⅜ ins thick. The bricks were irregular in surface, erratic in shape and varied in colour. Made almost entirely in clamps on the building sites (brickyards were few and short-lived) they suffered from the imperfections of this crude method of firing. Most bricks actually used tended to be red in colour, but a few yellow bricks are to be seen at Eltham Palace, for instance, and, perhaps around 1500, in the gatehouse at Jesus College, Cambridge. Although there are examples of first-class conventional brickwork, as at Holy Trinity, Hull, there are other examples of the mixture of bricks with other building materials, such as the stone and flint of Little Wenham Hall.

Irregular bricks were laid in irregular bonds. Again, there are exceptions showing the consistent use of English Bond, but generally one sees walls of many stretchers and the occasional part-courses of headers, or walls which start with a consistent bond and wander into irregularity. Vitrified headers are to be seen, but scattered among the other bricks. Where diaper patterns may be detected they, too, tend to be irregular and placed erratically in the walls.

Irregular bonds lead to thick joints and in this period the impression of a wall of bricks plus joints is stronger than in some other periods. There has, of course, been much repointing but lime mortar has survived intact to a remarkable extent.

This was a period of 'structural brickwork' in which bricks were used in place of stone and even plastered in imitation of stone. One finds this in complete walls or in mullions, tracery, transoms and jambs of windows. Related to structural brickwork is the use of winding staircases with continuous vaulting above, testimony to the skill of the bricklayers. It was also a period of decorative brickwork, moulded bricks being used in some places, cut bricks in other situations. There is a hint of Continental influence, but nothing survives to match the power and confidence of brickwork in contemporary cathedral cities of Germany, for instance.

The distribution of brickwork in this period is most characteristic. It is essentially a material of the East and South-East of England, but even in that substantial part of the country the surviving examples are localised, with a group in East Yorkshire, a group in Hertfordshire, a group in Lincolnshire, a group in the Thames Valley, and so on. Within these areas the surviving examples may be fragments of very substantial buildings. Two million bricks are reputed to have been used in the work at Eton College which began in 1451.

The distribution is as confined socially as it is geographically. There are no brick cottages or cowsheds from this period. Grandees built their imposing brick towers as at Tattershall, their partially fortified moated dwellings as at Kirby Muxloe, their episcopal palaces as at Hatfield. Rich towns adorned their walls with brick gatehouses as at Beverley. So we have in medieval brickwork a prestigious material used in the richest parts of the country on some of the most important building projects.

right
101. St Nicholas' Chapel, Little Coggeshall, Essex, c. 1225; brick dressing to windows and brick quoins.

opposite
102. St Botolph's Priory, Colchester, Essex, late twelfth century; thin Roman bricks; wide joints; structural arches and decorative interlaced arcading.

above
103. Thornton Abbey, Lincolnshire, gatehouse c. 1382; barbican and flanking parts of gatehouse are in red brick.

opposite
104. North Bar, Beverley, Yorkshire, ER, rebuilt 1409; thin bricks (2 ins) varying in width and length; irregular bonding; 'sqynchons' or chamfered bricks in jambs and arches; moulded bricks for cusped ogee arches over the niches.

overleaf left
105. Rye House gatehouse: all that survives of extensive buildings of c. 1443; English Bond generally, diaper work, relieving arch, corbelling in moulded brickwork, moulded brick dressings to windows.

overleaf right
106. Rye House gatehouse. Moulded brick handrail to staircase.

opposite
107. Tattershall Castle,
Lincolnshire, begun in 1434–5
by Ralph Cromwell; thin (2 ins)
bricks made at Edlington Moor
some nine miles away; elaborate
brick vaulting to the interior.

above
108. Tattershall Castle
guardhouse, Lincolnshire; an
original doorway on the first
floor; stone dressings to
windows a later alteration.

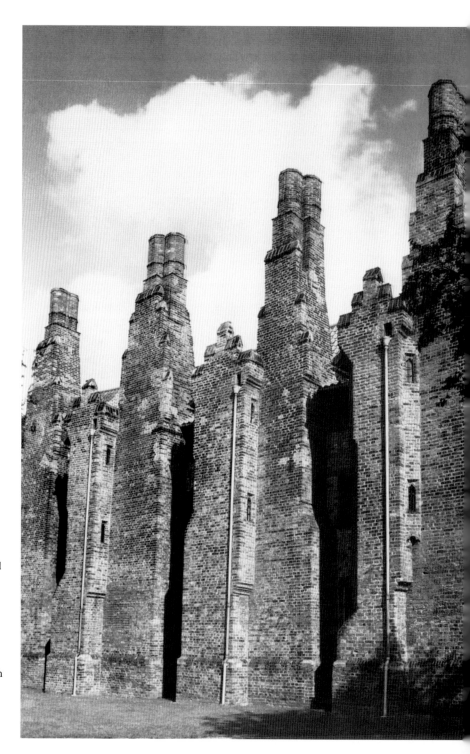

right
109. Gainsborough Old Hall, Lincolnshire, begun c. 1470; west range with boldly projecting chimney-breasts and lavatory blocks with crow-stepped gables; English Bond.

opposite
110. Pykenham's gateway, Northgate Street, Ipswich, Suffolk, c. 1471; arches probably in moulded brick with their mullions, jambs and label moulds; main walling English Cross Bond but with English Bond in the crow-stepped gable.

above
111. Kirby Muxloe Castle,
Leicestershire, 1480; English
Bond, thin bricks approx. 2⅜
ins thick; elaborate diapers.

opposite
112. Tower wall, Kirby
Muxloe Castle, 1480; detail of
brickwork, including gun ports.

left
113. Wainfleet School,
Lincolnshire, founded 1484;
irregular English Bond; some
moulded brickwork to doors
and windows.

above
114. St Mary, Polstead,
Suffolk; remarkable arcading of
large thin bricks, possibly
Norman.

Period II Tudor and Elizabethan 1485 to 1603

We now turn to the bricks and brickwork of the period of the Tudor monarchs, a period of great national self-confidence and rivalry with the European powers of France and Spain, a period when the use of brickwork, for display as well as utility, grew in importance.

Bricks continued to be made on the building site wherever possible. Itinerant brickmakers operating independently ensured that there was a great variety in colour and texture of clamp-fired bricks and some variation in brick sizes. Generally bricks continued to be thin with some little variation in length: at St John's College, Cambridge, for instance, the bricks 9 ins long were about 2 ins thick; on the Great Hall at Hampton Court bricks 10 ins long were almost 2½ ins thick; at Layer Marney Tower, bricks 9½ ins long were around 2 ins thick. The bricks were not precisely sized or shaped, clamp burning leading to twisting, and imperfect mixing of the clay leading to rough texture. Moulded bricks were used to produce masonry-like details as in four-centred arches and label moulds with Gothic cross-sections. Terracotta had a brief flourish both for purely decorative uses, as in the roundels at Hampton Court, and for partly structural use, as in the windows and doorways at Sutton Place.

The firing process in clamp or kiln produced flared headers and these were selected by the bricklayers for use in diaper patterns. Diamond and saltire cross shapes were the most popular, but heart shapes and symbols, such as the key, were also used. The difference in tone between headers and stretchers was often quite minimal and subtle effects were one result, though painted headers were another. Bonding steadied around straightforward English Bond, though English Cross Bond was used here and there, for example under Flemish influence at Bachegraig in North Wales. English Bond was modified to allow for patterns in the headers, and bricks in the less prominent walls were laid in an irregular bond with occasional headers or header courses. Where good stone was available it was used for quoins, window and door surrounds and dressings generally.

There continued to be an emphasis in the distribution of brickwork towards the eastern and south-eastern counties. London was seeing more brickwork and permanent kilns in brickyards are known from about 1540. Most of the well-known brick buildings of the period, such as Burton Constable Hall in East Yorkshire, Kentwell and Long Melford Halls in Suffolk, Layer Marney Tower and Hill Hall in Essex, Lambeth Palace in London, Hampton Court in Middlesex and Sutton Place in Surrey all show this distribution. But use of the material was beginning to spread to the Midlands, as at Kneesall in Nottinghamshire

below
115. Sutton Place, Surrey, south front c. 1530; English Bond with diaper work; terracotta dressings and panels.

overleaf left
116. St John's College, Cambridge, gatehouse c. 1520; diaper work.

overleaf right
117. Layer Marney Tower, Essex, c. 1523; gatehouse from inner side; diaper brickwork, moulded bricks, terracotta, all used with great virtuosity.

of 1522–7, to the North-West, as in Peover Hall in Cheshire of 1585, as well as making an exceptional foray into Wales in Plas Clough and Bachegraig, both built by Sir Richard Clough in 1567–9.

Brickwork was coming into use for engineering as well as ordinary building purposes. Henry VIII's artillery castles at Deal and Walmer are brick buildings though with stone envelopes. The brick fireplaces, chimney-breasts and chimney-stacks of the late sixteenth and early seventeenth centuries combined utility with display. Most characteristic of the period, however, are the great towering gatehouses which advertised various palaces and colleges. The Archbishop Morton gatehouse at Lambeth Palace is one; the eight-storey gatehouse at Layer Marney still dominates the landscape near Colchester. College buildings such as Jesus, Queens' and St John's in Cambridge are entered through gatehouses out of proportion to the college buildings they originally served.

It is at Hampton Court Palace, however, that all the characteristics of bricks, bonds, joints, ornament, colour and texture of the brickwork of the period may be seen in one whole composition.

opposite
118. St Andrew, Sandon, Essex, early sixteenth century; brick tower and porch added to earlier church; diaper work and quite elaborate corbelling; brick bonding in the tower varied between English Bond and English Cross Bond at stages up the tower.

below
119. Leez Priory, Essex, inner gatehouse, 1536–7; complex diaper patterns in blue headers.

opposite
123. Burton Constable Hall,
detail; detail of part of entrance
elevation showing consistent
English Bond and stone
dressings.

above
124. Burton Constable Hall,
Yorkshire, ER, general view,
late sixteenth century.

Period III Jacobean, Stuart and Queen Anne 1603–1714

The period from about 1603 to about 1714 witnessed the Renaissance in architecture in this country and a revolution in the use of bricks. What had been a prestige material, confined to a part of England, now became a material of much more widespread use down the social scale and across the kingdom.

Bricks themselves were still made by traditional means in clamps and updraught kilns, though coal was beginning to become a significant fuel. Individual bricks continued to be imperfect in shape though size was tending to settle at 9 ins long and 2½ ins in thickness. Colour and texture continued to vary quite widely by way of raw material, methods of manufacture and inconsistencies in firing, whether in clamp or kiln. The use of a frog in brickmaking became common from about 1690, at least in the south of England. Moulded bricks were used for classical details in buildings of the Artisan Mannerist style. Vitrified headers were deliberately provided and sometimes they were glazed with the introduction of salt during firing.

Diaper work was dying out. Sudbury Hall, Derbyshire, for instance, is unusual in having completely diapered main elevations in a classical building and here the diaper has a classical regularity. However, regular patterns of vitrified headers were used in plain walling in Flemish Bond.

There had been some tendency towards the use of Flemish Bond in the sixteenth century; some buildings had courses of alternate headers and stretchers, but separated by several stretcher courses. Regular Flemish Bond is believed to have been introduced in the Dutch House at Kew of 1631 and immediately became the standard bond for all locations of any importance. Pure English Bond became archaic, though variations on English Bond were used for inferior work or in insignificant positions.

This period was one in which gauged brickwork became important. As part of the decorative treatment of Anglo-Baroque buildings of the late seventeenth and early eighteenth centuries, pilasters of the classical orders and dressings to doors and windows were devised in brickwork. This work was created from cut and rubbed brick, the softer red or orange rubber bricks contrasting with the brickwork of general walling. The thin joints of lime putty between these sharply defined bricks contrasted with thicker joints in regular brickwork. Sometimes the whole elevation was constructed in gauged brickwork and the almost metallic precision of such brickwork foreshadowed its use in Georgian buildings, as at Chicheley Hall, 1719–23, for example.

During this period the use of brickwork spread widely: as far as the tip of Wales in the case of Bodwrdda in Llyn, Caernarfonshire, built in

1621, deep into the south-western peninsula in the case of Bridgeland Street in Bideford, Devon, of the 1690s. Its use in clay-bearing lowlands extended and its use in stone areas, such as the Peak District of Derbyshire, showed, in the Market Hall of Winster, that bricks were transported for the sake of an up-to-date effect. Even where timber-frame construction continued to be used, bold brick chimney-stacks dominated the houses; sometimes brick was used as a plinth; more and more brick was used as infill either from the first or as a replacement for wattle and daub. Counties from Essex to Shropshire bear witness to this.

Wren and the other great architects of the period were happy to change to brickwork either in conjunction with stone dressings or with different grades of the same material. Brick churches were built and, following the Act of 1689, neat and unobtrusive brick chapels were built by the Dissenters. Disastrous fires in the densely packed towns, culminating in the Great Fire of London, 1666, encouraged the use of brickwork for its fire-resistant qualities. Altogether the architectural revolution, the political revolution and the religious changes brought brickwork into prominence as a worthy rival to stone and timber for prestige or economy.

125. Burton Agnes Hall, Yorkshire, ER, c. 1601–10; brick with stone dressings; regular English Bond.

above
126. Sudbury Hall,
Derbyshire, c. 1613 and
1670–95; precise diaper
pattern.

opposite top
127. Bramshill House,
Hampshire, 1605–12;
south-west front in English
Bond with stone dressings;
blind windows at basement
level.

opposite bottom
128. Carr House, Bretherton,
Lancashire, 1613; a remarkably
early use of brickwork for this
part of the country; English
Bond generally but Header
Bond in the upper parts of
the wall (possibly to make
maximum use of bricks fired on
site); diaper work.

above
130. Balls Park, Hertford,
c. 1640; garden front; English
Bond generally, cut and rubbed
work as dressings.

overleaf left
131. Balls Park, Hertford,
corner of garden front; fairly
thin bricks (2¼ ins) with thick
joints used to make the pilaster
and quoins as well as main
walling; intermediate cornice in
moulded, rubbed and ordinary
bricks.

left
129. Wilberforce House, Hull,
Yorkshire, ER, c. 1630;
brickwork extravagantly,
though rather boldly, cut and
shaped so that the whole front is
modelled, bricks are thin (2 ins)
but with wide joints; English
Bond generally.

overleaf right
132. Winster Market Hall,
Winster, Derbyshire; it is
remarkable that the late
seventeenth-century hall over
the stone-built, covered market
was constructed in brickwork,
at that time still a foreign
material in this stone area.

opposite
133. Spraysbridge Farmhouse, Westfield, Sussex, 1690; plain walling in Flemish Bond.

above
134. The Old Hall, Aylsham, Norfolk, chimney dated 1689; Flemish Bond; rusticated quoins.

opposite
135. Detail of the Old Hall, Aylsham, showing the regularity in the Flemish Bond; moulded plat band; rubbed brick voussoirs and fine-jointed rubbed brick dressings around the door.

above right
136. Old Meeting House, Norwich, Norfolk, 1693; Flemish Bond generally, stone capitals and bases to pilasters.

right
137. Old Meeting House, Norwich; detail of sundial showing architraves (damaged) in cut and rubbed bricks, thin and with thin joints in contrast to the regular bricks used in the panel between plat band and sill.

above
138. Thornton Hall, Thornton
Curtis, Lincolnshire, c. 1695;
pavilions and upper part of attic
storey are later, possibly of the
1760s; the regular Flemish
Bond shows well on the
elevation.

opposite
139. House in Queen Anne's
Gate, London, SW1; what is
now Queen Anne's Gate was
first developed from 1704,
though there have been
restoration and additions in the
Queen Anne style; brown
bricks with white brick
dressings in some cases;
Flemish Bond.

140. Pallant House,
Chichester, Sussex, c. 1712;
brickwork of superb quality and
remarkable virtuosity in
handling of regular and gauged
brickwork.

141. Wickstreet Farmhouse,
Hailsham, Sussex, 1714;
confident use of brickwork in
timber-frame country; bold
chimney-stacks and projecting
chimney-breast; Flemish Bond.

Period IV Georgian 1714–1837

Many commentators regard the Georgian as the finest period in the use of brickwork. Whole towns and villages were faced or rebuilt in the material. A balance of variety and uniformity produced something like perfection in the use of brickwork. The quiet, restrained, Palladian version of Renaissance architecture seemed to be one for which brick was the most suitable material given the British climate. In all but colour the Georgian was a Golden Age for brickwork in this country.

Brick size and shape maintained the standard developed in the previous century and an Act of 1725 established minimum dimensions which were close to those in normal use. In the early years of the Brick Tax of 1784 some oversize bricks were produced but after the revisions of 1803 sizes settled down, except in the North and Midlands where depth was about 3 ins, rather more than that used in the rest of the country. There were some experiments in non-standard bricks, of which the Hitch Bricks of Hertfordshire were the best known. There was some reaction against red as being the universal colour for bricks: the yellow-brown London stocks were important; the so-called 'white' bricks found favour; silver-grey bricks of the Thames Valley were also characteristic of this period.

Flemish Bond and its variations continued to be the predominant way of bonding brickwork. Header bond had some popularity, es-pecially in the southern counties of England, and the colour contrast between the silver-grey of the headers and the warm red or orange bricks acting as dressings made for lively elevations. Among the cottages, Rat-Trap and similar bonds of brick-on-edge were found in southern and eastern counties of England.

Joints in exposed brickwork were generally becoming finer and, of course, in gauged brickwork they became very fine indeed. During this period tuck pointing was developed as a means of imitating these delicate joints. Mortar jointing was also related to the use of brick with other materials: brick lacing courses to flint or to inferior stone, as in Kent and Sussex, for instance.

This was a period of refronting of timber-framed buildings in the towns and villages both for fashion and for fire protection. Part of this was done in mathematical tiling. This technique was practically con-fined to the south-eastern counties of England though there were isolated groups, as in Cambridge, and isolated buildings, as part of Penrhyn Castle in North Wales. Generally the spread of the use of brickwork into all the British counties save the most rugged was maintained, and even there brickwork was used for special purposes, such as making fireproof floors or as a substitute for dressed masonry in mills and warehouses.

During most of the Georgian period brickwork was a material of high prestige as well as general utility. During the Regency period of the early nineteenth century, however, structural brickwork was hidden under plaster either to produce a uniform surface which could be painted or to provide an imitation of stonework. Exposed brickwork continued to be used in utilitarian circumstances and it is interesting that the railway station attracting passengers to the Manchester end of the Liverpool and Manchester Railway in 1830 was in rendered brick-work, while the adjacent goods warehouses and carriage sheds were in exposed brickwork and raised on huge brick arches and vaults.

142. Chicheley Hall, Buckinghamshire, 1719–23; entrance front; this and the garden front were faced entirely in rubbed bricks; it is reputed that altogether nearly one million such bricks were used in this one house; Flemish Bond.

above

143. Peckover House, Wisbech, Cambridgeshire; c. 1727; Flemish Bond; segmental arched windows; aprons, plat bands, pilasters.

right

144. House in South Street, Boston, Lincolnshire; moulded brick with initials IF 1726; Flemish Bond.

opposite

145. House in Castle Street, Farnham, Surrey; Header Bond; gauged-brick flat arches.

above
147. Great Ormond Street,
London, WC1; early
eighteenth-century street,
though with houses of several
periods and degrees of
restoration.

left
146. Holkham Hall, Norfolk,
1734–61, designed by William
Kent; light grey brick; Flemish
Bond; rusticated base and
voussoir blocks to doorway and
windows.

above
148. Stables at Burton
Constable, Yorkshire, ER,
c. 1760; simple but carefully
modelled elevation dependent
on plain brickwork; Stretcher
Bond generally with occasional
headers; gauged bricks for the
semicircular arches; Header
Bond in niches.

right
149. Bailey Hall, Hertford;
early eighteenth century; white
brick in Flemish bond (2½ ins
thick); red brick around
windows which have arches
slightly cambered in gauged
brick; pilasters in gauged
brickwork with thin joints.

opposite
150. Perrott House, Pershore,
Worcestershire; c. 1760;
Flemish Bond generally.

151. Sir John Leman's School,
Beccles, Suffolk; 1631 and 1762
with early nineteenth-century
extensions; principal wall of
flint diapered with brick
headers; some English Bond
brickwork in the gable wall.

right
152. Cottages in Spain's Court, Boston, Lincolnshire. Flemish Bond.

below
153. House of Correction, Newport, Essex, 1775; rusticated brick quoins and dressings to doorway; brick dentilation to pediment.

154. Farm building at
Seighford, Staffordshire; late
eighteenth century; Sussex
Bond; honeycomb brickwork;
corbelled brickwork to dovecot
in gable.

155. Union Place, Wisbech,
Cambridgeshire; presumably
dating from about 1800;
Flemish Bond.

above
156. Holy Trinity, Newcastle
under Lyme, Staffordshire,
1833–34; designed by
J. Egan; unusual use of
deep-purple near-glazed bricks
in a boldly panelled west front.

opposite
157. High Lighthouse,
Harwich, Essex; 1818; clever
bricklaying in taper to octagonal
plan.

158. Holy Trinity, Newcastle
under Lyme; detail showing
wide, thin, paving-type bricks
laid on edge with lacing courses
in a somewhat darker tone.

Period V Victorian and Edwardian 1837–1914

Probably more bricks were laid during this period than in all the previous periods put together. The huge increase in population led to great demands for houses, churches and public buildings of all kinds. The progress of the Industrial Revolution led to enormous demands for brickwork in railway bridges and continuous viaducts as well as for tunnels, mine shafts, factories and warehouses. At the same time new methods of brickmaking facilitated production of the material in unprecedented quantities. For much of the Victorian and Edwardian period architectural fashion favoured the use of bricks and terracotta in buildings ranging from the most prestigious to the most humble.

Traditional methods of brick manufacture continued, especially in the London area and the South of England generally. New demands were also met by production of bricks first from the Coal Measures shales and later from the Oxford clays of Bedfordshire. Mechanised manufacture led to the production of pressed bricks of precise dimensions, smooth texture, sharp arrises and uniform colour. Pressed bricks often had deep frogs on one or both sides. Engineering bricks, such as Staffordshire Blues, were now available for use in architectural polychrome as well as for their structural virtues. There was a tendency for large bricks, $3\frac{1}{4}$ ins deep, to remain in use long after the end of the Brick Tax in 1850 had removed one of the main reasons for their use. There was some return to favour of thin, hand-made facing bricks as part of the Vernacular Revival movement in architecture at the end of the nineteenth century and the beginning of the twentieth. Moulded bricks and terracotta blocks became popular, especially in relation to the application of the Gothic Revival style to buildings of many types and sizes.

There was a great variety of bonding in use during this period. Flemish Bond and all its variations continued to be used for main elevations, and, in the Midlands and South at least, for most utilitarian work. English Bond had a rebirth, partly for its strength in engineering structures and partly for its associations in Gothic Revival buildings. Variations on English Bond continued in use for utilitarian work in the North. There was a return to Header Bond in the north-western counties of England, especially in the Manchester area. The introduction of cavity walling entailed the use of Stretcher Bond though conventional bonds, including Header Bond, were also used with cavity walling.

Precisely formed bricks allowed the use of thin joints without the expense of cutting and rubbing. Conventional jointing in common bricks made use of ash to produce black mortar, popular in the industrial districts but also used on buildings in London. Cements, especially Portland Cement, began to supersede lime in mortar, though the changeover was far from complete by the early twentieth century. Tuck pointing continued in use both in white and in black mortar and especially in urban and suburban housing, but it was falling out of favour by the end of the period.

The use of brickwork continued to spread during the nineteenth century, perhaps because of the spread of branch lines and local railways in the second half of the century. Hard red, blue or yellow bricks are characteristic of the mining valleys of South Wales, for instance, whether for chapels and public buildings or as dressings in the long rows of miners' cottages. For major buildings the spread of the railway network cut the tie of brick to localities: Gripper's Patent Bricks of Nottingham, for instance, were used for the St Pancras Hotel rather than some clamp-burnt bricks from the Thames flatlands. The railway system made Bedfordshire Flettons widely available; engineering bricks from Staffordshire, terracotta from Ruabon in North Wales, 'Nori' bricks from Accrington in Lancashire all spread widely. However, regional variations did continue, such as the use of 'white' bricks in Cambridgeshire and East Anglia. In spite of mechanisation there were still huge numbers of local brickworks in the industrial areas as well as in the traditional brickmaking districts, some using continuous kilns but many still using intermittent kilns to fire bricks for local use according to local demand.

During the Victorian and Edwardian periods brickwork was represented in the work of major architects such as Butterfield, Street, Waterhouse and Shaw but it was also represented in the works of countless local architects influenced by these national figures. For utility or display brickwork predominated, notwithstanding the continued use of masonry in special circumstances.

159. Building, probably
maltings, Heytesbury,
Wiltshire; careful use of
ordinary brickwork with rough
brick arches and dentilation at
eaves; tie plates on main block;
tie plates and straps around the
kiln wall.

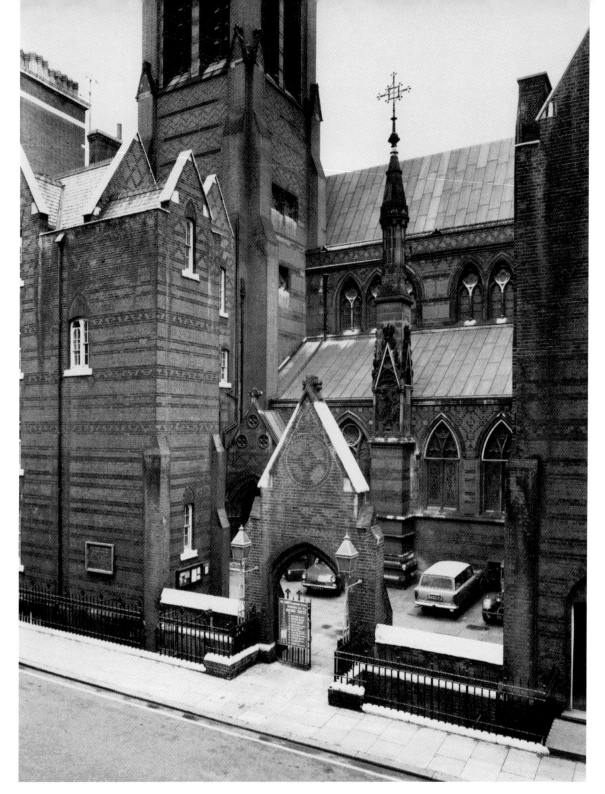

160. All Saints, Margaret
Street, London W1; 1849–59;
Butterfield; English Bond, but
with very elaborate polychrome
in red, yellow and blue bricks.

161. Digswell Viaduct,
Welwyn, Hertfordshire, 1850;
generally English Bond, arches
assembled in five layers; tie
plates with ends of tie rods
visible.

above
162. Keble College Chapel,
Oxford; 1868–82; Butterfield;
polychrome brickwork in red,
yellow and blue and with
sandstone dressings.

opposite
163. Granary at Welsh Back,
Bristol; 1869; polychrome
brickwork and English
Garden-Wall Bond.

164. Former Midland Grand
Hotel at St Pancras Station,
London NW1; 1873; Sir
G. Gilbert Scott, English Bond,
thin bricks (2¾ ins); black
mortar; polychromatic effect
with brick and stone.

above
165. Royal Holloway College, Egham, Surrey; built 1879–91 to designs by W. H. Crossland developing the Château of Chambord into hard red brick; English Bond.

right
166. House near Seighford, Staffordshire; Sussex Bond; polychrome; S-shaped tie plate.

overleaf left
167. Westminster Cathedral, Victoria, London SW1; 1895–1903; J. F. Bentley; red brick and some tile; stone dressings.

overleaf right
168. Detail of Westminster Cathedral; red brick and stone dressings; tiles as voussoir blocks; walls generally are in a variation of English Garden-Wall Bond in which the second and fourth stretcher courses are offset by a quarter-brick length instead of a half-brick.

Period VI Modern: 1914 to the present day

The ninety-five or so years since the outbreak of the First World War have seen many changes in the use of brickwork. At first there was some continuation of Edwardian Baroque, and its use of terracotta, and of the Vernacular Revival using thin hand-made bricks or common bricks concealed by rendering or tile hanging. After the war the campaign to build homes for heroes was at first hampered by a shortage of bricks so that many of the housing estates of the 1920s displayed common bricks rather than the facing bricks of Victorian and Edwardian housing. During the inter-war period the Neo-Georgian fashion was predominant and represented by banks, post offices, villas and council houses as well as by tall blocks of flats and offices in London and the major cities. Dutch influence brought the bold masses and geometrical details of Hilversum to British towns and cities. During the Second World War blackout restrictions and shortage of fuel and labour meant the closure of many brickworks, especially the smaller ones, some never to open again. In the immediate post-war years alternating shortages of steel and bricks affected the design and construction of all buildings.

From 1945 onwards experiments with tile-like bricks (V-bricks) and with prefabricated brick panels attempted to match traditional, or just acceptable, appearance to the assumed advantages of modular design and prefabrication. All are forgotten now. Reaction to the banality and crudity of much of the prefabricated concrete design and construction has led to a new interest in brick cladding and both Staffordshire Blue and Lancashire Red bricks abound. More recently an interest in bold brickwork form with the aid of corbelling and the use of special bricks, and in brick patterning with the interplay of two or three colours in one mass, has further developed the material and its techniques. This has been matched by the brickmakers with shapes, colours, textures, specials, mouldings, terracotta blocks and the revival of hand-making techniques all contributing to their responses.

At first bricks were standardised at 2, $2\frac{5}{8}$ and $2\frac{7}{8}$ ins thicknesses, though only the last two were widely used. Then there were changes to metric dimensions and limited experiments in the use of larger bricks. A brief use of long, thin bricks resulted from the influence of Dudok and the other Dutch architects in the 1930s. Many bricks were manufactured with perforations, if wire-cut, or deep frogs if pressed. Generally there has been a wide range of textures, artificial rustication, artificial sand facing as brickmakers competed for the attention of architects and other specifiers. Paving bricks have developed from their traditional shapes into interlocking shapes and patterned bricks with the spread of interest in brick paving, especially in pedestrianised town centres.

The use of Stretcher Bond has become almost universal in this period. Although in the inter-war years there was some continuation of the use of snap headers to make patterns and create the illusion of traditional bonds in the outer leaf, this was abandoned after 1945. Some interest in pattern-making from projecting or recessed headers was fostered by the Festival of Britain in 1951, but it did not last long. Except that corbelled brickwork goes with the use of headers, Stretcher Bond is universal, and even in this brick modelling, the stitching and hanging made possible by the ingenuity of designers and manufacturers has virtually eliminated the need to use headers for projections. There has been little interest in pointing techniques; plasticisers have given cement mortars something of the workability of lime mortars, but the monotony of deeply raked joints has drawn attention all too often to the brick rather than the brickwork.

Regional variation in brickwork has now all but disappeared. Concentration of production into a relatively small number of highly efficient brickworks convenient to motorways as well as railways, has meant that huge lorry-loads of palletised and carefully wrapped facing bricks now go straight from kiln to site. One is no more likely to see a dump of common bricks on a building site than a clamp burning away except to fire bricks for conservation work.

169. Shakespeare Memorial Theatre, Stratford-upon-Avon, Warwickshire; 1928–32; Elizabeth Scott; plain brickwork in boldly massed blocks relieved by soldier courses, pilasters, and other projections in brick; the illustration shows the original appearance.

opposite
170. St Martin, New Knebworth, Hertfordshire; 1914; Lutyens; thin bricks in Sussex Bond.

above
171. St Nicholas, Burnage, Manchester; 1931–2; Welch, Cachemaille-Day and Lander; brown bricks in English Bond.

right
172. Mond Laboratory, Cambridge; 1933; Eric Gill's representation of a crocodile has been incised into a wall with the regular rhythm of Flemish Bond brickwork.

above left
177. Robinson College,
Cambridge; 1977–80; Gillespie,
Kidd & Coia; doorway in the
Stretcher Bond wall shows neat
use of corbelling with the
recessed planes of brickwork.

above right
178. Office Building, Bow
Street, Manchester; 1971;
concrete bricks used in a boldly
modelled pattern to form a
non-structural screen wall; part
honeycombed.

above

179. Hillingdon Civic Centre,
Uxbridge, Middlesex, designed
by Robert Mathew,
Johnson-Marshall and Partners,
1971–6; a building of brick and
tile displaying a set of
interrelated blocks and making
use of simple brick ornament,
such as dentilation.

right

180. Detail of Hillingdon Civic
Centre showing the use of thin
bricks with fairly thick joints, in
Monk Bond.

Part Four:
Building in Cob, Clay, Mud, Wychert, Turf, and Mud-and-Stud

1. Introduction

It has been estimated that about one-third of the earth's population still live in houses made of earth. The proportion in the past was much higher, and one expects that in future the proportion will be much lower, especially in developed countries. Therefore, before too many of these buildings are lost to history, they arc bcing studied, and some repaired and conserved for the future.

In Britain and Ireland we are already at the point at which the survival rate of earthen buildings is small and rapidly diminishing, and so conservation of selected examples has begun. The study of examples and the history of their use is urgent so that the proper selection may be made. Fortunately there are reports of earthen buildings as curiosities from the nineteenth century and reports of buildings of sociological or archaeological interest from the twentieth century.

Houses of unfired earth are a branch of vernacular architecture and may be studied from the point of view of the period in which they appear to have been built, the location of the site and the status of the owner or occupier for whom they were intended. In Britain very few of the surviving houses were for people of even local importance; in the south-western counties many farmhouses were built of clay, but in the rest of Britain and Ireland most clay dwellings were cottages built for (and often by) the poor or even the destitute. It is hardly surprising that until recently such cottages had become an embarrassment to society and were vulnerable to decay and demolition.

Yet clay cottages always had their defenders. It was pointed out that earth was a universally available building material, free to acquire and cheap to extract. It could be utilised through community action, requiring cash for only a few items, such as roof timbers and window frames (when such an extravagance was expected), and was warm, dry, free from draughts, cosy and comfortable when covered with thatch, and was preferred to brick and slate.

There are several ways of using earthen materials: placing puddled clay in a series of layers whether in a slow or quick process; tamping a mixture of dry earth between boards rather as concrete nowadays is poured into formwork; making clay lumps in moulds and building walls as if out of over-sized sun-dried bricks; simply using turf pared from grassy fields. It is also possible to daub clay onto a light framework of studs and wattle-work. All these techniques have had their periods of popularity and their preferred locations. Techniques and locations are examined in the following pages (181, 188).

181. Diagram. Various ways of using clay or earth including relation to cruck trusses.

a Cruck truss with cob walls
b Jointed cruck
c Mud-and-stud with plaited withies between staves
d Mud-and-stud with closely spaced staves
e Shuttered clay wall under construction
f Wall of *pisé-de-terre* under construction
g *Pisé* walls with holes for frame
h Clay lump and mould (with brick for comparison)
i Earth wall with stone facing
j Stone-faced earth walls as found in the western Isles of Scotland

In the context of the world, earthen construction in the British Isles has been a minor contributor. Nevertheless, we have the Antonine Wall and part of Hadrian's Wall as our counterparts to the earthen Great Wall of China, and we have our cob houses of Devon as our counterparts to the multi-storey pueblos of New Mexico and Morocco; we even have the sod houses of Ireland as fore-runners to the houses built beyond the sod house frontier of the central United States.

The changeover from clay to brick construction in this country began early but intensified in the nineteenth century until clay cottages, however agreeable to their occupiers, fell foul of building regulations and moved into the categories of archaeology and conservation.

2. Variations in the use of the material

Cob (clob, clom, mwd, clay)

The technique of using cob is concentrated in the south-west counties of Cornwall, Devon, Somerset and parts of adjacent counties, such as Dorset, but it is also found in other areas of the British Isles.

The essence of the process is that the earth is available on the site or immediately adjacent, that additional items (such as timber and thatch for roofing, or wood for window frames) may be brought to the site from no great distance and, importantly, that the labour required is mostly unskilled with the minimum of craftsmen's work involved. In other words, the builder—or his friends and relations—can build the walls, supervised at most by a local mudmason.

The basic material is not necessarily clay, though clay would normally be part of the mixture, the remainder being aggregate, sand and lime where available, and dung and road sweepings where they could be obtained. Added to the clay mixture was some vegetable matter, normally chopped straw but alternatively hay, furze or broome. This helps to minimise and control shrinkage and cracking.

An essential ingredient is water. This is added at a preparatory stage to help complete the final mix; too much water, of course, would make the mixture too sloppy to make into a wall, too little and the material does not adhere and cannot be placed in position.

The process of cob building was carefully described by the Rev. Coppinger Hill in 1843 when he was building cottages for some of his parishioners. The description has often been quoted but may be summarised as follows:

1. On or beside the site, clay-marl was dug and, if necessary, mixed with chalk and road sweepings. Hill suggested a proportion of 7/10 clay, 2/10 chalk and 1/10 road sweepings.
2. The clay mixture was spread on hard ground, beaten with forks and cleared of stones.
3. A circular bed of the cleaned clay was then wetted and trodden by horses. At this point the vegetable matter was added carefully so that it was thoroughly assimilated by the action of the horses' hooves.
4. The completed mixture was piled up and covered with straw until dry enough for use.
5. In erecting the wall, the first stage was to raise a foundation wall or 'pinning' of stones, flints, bricks or whatever was available. Hill recommended a wall 14 ins thick and 12 ins high. This seems narrow,

and in many examples the wall is more than 24 ins thick, and the height may be as much as six or seven feet, and more in multi-storey cob structures.

6. One man then stood on the stone plinth and received the first clod of clay thrown up by his mate on the ground. Carefully trodden into position, a three-pronged fork is used to help consolidation. This process continued along the whole perimeter of the wall until a complete course or courses, making up about 20 ins in height, had been erected. At this stage the clay was to be left to dry for a few days, or longer, depending on the amount of water in the mix and the weather conditions.

7. Once the section of wall was dry, another course would be added, and so on (always allowing for the required drying intervals in between), until the desired height was achieved. In the superior work of Hill, door and window frames would be fitted as the work proceeded; in the inferior work of less knowledgeable families, door and window openings were cut out afterwards.

8. Hill recommended that the inner and outer faces should be pared smooth as the work proceeded and while the mixture was wet enough to be trimmed. Ordinary farming tools, such as spades, were sufficient for this work.

9. Finally, inner and outer surfaces were plastered with clay mortar or lime plaster (if it was available and affordable), ready to be whitewashed.

The procedure was conducted in stages that matched the weather. Clay was dug in the later Autumn to allow for frost action during the Winter. Building began in the Spring and continued into early Summer to improve the drying process, and so that family labour could take advantage of the long days after regular work was finished.

Bearing in mind that earthen walls could deteriorate and ultimately collapse, precautions in design and construction had to be matched with care over maintenance. Rising damp and splashes of rain around the base were countered by the plinth of stone or flint or brick—and the attacks of vermin were minimised. The vulnerable top of the wall was protected by a deep overhang of the thatch at the eaves, and by beam filling of good-quality clay between the rafters. The surface of the wall was protected by the clay or lime rendering, enhanced by the annual coat of whitewash (182, 183).

Shuttered earth and *pisé-de-terre*

Building an earthen wall with the aid of wooden shuttering was some-times described (and often recommended) by observers in the late eigh-teenth century and the nineteenth century, but was never a common practice—even on great estates with a programme of cottage building.

182. Cob walling, Stoke St Gregory, Somerset.

183. Detail of cob walling, Brightley, Devon; beam projecting with wedge through a slot to aid stability.

The clay was prepared as for cob walling, and the foundations and plinth were put in place. However, the clay was tamped into position, a clot at a time, into formwork or shuttering of wooden boards supported on brackets projecting from the wall. When the clay was dry, the shuttering was dismantled, re-erected further up the wall and the whole process was repeated, stage by stage, until the desired wall height was achieved (181). Supported by the shuttering, a drier mix of clay could be used and some time was saved by the shorter drying period. However, time was lost in dismantling and re-erecting the shuttering.

One advantage of this method was the greater neatness of the completed wall, as the corners of the building were squared off and the wall surface was smooth. To present-day eyes the rounded, moulded effect of a cob house is part of its charm, but to the landowner's eye of 200 years ago, 'neatness' of a cottage was much more desirable.

The process of *pisé-de-terre* is similar to the shuttered earth process. Wall construction still depended on wooden shuttering, but in *pisé* work this was usually much more carefully made and more precisely fixed. The mix was of dry earth, not moist at all, and the earthen mixture was energetically rammed into the mould to give a dense, carefully-shaped result. As no drying time was required, the process was relatively speedy, but of course time was spent in assembling and dismantling the formwork, and cost was involved in the design and construction of the mould.

Pisé-de-terre was devised in France and quite widely used there. Its details were extensively published in journals and encyclopedias, but the process was never widely used in the UK.

Clay daubing

There was a technique of building houses with solid clay walls that was rather different from that of cob construction. This technique was practiced on both sides of the Solway Firth: the Solway Plain in the north of Cumberland and the coastal areas of Dumfriesshire and Galloway in Scotland.

The extraction and preparation of the clay was similar to that for the clay in cob walling, but instead of raising the wall in stages, and allowing each stage to dry before proceeding, the wall was raised in courses of about 3 ins each, up to the low eaves of a single-storey building, and allowed to dry as a whole. This technique was clearly explained in the Second *Statistical Account of Scotland* (1830s), under the section on the parish of Dornock in Dumfriesshire on the Scottish side of the Solway Firth.

> The manner of erecting them is singular. In the first place they dig out the foundations of the house and lay a row or two of stones; then they procure from a pit contiguous as much clay or brick earth as is sufficient to form the walls and, having provided a quantity of straw or other litter to mix with the clay, upon a day appointed, the whole neighbourhood, male and female, to the number of 20 or 30 assemble, each with a dung fork, a spade or some such instrument. Some fall to working of the clay or mud by mixing it with straw; others carry the materials and four or five of the most experienced hands build and take care of the walls. In this manner the walls of the house are finished in a few hours after which they retire to a good dinner, and plenty of drink which is provided for them, whereupon they have music and a dance, with which and other works of festivity they conclude the evening. This is called a 'daubing' and in this manner they make a frolic of what would otherwise be a very dirty and disagreeable job.

A somewhat similar account for the English side of the Solway Firth was published in 1794. J. Housman, in his 'Parish Notes' to W. Hutchinson's *The History of the County of Cumberland*, writes of the houses in the parish of Orton in northern Cumberland:

> These houses are generally made up in a day or two; for, when a person wants a house, barn etc. built he acquaints his neighbours who all appear at the time appointed; some lay on clay, some tread it while others are preparing straw to mix with it. By this means building comes low in cost and expeditious, and indeed it must be owned that they have brought the art of clay building to some perfection. They generally ground with stone about a yard high; and a house thus built will stand (it is said) 150 or 200 years.

The construction of a home was especially appropriate as part of a village wedding celebration. In an article published in 1857–8, A. C. Gibson describes how after a wedding on the Solway Plain:

> Their friends would assemble about dawn on the appointed spot and, labouring with good will, each at an allotted task, would erect, long ere sunset, the clay walls of a dwelling for some young couple who had to rely on a bridewain [wedding presents] for means to finish it and furnish it. The walls reared and the floor laid of the same materials, the volunteer operatives would 'hansel' the cottage by a dance on the wet clay floor . . . Many cottages with clay walls and a thatched roof built by this method which was called 'a clay-daubing' are still to be seen in the northern parts of the country . . . this old custom has died out within the last 30 years or so [i.e. about 1820].

The walls at the end of the day's work clearly show the method of erection. Each course of clay, about 3 ins or 4 ins high, is topped with straw before the next course is placed on it. The ends of the straw would project until the whole inner and outer surfaces had been pared back to receive a rendering of clay mortar or lime plaster (184).

The structural loads carried on the purlins and rafters of the turf, straw, or heather roof are carried by cruck trusses. The members of the cruck truss being of rude construction, are much inferior to the carefully finished blades of cruck trusses in Worcestershire or Herefordshire. Several trusses found on the Solway Plain have been dendro-dated, through the initiative of Nina Jennings, giving felling dates of between the late fourteenth and very early fifteenth century and later. It is clear that some members of the cruck truss have been re-used. In the later clay houses walls have been accepted as load-bearing. The very few two-storeyed clay buildings are probably built in conventional cob construction.

184. Clay daubing, Cumberland; note the thin lifts of puddled clay and the layers of straw between each lift.

Clay lump (clay bat, clay block, mud brick, adobe)

A method of using earth in building, practised over much of the world and from deepest antiquity to the present day, was to make earth into blocks and so to build walls which were stable, long-lasting and capable of rising to considerable heights. This technique of making structural blocks was variously called in England clay bat, clay block, mud brick and adobe. Elsewhere in the British Isles they were usually called clay lump or clay bat.

Their use was quite widespread in these islands, but examples are concentrated in south Norfolk and north Suffolk. At one time they were thought to be, like cob in Devon, objects of some antiquity, but through the researches of John McCann the earliest reliably dated example has been found to be 1791. The chief period of use was about 1820 to 1840, which helped to meet a demand for cottages that resulted from the conversion of pasture into arable as part of the sequence of agricultural revolutions.

The clay of which the lumps were made was dug and prepared in much the same way as for cob buildings, except that proximity to the building site was desirable but not essential. In selecting the material, clay with aggregate of small stones was chosen, but with an admixture of chalk, which helps to explain the popularity of clay lump in East Anglia and its scarcity in, say, Wales and Cumbria where chalk is not found. Having been dug in the Autumn, the raw material was exposed to frost action, turned several times, and in the Spring received an admixture of short lengths of straw or other vegetable matter, whereupon a pile about 6 ins deep was trodden by horses and watered from time to time until the desired consistency was achieved.

Next, in the building season, dollops of the clay were thrown into a wooden mould, open at the top and bottom like that used by a brickmaker, except that its dimensions were much larger. The most common size of clay lump to be produced was 18 ins long, 8½ or 9 ins wide and 6 ins deep. Some were smaller, but few were larger as the common size weighed in the region of 55 lbs and anything heavier was very difficult to handle. The mould was usually placed on a piece of prepared ground rather than on a brickmaker's bench and, as it was filled, the clay was tamped into the corners of the mould and the surplus was struck off. The mould was then lifted to reveal a solid block, smooth-sided and sharp-edged.

When sufficient blocks had been moulded in a day's work, they were left in position to begin the drying process. After a few days the blocks were dry enough and solid enough to be turned and placed on edge. If necessary they were turned again to benefit from the best of the wind until they were acceptably dry. They could then be moved to the hack, which was a platform of flat and solid material such as waste brick covered with a temporary roof of thatch. The blocks stayed there until they were ready to be transported to the site. Again

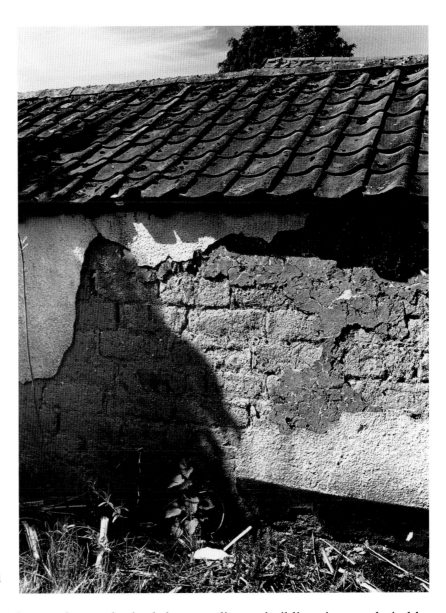

185. Clay lump, Oakley, Suffolk; note the size of each block and the clay rendering that would have concealed and protected the clay lump wall.

it must be emphasised that an adjacent building site was desirable, but a source of the best quality raw material might make it better to have a production run of clay blocks, which could be taken to various sites by horse and cart in a way that would be impossible for cob mixture.

In building the wall, stretcher bond was almost invariably used with the 9 ins width determining the wall thickness. The courses of clay lump would rise from a low brick or flint plinth sufficiently high to protect the base of the wall from splashes. Openings for windows and doors were left in the clay lump wall as if it were a brick wall. A timber wall-plate would be securely fixed into the top of the wall to receive rafters. Many cottages were single-storey, but two or more storeys were not too difficult to build in clay lump. The walls were finished internally with lime plaster and externally with a clay mortar or a lime rendering. The final finish of limewash was frequently renewed (185). In agricultural buildings a coal-tar finish was sometimes applied as a preservative. In cottage building the superior dwellings had a brick facing, which makes them difficult to identify as built of clay lump unless the brick is confined to the main elevation.

There have been questions as to whether clay lumps were subject to the Brick Tax. The questions arise because the Brick Tax was paid on the number of 'green' bricks in a yard, moulded but not yet fired, rather than on the actual number of bricks fired and used. However, the general impression is that clay blocks were not classified as bricks or tiles and so were not subject to the Brick Tax.

The pert, neatly built cottages of clay lump, especially when covered with a tile or pantile roof, rather than the soft expanse of thatch, give quite a different impression than their counterparts of cob, but they appear very much of their period—the middle years of the nineteenth century—and very long-lasting.

Wychert (witchert, witchit, chalk-cob)

Although only found in a comparatively small area, the use of wychert has attracted a good deal of interest. The name has been traditionally used for a variation of cob in which chalk has been incorporated. The soil is dug to a depth that includes the chalk deposits that lie a foot or two below the surface in the area where wychert is used. The material is broken and turned and watered as in making cob, but in cleaning stones care is taken to maintain the chalk mixture by simply breaking the pieces of chalk to an acceptable size. In the treading process, lengths of straw—rather than chopped straw—were scattered on the mixture, but the whole was thoroughly trodden by the hooves of carthorses supplemented by the boots of the builders.

The foundation of stone or brick having been erected, the two-man team of builders raised the first layer, or lift, of the wychert and carefully trod it into position. Three-pronged small forks with long handles were used. As with cob, the lift was allowed to dry until ready to receive the next one, except that the wall surfaces were pared with a spade wielded sideways so as to remove surplus clay, and chop projecting wisps of straw. Each lift was between 24 and 30 ins deep; the intended wall thickness was from 16 to 24 ins (186).

The quality of wychert was so good that it was not necessary to render the wall with clay or lime though it was still important to protect the head and foot of the wall from dampness and some builders preferred to apply a rendering.

The centre of wychert use was the small town of Haddenham in Buckinghamshire and many houses, cottages, other buildings and boundary walls still survive and remain in use. The material was still

186. Haddenham, Buckinghamshire: wychert wall raised on a plinth of small stones.

used as late as the 1930s and there has been a revival of making wychert, using debris of demolished walls for re-mixing—mainly for repair but also for experiments in new build.

Turf (sod) and peat

One of the most ancient building materials, whose use was continued in Scotland and Ireland well into the nineteenth century, is turf (called sod in Ireland) and its related material, peat.

Turf is the grassy top surface of a pasture field with growing vegetable matter, soil, and a set of roots. Indeed, the word encompasses the sward which makes up our cricket and football fields, our grass tennis courts, most of our horse-racing courses, the fine surface of the bowling greens and the treasured lawn in our domestic gardens. Peat is the decayed vegetable matter that has accumulated in bogs and mosses, which for centuries provided the domestic fuel when supplies of wood were scarce and before coal became cheap and readily available.

The turf used for building was not often of the quality needed for the purposes mentioned in the last paragraph. It is not long lasting, being susceptible to both excessive dryness and excessive dampness and therefore to structural collapse. However, turf was an ideal material for the swift erection of fortifications, and the western end of Hadrian's Wall in England and the full extent of the Antonine Wall in Scotland were built of turf. It was probably used as a facing to the walls of the swiftly erected marching camps of the Roman legions. It continued in use, in conjunction with earth, for fortifications throughout the medieval period, and as part of the deep earthen ramparts of the artillery period of fortress design.

Turf was also a suitable material for field boundaries. It did not survive as long as quickset hedges (such as hawthorn), but provided there was a good cap of stones or thatch it did not require much maintenance. For the walls of buildings it had the advantage of wide availability, cheapness and swift erection, not to mention swift renewal. However, it was difficult to make a stable wall of any length beyond head height unless buttressed or reinforced. It was difficult to raise into a gable and the triangle of a gable wall was usually made of some other material, such as mud-and-stud. It was not load-bearing in most circumstances, though it could carry its own weight, and so it worked best if there was a separate structure to carry the roof. It was always liable to collapse through buckling in plan or section.

Turf was also a useful material in thatching. Thin turf was used as an underthatch and sometimes as the thatch itself. It was said that in Ireland, the 'booley'—or summer shelter—could be covered with lengths of turf carried by animals as they moved from winter to summer pastures.

When turf was used in building cottages, a site was selected next to where the best available turf was growing, such as on clay loam or growing on top of a sedge or peat bog. The pieces and lengths of turf were cut with a flaughter spade or a breast plough. The flaughter spade had an iron blade forged in an L-shape so that the width and depth could be selected in one action of the spade. The proportions of each turf could be those of a brick, but were normally rather longer and wider—indeed similar to those of domestic garden turf. A variation of the turf block was a parallelogram in section, which helped the bonding of the individual turves. Having been cut, the turves were taken immediately to the building site, for it was best if they were used the same day. They were not stacked to dry like peat;

indeed, the uniformity of the turf wall was helped if the roots continued to grow after the turves had been placed in position.

The turves were usually laid with grass on top, but some builders preferred grass to grass, to make a wall about 18 ins to 24 ins thick. Sometimes they were laid herringbone pattern with scraps of turf to fill in the gaps when the builders thought this would add stability. Windows, if fitted, were cut out after the wall was complete.

Authorities differ on whether turf walls were rendered or plastered; some believe a turf wall could not take the surface finish while others point to actual examples. Stability was always a problem and some turf walls have reinforcement, such as short timbers lacing the corners, or pegs between the courses, or crude posts at the corners or at intermediate points in a long wall. However, any complication contradicts the essential economy and simplicity of the turf wall.

Peat was, in theory at least, an alternative to turf but it was a less satisfactory material than turf for building and presumably more valuable as fuel. One example is known in England, in a wheelwright's shop near Inskip in Lancashire; the peat wall is in short lengths between posts which carry the roof loads. A curious variation on the turf cottage was the peat house, which was actually cut out of a solid block of peat as part of peat extraction. Such a house did not last long, however. Peat houses were known in Ireland but none survive. A more orthodox variation was to have an inner and an outer skin either of wattle or of stones to protect the stability of turf walls which were thick but quite loosely packed.

The turf-walled cottage was acceptable if it had to be erected quickly and cheaply as a summer shelter or as a squatter's cabin. There is much evidence that exists in Ireland: from folk memories, the occasional survival of a cottage, or visitors' observations of sod construction. There is rather less evidence in Scotland and much less in England and Wales. But there was an experiment here and there, particularly that of building a new turf building in the open-air museum at Kingussie in Scotland with unskilled labour. The building did not last long, but it gave many insights into the problems their predecessors met and overcame.

Mud-and-stud (clam, staff and daub, wattle and daub, daub and stower, raddle and daub, rad and dab, stake and rice)

The term mud-and-stud represents several different forms of building, which share the use of timber as an armature on which clay was plastered. They can be thin clay walls reinforced with timber, or light timber walls given body by the application of clay. Mud-and-stud work extends from the familiar wattle and daub panels of half-timber construction to the timber palisade daubed with clay, and

187. Mud-and-stud, West Lancashire: the decayed clay rendering applied to the studs has been concealed by the lime mortar rendering.

there are variations in between. Mud-and-stud work includes partition walls in houses and cottages, chimney-hoods gathering smoke from the fire on the hearth, triangular panels extending a wall of any material to the apex of a gable, and storey-height panels consisting of closely spread timbers daubed inside and out and self-supporting if not load-bearing (187).

The mud-and-stud walling technique may have originated in circular houses of pre-historic periods in which the space between an outer and inner ring of wattle work contained a structural wall of turf, earth or clay.

Conventional wattle and daub includes the use of flat or inclined staves running between studs in a half-timbered building. The application of clay daub inside and out, slightly recessed from the surface of the studs and then plastered and limewashed made a weatherproof and draught-proof wall (at least until the timber members shrank and established cracks). Square panels contained wattle and daub consisting of osiers and split hazel, threaded in and out of staves held between holes in the under-side of a rail and a slot in the top of a rail or plate, with clay daubed in both surfaces and finished with lime plaster.

The mud-and-stud wall relies on quite closely spaced uprights around which were plaited split hazel sticks, osiers etc., or ropes of straw, heather or other vegetable material. The uprights might be earthfast, or nailed or held in some other way to a light beam or wall-plate, or they may be sprung between the underside of a wall-plate and the top of a sill beam. If the uprights were spaced apart, then some sort of wattle work was needed to provide a key for the clay daub. If they were closely spaced, only an inch or so apart, then no key was required. Quite a thick double coating of clay was expected in this case. A heavier version has been discovered in Scotland: a wall or palisade of closely spaced vertical poles has been thickly daubed with clay and neatly smoothed so that the wall appears to be solid clay and no sign of the poles is to be seen. This is called in Scotland 'kebber and mott', or 'caber and daub'.

The various techniques of mud-and-stud construction were widely used in Scotland and Ireland and the regions of England. Some techniques had a local name. In Derbyshire, the uprights were set about one foot apart, were one inch thick and provided the warp for a weft of unpeeled hazel twigs. In Lincolnshire the same technique was called 'stud and mud' and 'daub and stower'. In Scotland the term commonly used was 'stake and rice' or 'stab and rice' as an alternative to mud-and-stud. In Lancashire the local technique was recorded by R. W. Dickson in 1815:

A more ancient but much less durable method which is still not infrequently had recourse to in the tract from below Leyland to some distance beyond Garstang, and throughout most of the Fylde district, is that of forming them on wattled stud work with a composition of well-wrought loamy clay and cut straw or what is locally termed 'cat and clay' . . . These sorts of cottages have seldom more than a mean ground floor, which with their sombre brown gives them a mean hovel-like appearance, far from agreeable and affords but little accommodation.

The mud-and-stud tradition is to be distinguished from the timber-frame tradition and the cob tradition; the flimsy construction being quite inferior to the sophisticated carpentry work of the one and the heavy solidity of the other.

Map of regional variations

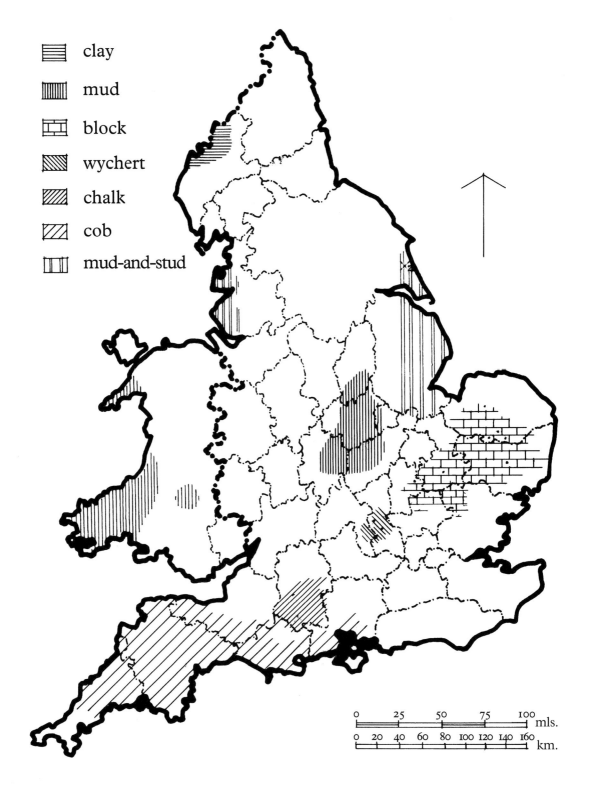

clay

mud

block

wychert

chalk

cob

mud-and-stud

0   25   50   75   100 mls.

0 20 40 60 80 100 120 140 160 km.

3. Regional variations

The South-West

Architecturally, the traditional counties of the South-West are not only Cornwall, Devon and Somerset but also Dorset, Gloucestershire and Wiltshire. Hampshire and the Isle of Wight, however, may be similar architecturally but regionally they are in the South-East. Cob construction stretches throughout the South-West.

Cob construction makes use of the varied but plentiful deposits of clay that surround the moors and crags of such areas as Dartmoor and Exmoor. The clay is deep red and red-brown in colour where it lies on the sandstone, but much of the clay has admixtures of limestone or chalk giving a grey colour that can be almost white. As in other cob areas, the clay mixture, having been sorted and weathered, was turned and pounded with hooves and boots while being watered and mixed with straw or other vegetable matter. The actual composition depends on the experience of the mudmason as well as on the nature of the raw material. Once ready, the clay was lifted by spade and fork onto a prepared stone plinth until it constituted a 'lift' or course of clay able to rest securely in position without slumping. The lift of 12 to 14 ins in

left
188. Diagram. Earth building in England and Wales illustrating zones of use of the various techniques. Individual examples surviving or known from records are not indicated.

right
189. Cob cottages at East Budleigh, Devon.

height was allowed to dry for days or weeks until ready to receive the next layer. Having been trimmed or pared, the wall was rendered inside and out with clay or lime plaster and was then ready to receive the thatched roof (189).

Within the region there are some variations on the standard technique. In parts of Devon, for instance, the quality of materials and constructional methods meant that two-storey or three-storey buildings were constructed even within the towns. In parts of Cornwall the stone plinth was taken to first-floor level before a second storey of clay was added. In this case the clay wall was rather thicker than the stone and projected slightly. Sometimes a single-storey house or cottage was extended upwards by superimposing a clay wall like this on the original stone wall.

Unlike other regions, the South-West retains many cob houses. It is estimated that as many as 50,000 cob houses are still inhabited. Far from being a feature dotted around here and there, the cob dwellings make up complete streets and whole villages, only gradually decreasing in number. Unlike other regions, the cob dwellings of the South-West represent several social levels, whereas in Wales, for instance, earth building was effectively confined to the cottages of the poor and often intended for a short life. In the South-West, cob is as likely to be used for farmhouses, indeed the whole collection of buildings on a farmstead, and even occasionally for manor houses.

There is a greater range of dates for cob building in the South-West than in any other part of England, indeed greater than anywhere else in the British Isles. Archaeological investigation has revealed evidence of cob building from the thirteenth century while actual buildings date back as far as a century later. There are farmhouses and parsonages from the sixteenth and seventeenth centuries, villas from the nineteenth century, urban houses and cottages from the eighteenth and nineteenth centuries, and even a house designed by Ernest Gimson and built of cob in 1912.

Earth building is not confined to cob construction. Ray Harrison has described a version of mud-and-stud construction found at Bowhill near Exeter. In this, staves were set horizontally between studs and daubed with a thickness of 3 or 4 ins of clay on each side. The technique was used both for internal partitions and for external walls.

West Midlands, North-West England and the Solway Plain

In this brief survey, the counties of the West Midlands (where clay buildings are scarce) have been considered with Lancashire and Cheshire (where evidence of clay construction is relatively plentiful), as well as both sides of the Solway Firth (where comparatively many

190. Decayed dwelling of mud-and-stud near Ormskirk, Lancashire.

191. Detail of end wall of 190 showing cruck truss members revealed by decay of clay-covering at the corners.

survive, at least on the English side of the Solway Firth, though in diminishing numbers) (190, 191).

Very little has been published about earth building in the Marcher Counties, nor has much been discovered as physical evidence of the practice. However, some observations have been provided from an unlikely source. Frederick Law Olmsted, the famous American land-scape designer, made a journey in the nineteenth century through parts of England, beginning with his landing in Liverpool and con-tinuing south along the Welsh Border. His observations were pub-lished in 1852. While travelling near Hereford he wrote:

> The walls of labourers' cottages are of stone or brick and timber or of clay. In making the latter which travellers frequently describe as 'mud walls' and which are very common, the clay having been well forked-over and cleared of stones is then trodden with horses and worked over until it becomes a plastic mass. The more it is trodden the better. A foundation of stone is first made; one man forms the prepared clay into balls, or lumps as large as bricks and passes them to another, who lays and packs them well and firmly together dressing off smooth and straight with a trowel. After the height desired for the wall has been attained, it is commonly plastered over inside and out with a thin coat of more carefully prepared clay and whitewashed. This makes an excellent non-

conducting wall equal in every respect except permanence, and almost in that, to stone or brick. Very respectable houses, such as villas and parsonages, are sometimes built in this way. The cost is about 30 cents a square yard.

These observations are quite comprehensive and convincing. We do not know how common were cottages made of clay in 1852, nor do we know how many other clay cottages with walls plastered and lime-washed have been mistaken for buildings of other materials.

Recent studies of vernacular buildings in Shropshire by Madge Moran and Eric Mercer make no reference to earth building. Extensive surveys and measured drawings, mostly unpublished, of houses and cottages in Cheshire and South Lancashire have not revealed much on the subject. However, S. O. Addy, in his book on houses in 1898, included studies of mud-and-stud dwellings in West Lancashire built on the stretches of dry land between the mosses and the sea, roughly between Ormskirk and Southport. The two dwellings near North Meols and the house at Burscough had cruck trusses and walls of mud-and-stud (Addy uses the local term 'clam-staff and daub') though partially replaced by brick. He also noted that field walls in the area were of mud or sods. Further north, in the Fylde, a number of mud-and-stud houses and cottages have been studied; the basic construction is of cruck trusses rising from a stone plinth and with mud-and-stud panels infilling between the trusses.

There is some evidence of the use of turf building, either turves from the fields or peats from the mosses. There is an actual survivor, near Inskip, of a peat wall in a wheelwright's shop. The peats are about 3 or 4 ins deep, separated by a thin layer of straw, and not plastered (except that there are remnants of a clay skimming).

Further south and inland there is a reference to turf houses in Dr Plot's *Natural History of Staffordshire* of 1686. Alec Clifton-Taylor also mentions in *The Pattern of English Building* the use of clay lump during the seventeenth and eighteenth centuries near to Stourbridge.

Moving north to the Scottish Border we pass the Lake District and Eden Valley where no evidence remains of a tradition of using earth in building. Here both timber and stone were available. Yet there was a long period in which transhumance was practiced and there are many place-names in which the suffix 'scale' in various forms, such as Summerscales, indicate the sites of summer cottages. The few sites that have been examined are on the north-east border and are of stone, but it is more than likely that summer dwellings of turf were widespread.

On the Solway Plain the clay dabbin, built quickly of thin layers of clay, is the characteristic house (192). Distribution maps have been published, most recently by Nina Jennings, showing the area of survival between Carlisle and Silloth. However, library work has shown that the area of use once extended into the hills in Bewcastle

192. Clay house at Great
Orton, Cumberland.

parish. Work in dendrochronology, initiated by Nina Jennings, has
shown that the techniques of timber support and a process of
quickly building a clay wall may extend as far back as the late fourteenth century, from their associated crucks or other timber work.
On the Scottish side of the Solway the destruction of clay dabbins
seems to have been complete, though buildings with clay walls have
been preserved further west, such as one or two associated with
Robert Burns.

The North-East, Yorkshire and Humberside

Of all the regions of England, this area has the least evidence of the
past use of earth in building and the least physical evidence of survival. Yet all the ingredients of clay construction are present and there
do not seem to be any major social circumstances that would
discourage use of the material in one form or another, so the lack of
evidence or survival may be simply accidental.

S. O. Addy, writing in 1898, believed that 'many of the poorer
houses were built of mud or sods' and he lived in Yorkshire. In
particular, he describes in detail a clay house in Mappleton, East
Yorkshire, with walls 19 ins thick and rising to room height but with
a chamber or loft occupying part of the roof space. The construction
was slightly unusual in that the courses of clay mixture were quite
shallow (between five and seven inches thick) with a layer of straw
between each layer, as on the Solway Plain. However, according to
local memory recorded by Addy, each layer had to be allowed
to dry before the next was laid, so it was not in fact the clay dabbin

technique. Addy also points out the place-name 'Sodhouse', which he takes to mean houses built of turf.

C. F. Innocent, another Yorkshire resident, quotes Addy's description of the house at Mappleton but makes the additional point that the clay wall was built on a clay foundation rather than on a plinth of stone. He also makes the interesting point that in Newcastle-on-Tyne bricklayers were once styled 'catters and daubers', and he explained, 'cats were pieces of straw and clay worked together into pretty large rolls and laid between wooden posts in constructing mud walls'. He also suggested that the idea of burnt bricks to be laid by bricklayers descended from the use of unburnt clay bricks.

East Midlands and Lincolnshire

This large region includes Leicestershire, Northamptonshire, Rutland, Nottinghamshire, Lincolnshire and, rather surprisingly, Derbyshire. It is crossed by the limestone belt with other geological formations, such as ironstone, running parallel to it. Apart from the Wolds, Lincolnshire is largely flat and low-lying with drainage through the fens into the Wash. Derbyshire, on the other hand, in the north-east of the region, includes the carboniferous limestone of the White Peak and the gritstone of the Dark Peak. Generally there are plenty of surface deposits, including clay, and so earth building was possible alongside stone and brick.

At one time there was plenty of construction in cob (here called 'mud'). The technique of preparing cob was the same as elsewhere: digging the clay, cleaning it of stones, mixing it with water, souring it with vegetable matter, treading it with hooves and boots, and then laying it on a stone foundation, layer by layer, with a drying period between each lift. Yet the detailed techniques did vary. For instance, in the Trent Valley and Rutland, where patches of stone could be found, there were tall foundation walls with a limited amount of cob added to make up the desired height. In this area the stone and cob walls were strong enough to carry roof loads, including tie-beams. Timber reinforcement at the corners of barns and in walls helped maintain stability (193).

In Leicestershire there are many references to the use of cruck trusses, along with clay walls. For cob (mud) walls generally, William Pitt in his *General View of the Agriculture of Leicestershire* of 1809 wrote of the southern part of the county:

> . . . mud walls are not uncommon . . . they are used not only for fences for yards and courts, gardens and homesteads, but also for hovels, outhouses and cottage tenements; as fence walls they are capped with clods or thatch, and in tempering the mud is mixed with chopped straw or stubble to hold it together; road scrapings are the best mud for walls; they are often constructed by labourers

193. Mud wall, Laughton,
Leicestershire.

who can both build the walls and thatch the cottages and when
well executed they are very durable.

Indeed, published glebe terriers show that the incumbents of lesser
livings lived in clay-walled parsonages; such terriers extend from
1605 to 1709. However, William Cobbett, writing after a visit to the
Lutterworth district in 1830 praised the parsons' houses, but was not
complimentary about clay-walled houses and cottages:

See the parson's house, large and in the midst of pleasure gardens,
then look at the miserable sheds in which the labourers reside.
Look at these hovels made of mud and straw, bits of glass or old
cast-off windows without frames or hinges, frequently but merely
stuck in the mud walls.

It is believed that cob walls with cruck trusses were in use at least as early as the fifteenth century but surviving examples appear to be of eighteenth- or nineteenth-century date. There seems to be the same technique in Northamptonshire, where a band of cob construction runs alongside the band of good quality stone. Malcolm Seaborne, in his study of clay houses in the county, mentioned the late fifteenth-century church at Cold Ashby built of cob faced with stone, but he also believed that most cob construction was of eighteenth- and nineteenth-century date and that cob cottages were especially numerous. In Nottinghamshire a portion of earth wall has been noted in a fifteenth-century aisled hall in Collingham; in Lincolnshire a farmhouse in Greetham has been dated by dendrochronology to about 1400. In the same county generally, cob construction where found is to be seen in the east with other building techniques in the west. Again, observers of the eighteenth and nineteenth centuries noted earthen buildings in significant numbers in the county as a whole.

Mud-and-stud construction was most characteristic in the east of Lincolnshire and was found here and there in other parts of the region. The earliest published date for a house in the county using this technique is 1683 but most examples are from later centuries; they were once very numerous but only about 350 such cottages remain in Lincolnshire. In mud-and-stud here, as elsewhere, the wall consists of a structural frame of earthfast posts with staves, earthfast or nailed in position, daubed on both sides to give a total thickness of between 8 and 12 ins. Properly maintained, a mud-and-stud cottage with a lime plaster finish whitewashed or colourwashed gives a very neat appearance.

Although brick has superseded clay, it is clear that in the East Midlands and Lincolnshire clay was in widespread and long-lasting use for houses, cottages, farm buildings, boundary walls and even, occasionally, for churches.

East of England

This region is rather more than East Anglia. To Norfolk, Suffolk and Essex are added Cambridgeshire and Huntingdonshire, Bedfordshire and Hertfordshire (which is not accustomed to being in the East of England). Generally it is not a region one immediately associates with earthen construction. Timber-frame construction with overall rendering, together with brick building, are more characteristic. The geology encouraged the growth of good quality timber (growth which was regulated in favour of the conservation of structural timber), and at the same time provided good quality clay, including bands of chalk, which led to the production of bricks from the medieval period right up to the present day.

However, there was one other way of utilising clay—that is in the form of clay lump. The clay was prepared as for cob but the puddled mixture was dumped into large wooden moulds, turned out and allowed to dry in the sun, or stacked towards the wind (both sun and wind being more plentiful than in other regions). The clay lumps were usually about 18 ins by 9 ins and 5 ins thick; they were laid usually in stretcher bond and rarely in herringbone fashion. At one time it was assumed that surviving examples were the tail end of a long tradition, but John McCann has recently demonstrated that, 'There is no reliable evidence of clay lump construction anywhere in Britain before the 1790s', and his first recorded example in the eastern counties was built in 1791–2. Clay lump is characteristic of the nineteenth century, when it attracted great interest, and was regarded as an experimental technique adequately proven and quickly adopted. It was especially appropriate for cottage building at a time when timber was scarce and bricks still expensive, not least because of the Brick Tax of 1784–1850. By the middle of the nineteenth century its popularity began to wane, except that cottages of clay lump with brick cladding retained the undoubted virtue of clay as a heat insulator.

South-Eastern counties

The south-eastern region comprises, for present purposes, London, Kent, Sussex, Surrey, Buckinghamshire, Berkshire, Oxfordshire, Hampshire, the Isle of Wight and the fringes of Dorset. Although it is rich in vernacular buildings, with examples from the early medieval period almost to the present day, it is poor in examples of earth building. This may be because an abundance of good timber fit for building, plus well-distributed building stone, meant that there was little need to resort to clay or turf; or it may be that any long-sustained tradition of earth building was lost during the eighteenth and nineteenth centuries, when earlier houses of quality had survived in good condition, and could be modernised with the aid of changes in planning and various forms of cladding to the timber base.

There is a record of mud building in London in 1212 and the place-name 'Mud-wall' was mentioned in London in 1395. In east Kent, Alec Clifton-Taylor notes that chalk was added to the mixture used in the occasional cob building; he also mentions that in the region there was an appreciable number of thatched and mud-wall cottages surviving at the beginning of the twentieth century. To this rather meagre collection, however, must be added the houses and farm buildings in Hampshire built using the cob technique—a technique that had strayed over the border from Dorset and the rest of the South-West.

The chief reason for an interest in the use of clay in the South-Eastern counties lies in their being the home to building in wychert, centred on Haddenham (194). The chalk beds in that area provided the essential ingredient for the material which could be built in layers like cob, but was less demanding of drying time, and whose neat cheerful appearance remains popular among residents and visitors to Buckinghamshire.

Wales

In Wales, the use of earth as a building material was a matter of status as well as geography and history. The manor houses and farmhouses of eastern Wales were traditionally built of timber-frame, with fireplaces and chimney-breasts of stone or brick. They formed part of a Border architecture with little to distinguish the houses of Cheshire, Shropshire, Herefordshire and Worcestershire in terms of construction from those of Flint, Montgomeryshire, Breconshire, Radnorshire and Monmouthshire. For most of the rest of Wales stone was the building material of houses and farm buildings, as well as churches and castles. However, there remains evidence from references, and survival, of earthen construction for cottages in many parts of Wales, with some concentration in Pembrokeshire, Carmarthenshire, Breconshire and Cardigan in the south, and Anglesey and Llŷn in the north. It must be stressed that these buildings were rude cottages or fragile farm buildings and especially squatters' cottages, representative of the period of population pressure and land hunger in the nineteenth century.

Many cottages were built on the undivided common land as squatter cottages, following the widely accepted, but generally unfounded, belief in the 'ty-unnos': the custom whereby a cottage, which could be built overnight so as to produce smoke from a fire in the morning, would acquire informal title to the land on which it stood, land which could gradually be extended to a few fields according to other customs of dubious authority. This building practice depended on the assembly beforehand of building materials, such as turf, clay, roof timbers, thatch and clay for plaster, and the visit of friends and neighbours for the night in question. The same procedure was adopted for some settled communities whereby a cottage for a newly-married couple was built by voluntary labour on whatever scrap of land could be found.

For more permanent cottages the cob tradition of the counties across the Bristol Channel was adopted; puddled clay being raised in 'lifts' with a drying period between stages, surfaces pared off, and clay plaster rendering applied. The cob was known as 'clom' or 'mwd' in Wales. Some of these more permanent cottages superseded the turf cottages of the squatters, though many of the squatters abandoned the roughly made cottages and unrewarding farm work for the mines and quarries of the coalfields with their regular wages and their brick terraces.

A variation on the house of clom or mwd was noted by an observer of 1812:

194. Haddenham, Buckinghamshire: house of several periods built of wychert though with gables of brick or weatherboard.

The peasants' habitations particularly in Llŷn consist of walls built of what in Devonshire is termed *cobb*, that is an argillacous earth having straw or rushes mixed with it while in a state of paste and then laid layer upon layer, between boards, till the whole are ready for the thatched roof.

Whereas in the South-West of England many cob farmhouses are two storeys or more in height, in Wales their counterparts are single-storey, with walls little more than 6 ft high, or one-and-a-half storeys at the most.

In the towns such as Conwy, Denbigh and Ruthin, many houses and cottages were built with a high-quality timber-frame—or at least for the most important houses, but with clay daubed on staves or laths or wattle-work with a minimal timber structure for the rest.

In town and country the practice of building in clay, let alone turf, had died out towards the end of the nineteenth century. Indeed, it was noted in New Quay, Cardiganshire, in 1903 that:

> The practice of building in clay is well-nigh forgotten. We learn that the red earth of which they were formed was mixed with water and made into a paste by treading it in the fashion in which culm is yet made and then the paste was mixed with straw.

It is worth mentioning the ancient practice among Welsh farmers of having the 'hendre' or winter house, and the 'hafoty' or summer house and dairy, where the younger members of the family lived while they tended the cattle in the summer pastures on the un-enclosed common land, and while they made butter and cheese for sale or to help sustain the family in the winter. The 'hafotai' were made of loosely piled field stones if available, or made of turf year by year if not.

Scotland

By the standards of the British Isles, Scotland is a large country and has various regions, which will be treated together here except that the border of the Solway Firth and eastwards will be treated with the Solway Plain of England.

Building with earth in Scotland has a long history of several phases. The earliest use of the material was in connection with the ancient tombs where the burial chamber was covered with an earthen mound. The greatest extent was the Antonine Wall built by the Romans in c. 140–146 as a turf rampart stretching from the Firth of Forth to the Firth of Clyde. Stone was available, but turf was presumably selected because of speed of erection by semi-skilled soldiers. There was a phase in the Middle Ages when tower houses were built as fortified dwellings, available for refuge during disputes between the clans and their chieftains. G. A. Neilson thought that, 'the more powerful Scots Borderers made towers of earth only which cannot be burnt, nor without great force of men of war down can be cast . . . called "pailles" [presumably "peels" as in "peel towers"]'. It is also possible that timber towers were clad with earth, similarly as a protection from fire, and so acquiring the pyramidal shape mentioned in records now and then.

A further phase was the construction of farmhouses and cottages over a long period, but especially in the eighteenth and nineteenth centuries. Evidence for this phase is confused by the Clearance Movement and the Agricultural Revolution, both leading to amalgamation or destruction of the traditional 'fermtouns' (or groups of farmsteads), and their replacement by a smaller number of superior farms and farmhouses on fresh sites with stone walls and slate roofs. During the same period, the practice of housing farm servants with the family was replaced by that of putting the labourers and their families in cottages, often with provision for domestic industry such as weaving. Thus, changing circumstances led to the traditional buildings of clay or turf being replaced by the new construction of superior dwellings by landlords.

Many travellers, such as Boswell and Johnson on their tour to the Western Isles of 1784, made notes of what they saw, condemning the old farmhouses of clay and turf, and praising the new ones of stone and slate (notwithstanding the preference of the tenants for their warm and cosy dwellings).

The complex geology of Scotland, combining many hard intractable rocks with different sorts of drift deposit available for use as clay, provided variety in clay-building techniques. Among those used in various places at various times were tempered clay (like Devonshire cob), shuttered clay and, with *pisé* for a brief period, clay and stone combinations, including broad earthen walls faced with stone as well as layers of clay alternating with courses of cobbles, some use of mud-and-stud, and finally extensive use of turf, especially for ephemeral structures.

The familiar cob construction was called 'mudwall' in Scotland and the more expert workmen were called 'mudmasons'. The material has been used at one time or another in half the country, mainly the eastern half, from Easter Ross, through the Carse of Gowrie to Berwickshire. The technique is the same as in other parts of Britain, though it is sometimes called simply 'tempered earth', with the practice of interspersing layers of earth with layers of straw or other vegetable material known as 'cat and clay'. At first the walls were not considered load-bearing, though they rarely exceeded 6 ft in height, and the loads of the thatched roof were carried by crucks or jointed crucks, including half crucks at the hipped ends.

As in other regions, there are references to the use of shuttered earth (whereby the moist tempered clay was thrown into shuttering temporarily fixed to the wall, allowed to dry, and then the shuttering was moved up, a layer at a time). Dependent on sawn timber to make the shuttering, this technique was probably only used for a short time in the late eighteenth and nineteenth centuries. Its other version, *pisé-de-terre*, dependent on even better quality shuttering, was most often associated with programmes of cottage building by reforming landlords.

Combinations of clay and cobble made use of rounded stones taken from river beds, or cleared from the fields. In the 'black houses' of the Hebrides the very thick earthen walls were consolidated and protected with stones that were difficult to lay in courses, even in clay mortar. Rounded corners and thatch set back from the eaves are characteristic. Alternatively, and as found on the mainland, rounded cobbles were combined in courses with tempered earth, in a technique which led to quite thick walls that were stable enough to reach the height of a man.

Mud-and-stud, or 'stake and rice', was not a technique well suited to the Scottish climate, but was suitable for closing the vulnerable triangle in gabled walls between eaves height and the ridge, and also for partitions and chimney-hoods.

Turf was universally available, but as the best turf came from the best pastures its use was not popular among landlords. However, it was cheap, allowed walls to be quickly erected by an unskilled family labour force, and could be spread as manure on the fields when its short life came to an end.

On the Scottish side of the Solway there is documentary evidence, but no longer any physical evidence, of clay construction as a communal activity. Further east, on the route taken by English travellers going north and Scots travelling south, there is documentary evidence of clay and turf construction.

William Pennant, travelling north in 1769 and 1792, noted that in Canonbie (east of Carlisle) 'most of the houses were built of clay', and that 'the person who had building in view . . . then summoned his neighbours on a fixed day, who came furnished with victuals at their own expense set cheerfully to work and complete the edifice before night'. Sir John Clerk, travelling south in 1731, noted on passing through Gretna that 'both on the English and Scottish sides the farmhouses of clay without any mixture of stone and these stand the weather pretty well'.

The surviving clay-walled barn at Canonbie has been well conserved and is a standing reminder of the use of earth in construction in Scotland over a long period and in a large part of the country.

4. Earth building in Ireland

Introduction

The significant events affecting vernacular architecture in Ireland were the long late-medieval period of local warfare between clan chiefs, when dwellings were mainly defensible or expendable; the period of plantation of English and Scottish settlers in the north, especially during the seventeenth century; the changes in agriculture during the eighteenth and nineteenth centuries; the great increase in population in the eighteenth and early nineteenth centuries followed by a decrease during the famine years of the 1840s; and including large-scale emigration for the rest of the nineteenth century.

The late medieval unrest led to the building of stone tower houses alongside small farmhouses and cottages built of earth, quickly and cheaply, by the common people and capable of being rebuilt if necessary equally economically. The plantations brought English-style timber-framed houses erected for a few decades while timber supplies lasted. Changes in agriculture broke down the tradition of transhumance, with the more permanent houses in communities among the fields, and the ephemeral booths and cabins occupied by those tending the animals on the moors and waste land. The failure of the potato crops in the 1840s led to some rural depopulation, accompanied by amalgamations among the many tiny farms, resulting from partible inheritance customs, and replacement of clay walls and thatched roofs by a smaller number of stone-walled and slate-roofed farmhouses and cottages. Throughout the late eighteenth and nineteenth centuries travellers and boards of inquiry commented on the traditional way of life of the Irish poor and described, usually in unfavourable terms, the cabins in which they lived.

The geology and landscape of Ireland meant that timber for building was always scarce, stone was plentiful within certain areas (but not necessarily of masonry quality), while the widespread availability of clay and turf meant that these materials were always to hand for walls and underthatch.

Information on the characteristics of small houses and cottages built before about 1600 is scarce, and unlikely to be made much more plentiful as a result of archaeological investigation. The records related to the plantations are helpful, while the comments of English and Scottish visitors in the eighteenth and nineteenth centuries are also informative though biased in their assessment of quality. The *Ordnance Survey Memoirs*, and the reports of commissioners of the later nineteenth century, are also observant and generally impartial, but they do see the Irish and their housing through English eyes.

Ireland, like many other parts of Europe, recently experienced a period when traditional houses were under threat, not least because of their association with an unhappy past, but is currently experiencing a period in which the surviving vernacular buildings are cherished and conserved.

Apart from stone the principal walling materials have been clay (mud), turf (sods), mud-and-stud (cat and clay) and stone-faced earth. Apart from slate, the use of which tends to be late in date, the principal roofing material was thatch, including turf, reeds and heather, as well as straw. Roof construction was for a long time dependent on crucks, which would not impose loads on the walls and which had a crudely curved shape, or were jointed, having posts joined to the principal rafters. Supplies of timber were increasingly dependent on what could be retrieved from the bogs, and the quality of Irish cruck trusses is not to be compared with those of Herefordshire or Worcestershire.

For many years Irish agriculture, like Scottish, was based on 'rundale', whereby the farmed land was divided into two: the 'infield' in the heart of the townland, and the 'outfield' surrounding. The infield, which was in joint or co-operative occupancy, was subdivided between descendants, and allocated in narrow strips that changed from time to time. The infield received whatever manure was available and was more or less continuously cropped with occasional fallow periods. Surrounding the infield was the 'outfield' or undivided waste land. Animals were moved between infield and outfield according to the season and with them moved the younger family members. The winter quarters had farmhouses and barns of the better materials (including clay), while the summer quarters were much cruder structures of less costly materials (including turf). In some communities various materials, such as timber and rolls of turf, were moved from winter to summer quarters and back again according to season. The winter quarters constituted the 'bally' and the summer huts were called 'creats' and hurriedly erected outside the 'booley' or milking enclosure.

Clay (mud, tempered earth/clay)

Buildings of mud were the Irish version of cob and were widespread in the island—only the counties of the western seaboard, such as Donegal, Mayo, Galway, Clare and Kerry, lacked a large proportion of such buildings. The city of Cork was noted in 1622 as being full of mud cabins and it is likely that mud walling was used in much earlier periods. Mud construction continued practically into the twentieth century, and many buildings survived until recently and many more may be undetected, concealed behind plaster coatings or claddings of other materials.

The methods of preparation and erection were similar to those of the cob of Devonshire. A bed of suitable clay was selected near the house site. The clay, having been dug, was forked over and stones extracted. Water was added and the mixture was kneaded like dough with pitchforks and shovels. Next, the clay was trampled with hooves and boots as vegetable matter was added, and this consisted of straw, reeds, lime, dung and animal hair, and, no doubt, road sweepings. The whole was allowed to 'sour' or 'temper' for a few days until it was judged ready for use. A rough foundation was prepared on the site consisting of such loose stones as could be assembled. Then the mud was forked into place and trodden into position. Each layer was raised to 12 or 18 ins, pared flat and covered with straw as it was drying. Having been left for a few days (or even weeks) until it was judged ready, about four lifts were raised to give a height of between 4 and 6 ft before wall construction was complete. A thatched roof carried on rough rafter poles between eaves and ridge purlin completed the structure, except for cutting out door and window apertures and adding a chimney flue. Finally, the finishing coat of best clay mortar was added and completed with whitewash. Some of these buildings were raised to two storeys but the majority were of a single storey and many had only a single room.

Many observers regarded the houses as little more than hovels but others, such as Arthur Young, visiting in the later eighteenth century, acknowledged the comfort of warm and cosy homes with draught-proof and well-insulated clay walls and thatched roof, comparing them with the thin and draughty panels of half-timbered houses in England, or the damp and chilly stone walls and slated roof cottages provided by reforming landlords in Ireland.

Shuttered clay and *pisé-de-terre*

The vast majority of clay-walled houses were built by the cob process in spite of the delays in completing such a house. The alternative—whereby clay was rammed into shuttering in a fairly dry state so that the shuttering could be moved up the wall, stage by stage—helped to give the cottages a neat finish in a shorter time. This method was generally used by landowners with a programme of work, rather than by individual farmers who were perhaps replacing a single decayed cottage.

The superior version of *pisé-de-terre*, with dry clay rammed energetically into good quality wooden formwork, was rarely mentioned, even though it was widely advertised in journals and encyclopedias that would have circulated among the landowners.

Reinforced clay

Although true cob construction was load-bearing, it was still considered desirable by some, and necessary by others, to have timber reinforcement to carry roof and floor loads. The usual way in England and, to some extent in Ireland, was to incorporate cruck construction. An alternative was to have earthfast timber posts at each corner. A variation was to have, in addition, forked posts in the end walls that could carry a rough ridge purlin and so support the rafters, which would also rest on the top of the clay wall.

Clay lump, unfired brick

This technique was almost unknown in Ireland. Where used, there were two main variations. In one, a layer of puddled clay was spread on a flat piece of ground, allowed to partly dry, and then cut into slabs of about 18 ins by 12 ins and about 4 ins thick; the slabs were then allowed to dry completely until they were ready to be built into walls. In the second variation, the clay was poured into wooden moulds, turned out, air-dried and then used like bricks.

Mud-and-stud (cat and clay)

Clay walls, dependent on a wooden armature, were at one time quite common in Ireland. Heavier earthfast timbers were used as corner posts or at intermediate points along a wall, but lighter staves provided the actual armature for clay daubing. The staves or poles were at first set in the ground and later, as nails became cheaper, the staves were nailed to a wall-plate or another beam. Pliable lengths of osiers, briers or twigs were woven into place, usually covering two staves at a time; alternatively, straw rope was woven into place. The wattlework was then liberally plastered, inside and out, to produce a wall 6 or 8 ins thick, or even more. The technique was called 'cat and clay' and is to be distinguished from the small square panels of the 'English' houses, built in towns and by settlers in northern Ireland. It is probable that the technique survived from medieval times, but by the early eighteenth century the pressure on supplies of timber, even of the rude variety used for staves, meant that landlords discouraged the practice.

An early version of the technique was to build circular houses and cottages with low walls of mud-and-stud as illustrated in a sketch of the city of Armagh in about 1600.

Stone-faced earth

It was recorded in 1838, on Achill Island off the west coast of Ireland, that the walls of houses were of earth or clay faced internally and externally with stone gathered from the fields. The total wall thickness was about 3 ft. Such houses were probably similar to the 'black houses' on the west coast of Scotland where conditions were similar. It is not known how widespread was the practice but it is likely to have been confined to the coastal region.

Timber-frame

Houses and cottages of timber-frame construction were recorded as having been built within the walls of Dublin and Limerick. The most reliable evidence of such construction, however, comes from drawings of houses built by English settlers in Londonderry and its vicinity included in Sir Thomas Philip's *Survey of Londonderry Plantation*, in 1622. The houses illustrated were rectangular, two storeys high and with a central chimney-stack and walls of timber-frame and square panels of wattle and daub. They were called 'English' houses to distinguish them from the low earth or mud 'Irish' houses with solid walls. Few English houses seem to have been built in Ireland much after the plantation period.

Turf (sod)

The use of turf, rather than clay, was at one time the main form of earth building in Ireland. A report of 1787 stated of Irish 'cabins' that: 'Their houses are of several sorts but the most common is the sod-wall as they call it.' A small number were reported as surviving into the twentieth century, and, indeed, were photographed, but it is unlikely that any remain nowadays.

Turf was cut into large slabs, about 2 ft by 3 ft. Thickness varied between about 2 ins and 6 ins, depending on how deep and how matted were the roots. The sods were laid grassy side up to form walls, mostly coursed and laid like stretcher bond brickwork, but sometimes laid herringbone fashion. It was noted that sometimes the turf was brought to the site rolled as it was cut, rather like the familiar garden turf, and then unrolled on the wall speeding up the construction process. Several sources quote an hour as the time taken to raise a turf wall to man height. The inner surface was pared smooth but the outer surface was often left rough and lacking any clay mortar rendering. Sod walls were made thick in proportion to height: 2 ft or 3 ft thick.

There were limitations in the use of turf as a walling material. If raised too high it was liable to collapse, if extended too long it was liable to buckle sideways. It could bear its own weight but was unreliable in carrying roof loads even if the walls were capped with flat stones. Because of the vulnerability of a gable triangle the thatched roofs were usually hipped rather than gabled. In order to carry principal rafters, earthfast posts were sometimes placed at each corner. Any partitions in the small cabins were made of brick-sized turves but were even less stable than the walls. The blocks of turf were sometimes bonded with viscous clay, or bound with wooden pegs or twigs, or reinforced with horizontal timbers at the corners.

So-called 'soot houses' were small one-roomed cabins, about 10 ft by 8 ft and 8 ft high to the ridge, located in the outfield near the 'booley' settlements. They were regarded as expendable, taken down each year, and the materials scattered on the ground as fertiliser, and quickly replaced if needed. When peat workings were being excavated, sometimes a block of peat was left and then hollowed to produce a rude shelter, hardly a dwelling. This would be occupied for two or three years and then dismantled.

Turves, either in lengths or in slate shapes were used in thatching, either as an underthatch with straw or heather-thatch finish, or as the roof covering itself. Because of the speed of erection and cheapness of the material, which required no transport to the site, turf walling was appropriate for the dwellings of the poor and especially for squatters on the 'waste'. Sod walls were especially popular in the southern counties of Ireland and for 'creats' and 'booley' houses in the summer. In spite of the lack of surviving examples, the turf or sod house will always be regarded as an important part of the Irish heritage, and it is hoped that examples will be discovered, and recorded, and conserved for the interest of future residents and visitors.

5. The international context

The ubiquity and variety of the use of earth in building, as seen in the British Isles, is fascinating enough, but it is just one small sample of the use of earth in the world as a whole. Every continent retains current employment or surviving evidence of the use of earth in building, over centuries in some cases and over millennia in others. In some parts of the world, earth is still the principal material for walling (at least for minor domestic buildings), in other parts of the world the march of other materials (natural or manufactured) is unceasing, while generally the widespread availability of Portland Cement means that the appearance of earthen walls can be created where the earth-building tradition was strong.

The traditional varieties of earth-building techniques in the British Isles have their counterparts in other countries. Here we have seen in various techniques the use of cob or clay construction, clay in shuttering or dry earth in pisé, clay lump in various forms, turf, and mud-and-stud. Elsewhere, one or other of these techniques may be found but the scale may be quite different: the huge clay blocks which mark the solidity and the overwhelming dominance of the fortresses of the Atlas mountains in Morocco, notwithstanding their highly decorative detailing, seem a far cry from the modest clay-lump cottages of Norfolk.

The timescale, which sets the use of earth by our ancestors in assembling earthen mounds as tall as Silbury or as small as the graves which cover the Isles of Scilly, is impressive enough, but on other continents the choice of earth as a material suitable for the commemoration of the dead in tombs, and the living in palaces, stretches back 4000 years to the mastaba tombs of Egypt. So the use of earth building in the British Isles can be the better understood if it is put into the context of the world-wide choice of earth as the material for religious and secular structures almost everywhere.

Taking the world as a whole, the materials for most periods of history and pre-history were stone, timber (including palm fronds and reeds) and clay (unbaked or fired as bricks), as well as the steel, aluminium, glass and plastics of our own time. Where found, stone quarries are virtually inexhaustible, but natural materials, such as timber, tend to be used and not replaced, while manufactured materials, such as brick, metals and plastics require expensive energy resources for their production. Earth is almost universally available, inexhaustible in supply and requires little more than manual labour in its use. It is the material of necessity where other materials are not available or are unsuitable. However, it is normally not chosen where

permanence or high status is important, and the high cost of transport of materials from source to site is affordable.

This world-wide choice extends to six continents. In some regions, such as the British Isles, the practice has ceased and the evidence is diminishing; in others, such as Egypt, the earth-building tradition has been maintained.

In Europe there was a long-standing tradition in Brittany of the use of cob or *torchis* in conjunction with a stone plinth, as well as a more recent tradition of the use of shuttered clay and pisé, just like the work in Devon and Cornwall across the Channel. Elsewhere, in northern France, mud-and-stud work survives. In central Spain clay lump or adobe was widely used.

In northern Africa large numbers of Moroccan and Algerian people still live in the tall, massive, fortress-like blocks built of clay lump laid in patterns and often brightly coloured. The use of cob and sun-dried mud brick has survived to the present day in the Nile valley, at least for the construction of small, single-storey dwellings. In central Africa mud-and-stud construction remains in use in the hot, wet, climate of Nigeria and the adjacent coastal states.

In Asia there are several concentrations, such as Arabia, Iraq and western Iran, where mud-brick, a miniature version of clay lump, was used. The most spectacular of such buildings are on the fringes of the Arabian desert and include the thousands of closely-packed tower-houses in Sana'a, the capital of the Yemen. In Iraq archaeologists have traced the use of mud bricks, either of regular shapes or of crude turnip-shape, in the great palaces and religious compounds of pre-Christian civilisations, often with brightly coloured tiles or fired bricks as cladding. Elsewhere, cob and mud-and-stud have been used. The most extensive survival is the Great Wall of China, which is built mostly of earth notwithstanding the use of stone in the best-preserved and most accessible stretches.

In North and South America the indigenous people tended to live as wandering tribes with tents for shelter, but during the Inca civilisation, which preceded that of the Spaniards, earth construction was developed. In the extensive tracts of both North and South America, colonised by the Spaniards in the sixteenth to nineteenth centuries, the Spanish tradition of using sun-dried adobe blocks was introduced and merged with any indigenous tradition. Most mission churches were built of stone but some in California were of adobe or cob construction. Such is the strength of the adobe tradition in California that examples are cherished or copied in towns such as Monterey, while modern imitations are added to the surviving examples in the tourist hubs of New Mexico. Generally, immigrants from elsewhere in Europe were able to use the native stone or timber but there is a stretch of the west-central states, including Nebraska and the Dakotas west of the so-called 'sod-house frontier', where only earth was available and where single-storey buildings of turf were formerly plentiful.

left
195. Diagram. The international context.
a Fortress in Oman, mud-brick walls, rendered
b Houses with adobe walls, Syria
c Rammed earth – *pisé-de-terre*
d Taos Pueblo, New Mexico, USA
e Moulds for mud-brick, half awaiting clay mixture, the other half showing mud bricks drying
f Mud-and-stud, Kenya
g Mud-and-stud, Mexico
h *Pisé* walls, rendered, South Australia, with detail of lifts of *pisé*
i Turf (sods) walling, house in Nebraska, USA

In Australia the nomadic aboriginal people sheltered in tents and windbreaks but immigrants made use of familiar materials, such as timber and stone. However, in South Australia farmers from Devon, miners and quarrymen from Cornwall and congregations from Germany built house and farm buildings in their familiar cob construction.

The use of earth is not simply a matter of availability. Even where neither stone nor timber is on the site, earth may be neglected and other materials sought. Nevertheless, in most parts of the world (and for most uses) earth is or has been the obvious choice. The counterpart of every technique found in the British Isles may be found somewhere else in the world, but by the same token nowhere else can examples of all the world-wide techniques be found in such a small area as the British Isles.

Part Five:
Special Topics

Special Topic 1
The Brick Tax

The several wars of the eighteenth century, requiring as they did direct payment of the royal forces and indirect subsidy of the forces of the allies, were hard on the Exchequer. In the absence of an income tax and with limitations in revenue from customs duties, successive governments looked increasingly to excise duties for their support. Among those considered in the Plan for Supplies and Taxes of 1756 was one on bricks and tiles. This was rejected at the time on grounds which included the geographical and architectural points that fashionable houses built in stone would avoid the tax, while bricks for cottage-building would be taxable. However, in 1784, at the conclusion of the expensive War of American Independence, the Prime Minister, Pitt the Younger, secured the passage through Parliament of 'An Act for granting to His Majesty certain Rates and Duties upon Bricks and Tiles made in Great Britain and for laying additional Duties on Bricks and Tiles imported into the same'. Pitt was reported in *The Gentleman's Magazine* for 1784 as saying that 'a tax on bricks and tiles had long been talked of . . . The rage for building was now universal. It had been stated that more than 205 million bricks had been manufactured for years in the neighbourhood of London only, and it was reasonable to suppose as many more in the rest of the kingdom. These then at 2/6 per M [i.e., per 1000] only, added to the number of tiles, would, he observed, produce £50,000.' By the time the Brick Tax was repealed, in 1850, the yield was more than ten times that amount.

The Act came into force on 1 September 1784 and imposed duties to be paid by brick and tile makers as follows:

> for all Bricks, 2s. 6d. per 1000
> for all plain Tiles, 3s. per 1000
> for all Pan or Ridge Tiles, 8s. per 1000
> for all Paving Tiles, not above Ten Inches Square, 1s. 6d. per 100;
> and for all Paving Tiles, above Ten Inches Square, 3s. per 100
> and for all other Tiles, 3s. per 1000.

A 'sweeping-in' clause required 'For and upon all Tiles other than such as are hereuntofor enumerated and described by whatever name or names such tiles now or hereafter may be called or known, a duty of 3s. per 1000 and so in proportion.'

The brick or tile maker was required to give notice to the local excise officer before making the items. The excise officer was then to be given the opportunity of counting the bricks or tiles after they had been turned out of the moulds, while they were drying and before they had been carried to the clamp or kiln. An allowance of 10% was given for bricks spoiled in the firing. There were various penalties for failing to give notice, concealing bricks or tiles, failing to pay the duty within the specified time and so on. The brickmaker was, however, not to be blamed if the excise officer did not appear after due warning.

In 1794 the duty on bricks was increased to 4s. per 1000 and in 1797 to 5s. per 1000 with corresponding increases on tiles. Since the tax was levied by number of bricks there was every incentive to make bricks larger than normal, whereas previously brickmakers had some commercial advantage in making small bricks. The Treasury was warned by the Commissioners of Excise of the danger to the revenue from the practice of making larger bricks. Arthur Young, in his Tour of England and Wales, had already come across a leading exponent of this practice, Mr Wilkes of Measham in Leicestershire: 'in brickmaking Mr Wilkes has made a very great and, since the tax, a very obvious improvement which is considerably increasing the size; he makes them of various dimensions for different purposes, some to 22½ inches long, but all double the size of common ones; with these bricks he builds his cotton mills, steam engines, weaving shops and his numerous houses by means of which he is filling this country with industry and population.' The Treasury counter to this was to introduce a size bar. By an Act of 1803 bricks with dimensions exceeding 10 ins by 5 ins by 3 ins were charged double duty. It should be noted that dimensions were taken of the bricks as they came out of the mould; shrinkage in drying and firing meant that a brick at the statute limits when assessed would be appreciably smaller when it was built into a wall.

In 1805 the duty was increased to 5s. 10d. per 1000, a rate maintained throughout the remaining life of the Act. Since the dimensions given in the Act of 1803 were unintentionally restrictive on the designs and sizes of shaped bricks, the size bar was changed in 1839 to one of volume. Only bricks in excess of 150 cu. ins in volume were to be charged double duty. Each brickmaker was expected to keep a mould with inside measurements of 10 ins by 5 ins by 3 ins so that if there were any dispute the exciseman could take up a green brick of any size and squeeze the clay into the mould: any surplus would show that the 150 cu. ins volume had been exceeded. Bricks or blocks made as part of a drainage scheme were exempt from duty provided they were stamped with the word 'Drain' before firing. In spite of the rules it might be worth while for a brickmaker to pay the double duty and still give a saving to the bricklayer. Any brick of more than 300 cu. ins volume, say more than 10 ins by 10 ins by 3 ins dimensions, would cover more wall than two maximum-sized bricks.

Inevitably, the Brick Tax became no more popular as years went by than it had been in 1784. Even after tiles were exempted from tax in 1833, balancing the elimination of the duties on coastwise shipping of slates, it was felt that there was discrimination against bricks and so in favour of stone. It was claimed that the requirement to have the excise officer visit the site of the brickmaking to count the bricks and assess the duty militated against the ordinary farmer or villager wanting to make bricks to build a house in the country far from the excise offices. It was, of course, claimed that the tax added substantially to the cost of bricks though an addition of about 15% on good-quality bricks was about the rate in 1850. The government accepted the criticisms and the Brick Tax was repealed in 1850.

It is hard to gauge the effects of the Brick Tax on the use of bricks generally. It did bear disproportionately hard on the cheapest bricks intended for the humblest dwellings and to that extent it probably encouraged the new use or revival of substitute materials, such as clay, and the continued use of obsolete construction such as timber-frame. On the other hand the graph of the consumption of bricks continued upward throughout the nineteenth century. The period of the Brick Tax coincided with the first considerable spurt of railway-building and the tax did not prevent the use of millions of bricks in the great viaducts and tunnels. Similarly, the price of bricks increased, but at the general rate of inflation. There may have been some levelling-off in the second half of the nineteenth century, but there was no sudden and steep rise in brick production immediately following the repeal of 1850. Nevertheless, there was a feeling that taxes on bricks, like taxes on windows or glass, were taxes both on health and progress; the repeal was greeted with general satisfaction and the revenue proved adequate without it.

Special Topic 2
Cavity walling and damp-proof courses

The cavity wall is, surely, the most familiar of all types of brick wall. Its endlessly repetitive Stretcher Bond extends for miles between the picture windows and false dormers of suburbia from Carlisle to Cowes. But the cavity wall deserves special attention in any study of brickwork because, in spite of its recent widespread use, it only came into general favour in the 1920s and passed out of use in its most familiar form in the 1970s. It is, therefore, a type of construction which has flourished and then been abandoned in the lifetime of some readers. Yet its origins and occasional use go back to the early years of the nineteenth century.

The brick cavity wall consists of three elements: an inner and an outer leaf of brickwork and an air space in between. The outer leaf of facing bricks deflects the rain and carries some of the loads; the inner leaf of common bricks provides a key for the plaster finish, gives stability to the outer leaf and carries the rest of the load; the air space prevents moisture which may pass through the outer leaf from being absorbed into the inner leaf, allows for the evaporation of moisture from either of the brickwork leaves, and provides some heat insulation. The two leaves are tied together and the cavity bridged by metal ties, nowadays usually of galvanized steel wire, but otherwise the three elements are kept separate and the cavity is maintained unbroken and continuous throughout the wall.

There seem to have been four possible origins for the cavity wall:

1. the various bonds, principally Rat-Trap Bond, which use bricks laid on edge to produce a discontinuous cavity in a 9-in (229 mm), or 11-in (279 mm) thick wall;
2. the use of a separate layer either outside the main structural wall to deflect driving rain or inside the main wall to conceal dampness;
3. the impression that a cavity would act as a heat insulator and might be used to distribute hot air;
4. the experiments with hollow blocks of various sorts which, combining damp-resistance and light weight, could be as easily handled as conventional bricks, but with greater economy.

Of these four possible origins, the first was abandoned largely because of the poor damp-resistance of walls in which bricks acted as cavity ties, the fourth has continued intermittently as a series of experiments the results of which have never found real favour, while the second and third have combined to produce the cavity wall with which we are familiar.

There is no mention of hollow-wall or cavity-wall construction in the few seventeenth-century technical works such as Moxon's *Mechanick Exercises* or in the eighteenth-century architectural pattern books such as that of Batty Langley; and it was not until the early nineteenth century that the idea was introduced in print. In his *Views of Picturesque Cottages with Plans* published in 1805, William Atkinson recommended that 'in constructing walls for cottages or other edifices in brick a great saving might be made in materials without sacrificing much in regard to strength by leaving the walls hollow'.[1] Two leaves with a 6-in (152 mm) cavity and brick ties were suggested, and it was pointed out that a 'hollow wall will be much warmer also than any other kind in consequence of the air confined in the cavity which is one of the best non-conductors of heat and cold'. Thus stability, economy and insulating properties were linked as advocates for the cavity wall at this early date, and its connection with very small dwellings—cottage property—was established. Advantages in preventing damp penetration were not mentioned. At the moment it is impossible to tell how far, if at all, Atkinson's recommendations were followed by his readers and yet a hollow wall in a house at Bitterne, Southampton, reportedly dating from 1804, has recently been discovered when its cavity ties were found in need of repair.[2]

Thomas Dearne recommended a somewhat similar form of construction shortly afterwards in his *Hints on an Improved Method in Building* published in 1821, but with the modern 11-in width of two 4½-in brick leaves and a 2-in cavity, the two leaves being tied by headers with 2-in closures in the inner leaf. Again one cannot be sure how popular this technique proved to be,[3] except that the author has given his name to Dearne's Bond, one version of which is described in the Glossary. Pasley noticed in 1826 that 'hollow brick walls are sometimes adopted as security against damp. Nicholson of Rochester has adopted this expedient in those two external walls of his house in St Margaret's which were most exposed to rain. These walls are one brick thick, divided by a space of 4 ins and connected together chiefly by the sills, jambs and soffits of doors and windows, with in other parts heading bricks occasionally thrown across.'[4]

In 1839 an ingenious variation of the hollow wall idea was suggested by S. H. Brooks in his *Designs for Cottage and Villa Architecture* (the book is undated, but the plates are dated 1839). In a design for a cottage 'in the Italian Style' it is proposed 'to erect the walls hollow by carrying up 4½-in brickwork externally and internally, leaving a cavity between them of 5 in. The bond of the brickwork is to be made by bricks 14 in by 9 in, which may be placed at every fifth or seventh stretcher course horizontally and in every third or fifth course vertically. In this way an excellent bond may be obtained, and if the sides of the openings be pargetted in the same manner as fireplace flues they may be made to carry rarefied air to all apartments; and with suitable ventilators the rooms may be kept at an equable temperature, which cannot be done with a common English fireplace.' The cool air was to be admitted by way of grilles near the base of the wall and heated by means of a hot iron plate behind the fireplace.[5] The idea is reminiscent of the Gravity Warm Air Heating System officially recommended after 1945, and would probably have been no more successful. The diagrams included in Brooks's book also show the use of 'bonding timbers' running horizontally at various levels in the inner leaf. It is also noted that 'it is not necessary to have all the bricks laid as stretchers ... but the headers and stretchers may be laid, if considered more ornamental, in imitation of Flemish bond, and be equally as secure as the method we have particularly described'. It is worth noting that the idea of using a wide cavity as a warm-air duct was applied to the 'hot wall' or 'peach wall' found in

some late nineteenth-century gardens in which air from a furnace at one end was drawn along a garden wall to heat the surfaces against which the fruit trees were trained (90).[6]

In the second half of the nineteenth century more advocates of the cavity wall emerged. In H. Roberts's report on *The Dwellings of the Labouring Classes* (1850), as well as various hollow bricks, the use of 11-in cavity walls with brick ties, and 2-in (50 mm) 'closures' as in Dearne's Bond was recommended.[7] The cavity wall idea was understood in America at this time; its introduction was credited to Ithiel Town, who trained under Asher Benjamin and who used the construction widely in New Haven, Connecticut.[8] There it attracted the attention of A. J. Downing, who was an enthusiastic advocate of a technique which he believed would save materials, avoid dampness, conserve heat, and eliminate the need for furring and lathing for interior plasterwork. His contemporary, Gilbert Vaux, continued the advocacy in *Villas and Cottages*, 1857, but was more cautious: 'a wall eight inches thick with a hollow space of 3, 4 or 5 inches and an inner wall of 4 inches is the thinnest hollow wall that can properly be built.' He understood the value of a slate damp-proof course and iron ties and insisted that 'the two thicknesses of brick must be entirely and totally distinct if a satisfactory result is to be aimed at.' It is curious that he made the outer leaf load-bearing and the inner leaf simply damp-excluding, whereas we tend to transpose the two roles.[9]

A lively correspondence in the pages of *The Builder* for 1860 was initiated by an anonymous engineer who advocated completely sealed cavities because of their virtues for heat insulation. Other correspondents related accounts of the use of cavity walls to avoid damp penetration in exposed situations, and how the purpose was thwarted by builders who bridged the cavity with header bricks at the sills.[10]

In his book *House Architecture*, Vol. II, published in 1880, the architect J. J. Stevenson advocated the techniques he had already used in the house at 8, Palace Gate, London sw7. The 'hollow space' gave dry walls, provided the two leaves were not tied together by 'absorbent bricks or stones which would concentrate the moisture on the inner wall on the spots where they occur', and kept the house cool in summer and warm in winter especially if the inner leaf were only half a brick thick and the outer as thick as possible beyond the air space.[11]

The Papworth edition of *Gwilt's Encyclopaedia of Architecture*[12] summarised and illustrated cavity-wall construction as understood in the 1860s:

a. Rat-Trap Bond employed for some two-storey cottages since early in the century;
b. English Bond with stretchers cut in half longitudinally so as to give a 4½-in cavity in each alternate course (a most unsatisfactory and improbable form of construction);
c. cavity-wall construction as we know it, with wrought-iron cramps, a technique used, apparently, in Southampton.

The general use of cavity walling in Southampton was mentioned in a letter to *The Builder* of 19 April, 1862, in which the correspondent asserted that he found 'the hollow-wall system prevailing to such an extent, that at least 80 per cent of the dwellings of the working classes erected there within the last ten years have their external walls hollow'.[13]

The debate about ventilated as opposed to unventilated cavities had already begun. The anonymous engineer already mentioned had realised the significance of condensation within the cavity: 'Dampness does not come from without through the wall, but is deposited from the air within when it comes into contact with the walls which have been made cold simply because they are not thorough non-conductors. The greatest care should be taken to stop all holes, however small, especially between the outside atmosphere and the enclosed non-conducting stratum.' Nevertheless, Wm. Peachey, in reply, quoted an instance in which he had built a house with a hollow wall in a damp situation and air bricks at the bottom and top of the wall sufficient 'to give a current of air through the walls.' Although headers crossed the cavity to bond the two leaves there was no penetration of dampness. He wrote: 'I therefore infer that the above experiment is successful and that the damp does not find its way through the headers, neither does the admission of a current of air cause the inner portion of the wall to become damp; but on the contrary, I think the admission of air would keep it dry. . . .' The debate continues.[14]

By the beginning of the twentieth century the use of cavity-wall construction in small houses was fairly common, but not yet normal. In 1905 Rat-Trap Bond ('what is known in Surrey as garden-wall bond') was recommended for economy, but the specification for a cottage costing £110 called for 'the brickwork of external walls to be 11-in hollow walls with galvanised iron ties at proper distances'.[15] Sometimes, as in plans for workers' cottages to be built at Penshurst, there were to be 'walls of double brick with air spaces between up to the first floor, with tiles hanging on 9-in brick above.'[16] Generally the popularity of rendered walls at this time meant that the 9-in solid wall could remain in use with the added protection of the rendering, while presumably the low cost of coal meant that insulation was relatively unimportant.[17] The cavity wall was still regarded as a cheap substitute rather than a scientific design for economy. In *Cassell's Building Construction*, published in weekly parts in 1905, Professor Adams was unenthusiastic about cavity-wall construction: 'cavity walls can hardly be said to be much used, when the number of buildings erected with solid walls is taken into account; but for detached country residences of two floors cavity walls are fairly frequent. It will be noted that the 4½-in wall is in addition to the ordinary thickness; it would not answer to have two 4½-in walls 2-ins apart, connected by wall ties; these would certainly not be as strong as one 9-in wall.'

Rivington's Notes on Building Construction was no more encouraging; the whole brickwork section in the 1915 edition had no illustration or description of cavity walling except a note that 'hollow walls of two 4½-in thickness should be used only in single storey construction and with cement mortar'.[18] Even in the widely used Jaggard and Drury *Architectural Building Construction*,[19] hollow walls were only mentioned in connection with damp-proofing stone walls in exposed situations. Local bye-laws must have remained unhelpful, for as late as 1923, in Edwin Gunn's *Little Things that Matter for Those Who Build*, it was acknowledged that 'cavity-wall construction' was being largely adopted in cheap building 'owing to the sanction of this form of construction by the latest model bye-laws'.[20]

The great wave of small-house building between the wars, both for council tenants and for private clients, depended on cavity-wall construction. The technical section of the Tudor Walters Report, published in 1919 and forming the basis for the official housing manuals and much private housing policy, gave details of cavity-wall brickwork. The 1920 edition of *Mitchell's Building Construction (Elementary)* said that cavity walls 'are considerably and successfully used in many parts of England'.[21] The recently published specification for a house at Chigwell, Essex, designed by Sydney Castle, allowed for cavity walls to the habitable rooms only, with the outer leaf in Flemish bond but 'No more bats to be used than those necessary for bonds'.[22] By 1939 it was acknowledged, as in the article by L. H. Keay in Abercombie's *Book of the Modern House*, that 'in general the 11¼-in. brick cavity wall is the most satisfactory'.[23] The theoretical basis of cavity-wall construction was examined in the official *Principles of Modern Building* published in the previous year, by which time the advantages were clearly understood and the precautions to be taken in design and construction using this technique were familiar to architect and builder alike. The cavity must be maintained; the base must be protected by a damp-proof course; the head must be open for ventilation but protected by the roof; where bridged by ties the cavity must be kept clear of mortar droppings; where interrupted by windows and doors the cavity must be protected by vertical and horizontal damp-proof courses and flashings; enough air bricks must be included to allow for evaporation of moisture, but few enough to preserve the insulating properties of the air in the cavity.[24, 25] Only the aesthetic problem remained insoluble, as the committee preparing the Post-War Building Study No. 18, *The Architectural Use of Building Materials*, reported in 1946, 'Stretcher Bond is commonly used for the outer 4½-in leaf of a cavity wall. It has a stupidly monotonous appearance and there must be many square miles of it all over the country.' But their solution of using a bond of one snap header to three stretchers (i.e. Sussex Bond) never found favour.[26]

After 1945 cavity-wall construction once more became the basis of a housing drive, but by now both bricks and bricklayers were scarce, supplies undependable and skills expensive. Apart from experiments in eliminating brick walls altogether, there were less publicised but more significant experiments in using a cheaper, more quickly laid material for the inner leaf, where the bricklayer's skill was in any case less in evidence. Large 4-in thick blocks of coke breeze and cement, made hollow to increase insulation and decrease weight, began to replace bricks in the inner leaf, and other comparable materials were also tried, so that by 1969 a cavity wall composed entirely of bricks was becoming unusual. Rising fuel costs and improving standards of comfort meant that the heat-insulating properties of these blocks were at least as important as their quick and easy laying. Even this change was not sufficient and the cavity fill of foamed plastic or blown mineral wool became popular, gradually at first and swiftly after the 1973 increase in oil prices.

At all times the problem of stabilising the wall by tying the inner and outer leaves together without allowing moisture to penetrate from one to the other has dominated the design of cavity walls. In the early days of cavity walling header bricks were used; these were either 9 ins in length with a 2-in closure making up the required 11 ins usually in the inner leaf, or they were purpose-made bricks 11 ins long. Brooks's design called for such bricks with stretcher dimensions at each end and the width of the cavity wall as the length.[27] Because of the danger of damp penetration, especially in exposed situations, the use of headers as cavity ties passed out of favour. As an improvement, various sorts of salt-glazed hollow brick ties were invented. The best known are Jennings Patent Bonding Bricks. An early version, illustrated in Gwilt's *Encyclopaedia of Architecture*, was glazed and perforated to prevent transmission of moisture but had grooves to help mortar bonding. A variation had a slope in the portion which crossed the cavity to direct moisture to the outer leaf.[28] The Jennings Improved Patent Bonding Bricks, often illustrated in late nineteenth- and early twentieth-century textbooks of building construction, were cranked so as to direct moisture in the cavity back to the outer leaf of the wall. Both versions were produced in several lengths and allowed for a brick slip of facing brick to maintain the appearance of the outer wall surface. It is virtually impossible to tell that these bonding bricks have been used in a wall until it is demolished.[29] The most commonly used cavity ties were of metal, or so it seems at the moment. Wrought-iron ties forked at each end to be held in the mortar joints and twisted in the middle to drip away moisture were often illustrated. Cast-iron butterfly-shaped ties had a bead in the middle for the same purpose.[30] A variation in common use in Southampton was described by a correspondent to *The Builder* in April 1862: 'Two 4½-in walls are built with an intervening space of 2 inches, and connected by means of light cast-iron clamps, shaped somewhat like the letter H, the two parallel bars being about 3 inches by 1 inch by 1¼ inch, and the connecting bar from ⅜ to ½ inch diameter, and of such length as to allow the parallel bars to rest in the frog of the brick. There is a boss or moulding cast on the connecting bar in the centre of its length which prevents the passage of moisture

along the clamps. These clamps are usually built in every fourth course in height, and about 3 feet apart in length of the wall. . . . So common is the use of these clamps in Southampton and its neighbourhood, that they form part of every local ironmonger's stock-in-trade . . .'. Galvanised steel-wire ties eventually triumphed.[31]

By now the all-brick cavity wall has virtually passed out of use. One technique used nowadays is for the outer leaf to be of brick and the inner of insulating block. Another is for such construction to be supplemented by a complete fill of the cavity with a third leaf of insulating material, a fill of foamed plastic, pelleted plastic or mineral wool located in effect between two walls of permanent shuttering. A third is for the cavity to be partly filled with bats of rigid insulating material tied back to the inner leaf. All these techniques rely on workmanship and supervision of a high order. It may be that in future the cavity will be restored as the barrier against dampness with reliance on some superior form of inner leaf to combine new standards of insulation with the essential stability, or the inner leaf and cavity may be replaced by some insulating and stabilising material which is both impervious in itself and not prone to cracks which allow moisture to penetrate. In either case the brick cavity wall as we have known it, and as it was advocated for a century before it came into general use, will have gone for good.

Damp-proof courses

The matter of preventing damp from rising up brick walls exercised the minds of Victorian architects and builders more than a little. The arguments for the various solutions to the problem were summarised in Gwilt's *Encyclopaedia*.[32]

One solution was to lay three courses above the footings and below the ground floor in cement mortar—but it was admitted that this did not appear to have the slightest effect. Another solution advocated for small cottages was to build the subterranean parts of the wall 'dry', not using any mortar until clear of the earth. This, it was believed, left the wall above quite dry, though one doubts its benefits in other respects.

A better solution was to include two or three courses of slate in cement mortar as a damp-proof course in partition walls as well as in the main walling. This had rather fallen out of favour after about 1860, probably because of the tendency for the slates to crack under load and as a result of small foundation movements, but continued to be recommended in textbooks for another sixty years.

Sheet zinc bedded in loam was found to decay while 4-lb mill lead was reported as effective but expensive.

One recommended procedure was to include in the outer walls a course of brown stoneware perforated slabs laid flat so as to give a circulation of air right through the slots. The Jennings version was often illustrated in late Victorian textbooks (such as Longman's of 1893) and Cassell's textbook of 1905 illustrates a similar design of Royal Doulton. Such a damp-proof course may be seen in the Wyggeston Hospital Boys' School of 1876 in Leicester.

Another technique tried in the nineteenth century was the use of a layer of asphalt about ½ in thick. Philip Webb liked to use a ½-in thickness of tar and sand; the specification appeared in a notebook of 1849–50 kept by Webb when he was a pupil with John Billing of Reading. He used such a damp-proof course in his well-known house at Standen of 1892–4; the outer edge of the course was protected by pointing.[33] The asphalted or tarred roofing felt which is the basis of most damp-proof courses at the present day figured in Cassell's textbook of 1905.

However, one technique which remained popular until the early twentieth century was the use of two courses of blue bricks in cement mortar, demonstrating that in the right circumstances bricks themselves could provide damp-proofing.

Special Topic 3
Header Bond brickwork

As we have seen, the two principal bonds used in this country are English Bond and Flemish Bond. In the former the bricks are laid in alternate courses of headers (with the end of the brick exposed) and stretchers (with the side of the brick exposed); in the latter headers and stretchers alternate in each course. There are variations in each bond—such as English Garden Wall Bond where several courses of stretchers are laid between the header courses—and Sussex Bond where three stretchers are laid between the headers in each course. English Bond is associated with the period from the emergence of regular bonding to the early seventeenth century. Flemish Bond is associated with the period of Dutch influence from the early seventeenth century, flourished in the Georgian period and lost some, but not all of its popularity in the nineteenth century. Header Bond (sometimes called Heading Bond), in which all exposed bricks present the header face, was much less common and was confined to the period c. 1725 to c. 1800. However, both English Bond and Header Bond were revived in the nineteenth century and joined by the Stretcher Bond that we see all around us nowadays.

The Header Bond of the eighteenth century is mostly to be found in central Southern England, in counties such as Berkshire, Buckinghamshire, Dorset, Hampshire and especially Oxfordshire, but also Kent.[1] Small market towns, such as Marlow, Henley-on-Thames, Hungerford and Wallingford, have a fair sprinkling of Header Bond brickwork. Scattered examples are present in towns such as Arundel, Newbury, Marlborough, Poole, Rochester, Winchester and Salisbury, together with Carisbrooke and Yarmouth on the Isle of Wight. Further north few have been noted: one in Louth in Lincolnshire (57) and a couple in Towcester in Northamptonshire for instance. In the Manchester area there remains one example in Altrincham and there was one eighteenth-century example in St James's Square, Manchester, now demolished. Nearly all examples are in small houses whose elevations would otherwise be in Flemish Bond. A survey by Anthea Brian of the bonds used in some 12,000 houses in England and Wales revealed only 120 or 1% in Header Bond and yet where used Header Bond is distinctly prominent.

Most examples display grey headers; these result from the method of firing and the position of the brick in the flue gasses during firing. The grey is rarely uniform and so the bricks present a 'brindled' appearance, heightened through weathering. The pattern of joints gives a network effect sometimes enhanced by lime putty tuck pointing. The walls are visually stabilised by the use of red bricks as dressings: at the quoins, in horizontal flush or projecting string courses, in vertical stripes recalling pilasters, and in door and window surrounds. Often Header Bond is confined to the front elevation with more utilitarian bonds such as English Garden Wall Bond used on the side and rear. In some parts of England flint is a utilitarian material used on the side and rear walls, but where used decoratively the square ends of knapped flints match the almost square proportions of header bricks used in Header Bond brickwork.

It is worth mentioning that the area of use of Header Bond marches with that of mathematical tiles. This subject has already been covered (see pp. 64–8).[2] Mathematical tiles can be seen in such cities as Canterbury, Salisbury and Winchester and in abundance in some smaller towns, most noticeably Lewes. Isolated examples are found elsewhere, as in Cambridge. With such a distribution pattern it is not surprising to find the use of Header Bond in the tiling, most spectacularly in the glazed black headers of Brighton.[3]

Header Bond was also used in curved work as in the rounded corners of buildings, in bay windows, in spiral staircases (106) and in garden features such as tanks or ponds. It was also used in decorative panels, such as blind windows (13, 18) when other bonds were used for the main walling.

The use of Header Bond brickwork was a dying practice at the end of the eighteenth century, but it did survive, and in the Manchester area into the nineteenth century—a pair of cottages in Mobberley, in Cheshire, have a worn date stone of what appears to be 1835. Edgar Wood, a leading architect of the Arts and Crafts period, could possibly have seen Header Bond brickwork on his sketchbook wanderings. However, there were architects of an earlier generation who adopted the technique with enthusiasm, the most prominent of these being J. S. Crowther[4] (1821–93), the major Gothic Revival architect. His first main commission was St Mary's Church, Hulme, Manchester, built 1853–8. It was largely a work of masonry, but the ancillary buildings are brick and involve a parsonage, 'a neat piece of domestic gothic in header bond', as Mathew Hyde put it. A school in polychromatic brickwork including Header Bond was added to the group in 1875. Crowther had sufficient early success as an architect to build himself a house in 1855 among the cotton barons on the slopes of Alderley Edge in Cheshire, and this was in Header Bond brickwork. About this time Crowther was responsible for St Philip's Church in Alderley Edge, 1851–2. The church is in stone, but the school alongside, equally Gothic in inspiration, is in Header Bond brickwork (196). Crowther was probably the designer in Header Bond brickwork of the Gothic villa, Gartness in Victoria Park, Manchester, c. 1865. Rather later, in 1877–8, Crowther built St Benedict's Church, Ardwick, Manchester, in Header Bond.

Another of Manchester's great architects of the Gothic Revival was Thomas Worthington.[5] Among his Header Bond brick buildings are Gorton Hall, Manchester, New Chapel, Altrincham, 1872, and probably Chorlton House, 1866, in Prestwich, a north Manchester suburb. Thomas Worthington had been articled to Henry Bowman in 1841 and was heavily involved with the practice until he established his own firm in 1849. J. S. Crowther had collaborated with Bowman on a book about Gothic architecture and became a partner in Bowman's practice. It is possible that Bowman's scholarly work suggested to Crowther and Worthington the use of Header Bond brickwork as a nod to Gothic architecture.

Other Manchester architects became fond of Header Bond:[6] Poulton and Woodward used it in the Congregational Church Sunday School, Stretford in 1860; Blackwell and Booth in the extravagant Barnes Hospital, Cheadle, Cheshire of 1871–5; H. F. Slater in the Wesleyan Chapel, Northenden, Cheshire; G. T. Redmayne in Dalton Hall of 1881–2 in Victoria Park; and R. B. Preston, another architect associated with Crowther and Bowman and Worthington, designed St Andrew's, Levenshulme, Manchester in Header Bond in 1907–8.

Notable dated buildings in Header Bond brickwork also include the Union Club building of 1874 in Bury, north of Manchester; of the same date Elm Road School, Didsbury, a southern suburb of Manchester; of 1896, St Paul's School in nearby Withington, and of 1899 the school opposite St Anne's Church in Wilmslow, Cheshire. Finally in this list comes the Queen's Road Bus Garage, off Cheetham Hill, Manchester, 1901–2, by J. Gibbons, with probably the most extensive range of Header Bond in the area.

Edgar Wood was responsible for a major group of buildings in Header Bond brickwork, the Long Street Wesleyan Church and School in Middleton, north of Manchester. It stands opposite the ornate Public Library in the same bond and the broad sweeps of brickwork massed in a sculptural purity in the same bond contrast with the broken surfaces and polychromatic busyness of the library. Mathew Hyde makes the fascinating point that Edgar Wood grew up in a house, Sunny Brow, of 1865, in Middleton, possibly designed by J. S. Crowther and built in Header Bond brickwork.[7]

The great flourish of Header Bond in this period, however, took place in minor buildings, such as modest dwellings in the Manchester suburbs. A rough transect between Alderley Edge in the south and Prestwich in the north has produced many instances of the use of the bond in small villas, shops and terraced cottages.

In Alderley Edge, as well as the buildings already mentioned, there are examples of Header Bond in Duke Street and there are three parallel streets—Clifton Street, Stephens Street and Chapel Lane—full of small houses using the technique, while on the outskirts of the village there are a house and a restaurant on Brook Lane, and two farmhouses on Hough Lane, one with stone dressings and bearing the date 1873. There are many substantial villas—detached, semi-detached and in short rows—displaying the technique in Wilmslow, especially in the Hawthorn Park area, in Chapel Lane, Water Lane and Fulshaw Park.

The Altrincham/Hale area is particularly rich in examples. In Railway Street, one of the main shopping streets in late nineteenth-century Altrincham, for instance, there are shops and offices, including one building with a date stone of 1896 and two others with date stones of 1894. In Hale the most prominent building in the main village street is the Railway Station, probably of 1902, in Header Bond.[8] There are villas in adjacent streets, and many shop buildings and domestic buildings, including conversions, in Ashley Road, while there are countless examples—including terraced cottages—in Hale Road, leading from Altrincham, via Hale, towards Wilmslow.

Moving towards Central Manchester one passes numerous small houses or terraces of cottages in Handforth, Heald Green and especially Northenden with examples of the technique. There is one particularly striking example in Cheadle: The Beeches, Mill Lane. It was built as a detached house with all four elevations in Header Bond of a hard blue brick pressed to precise dimensions and laid with thin joints so that it has a powerful mechanical appearance somewhat at odds with its rather romantic design. Continuing north through Didsbury and Withington one remains in Header Bond country. Notable examples include the ostentatious villas on Plymouth Grove and Stockport Road in Longsight, now converted into hotels or public houses. What remains of the inner suburbs, such as Chorlton-on-Medlock, show the developments of the Regency and early Victorian periods before the second phase of Header Bond brickwork was introduced.

196. Alderley Edge, Cheshire: school alongside St Philip's Church, designed by J. S. Crowther and built in Header Bond brickwork.

197. Hughenden, Buckinghamshire showing the Georgian house reclad in Header Bond brickwork.

Central Manchester has lost through bombing and reconstruction many of the commercial buildings built during the reigns of Queen Victoria and Edward VII, but substantial brick warehouse and office buildings survive in Whitworth Street West and Albion Street near the former Central Station. Beside the River Irwell there is a warehouse on the corner of New Quay Street and Stanley Street in Header Bond. Central Salford has suffered even more than its larger neighbour, but villas in Header Bond survive on Great Cheetham Street and Great Clowes Street. Moving north into Prestwich there is the large Friendship Inn of Holt's Brewery in Header Bond on Scholes Lane and there are several late nineteenth-century small villas and cottages in the centre of the former village. Outlying examples include two buildings in Bury and Heywood, two shops in Princess Street, Knutsford, and two buildings in Leigh, Lancashire, the only known examples in the Wigan area.

In the Manchester region over 200 examples of Header Bond brickwork have been noted in a very limited survey— about half of them individual buildings and the other half semi-detached and terraced cottages. They range in size from churches and schools, warehouses and offices, through large villas to streets of small terraced cottages.

There are concentrations in the Alderley/Wilmslow area and in Altrincham/Hale.

No comparable surveys have been made in other cities built largely of brickwork, such as Birmingham and Leicester, while casual observations over many years in Central London and several London suburbs have only revealed one piece of Header Bond brickwork of the late period: that is a section of the west front of Holy Trinity Church, Sloane Street, Chelsea by J. D. Sedding, completed in 1890. Outside London the resurfacing of Hughenden Manor for Benjamin Disraeli by E. B. Lamb in 1862 may be mentioned, but it is difficult to be sure what survived of the eighteenth-century core and what of the brick face belongs to Lamb (197).

Generally in this second phase Header Bond was confined to the front elevation or visible side elevations of the different types of buildings while some more utilitarian bond, such as English Garden Wall Bond, was used elsewhere. Sometimes, however, the bond was used on all elevations. Often the Header Bond in one colour was relieved by dressings in red brick and string courses, flush or projecting in red or blue brick. Occasionally the brick-layer would indulge in a conceit whereby a sort of reverse English Garden Wall Bond was created with one course of stretchers to four courses of headers. Variations such as these could extend to full polychromatic treatment inspired by Ruskin. The St Anne's Church School in Wilmslow, for instance, has three different colours for main walls, dressings and diaper work.

One would expect a wall of Header Bond brickwork to make use of full bricks laid across the wall and with the header faces exposed. In minor buildings, especially of the eighteenth century, with simple 9-in walls, no doubt this was commonly done. Such a wall would be strong, as it would have no uninterrupted joints running up the wall, in contrast to Stretcher Bond where a joint runs between the inner and outer skins. This strength is obtained at a price, because headers are slower and more expensive to lay than stretchers, half of the valuable flared headers would be lost, while the scarcity of Header Bond in engineering work, such as railway viaducts, suggests that this strength was more than was actually needed.

In eighteenth-century Header Bond it is likely that in addition to solid walls the bricklayer's trick, popular at that time, was employed of laying an outer face of better quality bricks and fine joints in front of a backing of common bricks, laid by a less skilful but cheaper bricklayer. This practice was commonly used in the Flemish Bond brickwork of the Georgian period, especially in the towns where the better quality bricklaying and the more expensive facing bricks could be confined to street frontages. The problem was that the courses of fine quality facing bricks laid with thin joints were incompatible with the courses of thick, irregular, common bricks laid with thick joints. At the best certain headers could run through now and then in the height of the wall, but actually most visible headers were 'snap headers', being half bricks whatever the bond. These were bricks cut in two giving two usable header faces from the one brick. Bricks moulded as half bricks were too expensive.

The technique was condemned by some technical authors and accepted by others. Batty Langley pronounced Header Bond 'the most beautiful and the strongest'[9] and noted that heading half bricks, with occasional whole heading bricks, was cheaper when facing bricks were being used. The Papworth edition of the *Dictionary of the Architectural Publication Society* (1853–92) observed 'such work is now very unusual and it might be considered to cause the bond of the brickwork to be much reduced in strength'.[10] However, in Longmans' *Advanced Building Construction* of 1893, the author wrote of the 'evils of facing with superior bricks . . . this leads to unsound work and should not be allowed.'[11]

The use of snap headers to make up the exposed face of Header Bond brick walls was significant as cavity wall construction came into use in the late nineteenth and early twentieth centuries. The rate of adoption varied in different parts of the country, but it seems to have been early in the Manchester area. In the inner and outer suburbs, where Header Bond has been noticed, the alternative was generally Stretcher Bond: the use of this bond together with tell-tale air bricks at the base of the wall implies cavity wall construction. This means that the terraces of inexpensive cottages in Header Bond brickwork were in fact constructed of snap headers, the decorative effect being obtained at the expense of hard and skilful work by the bricklayers busily cutting bricks in two. Although the outer and inner leaves were linked by cavity ties of cast-iron, lead or wire, what looks like a strong bond is actually rather weak.

No survey of Header Bond brickwork would be complete without reference to North America. In the Chesapeake Bay area of Maryland there was a flourishing school of bricklayers making use of the technique between about 1740 and 1780. Most surviving examples are to be found in Annapolis, the state capital; another group is in Charlestown and the remainder are scattered near the shore of the bay. As in England the use of the technique in Georgian houses died out generally before the turn of the eighteenth century. Although brickwork continued in use for official buildings, churches and commercial buildings, as well as domestic ones (usually in houses as a cladding to timber-frame), there was no recorded revival of Header Bond brickwork in the middle or late nineteenth century as had occurred in the Manchester area.[12]

Over the past ten years or so various holidays in European cities have presented the opportunity to note the use of Header Bond brickwork in buildings mostly large but sometimes small.

In the Baltic region, examples can be found in Stockholm, mainly in substantial office or apartment buildings rather than the great public buildings. Dated examples range from 1882 to 1891. Elsewhere in Sweden, on the island of Visby—a former Hanseatic seaport—can be found dated buildings ranging from 1890 to 1903, but no indication of the use of the technique in earlier buildings. In St Petersburg the great buildings are of stone or stuccoed brickwork, but there is a building in Header Bond brickwork dated 1905 opposite the Revolutionary Museum, and nearby there is a little chapel opposite the famous Church of the Spilled Blood; this is in red brick, but there are others nearby in yellow brick. Wartime destruction and post-war reconstruction have cleared buildings in the suburbs, which might have added to the total. In Tallin, the capital of Estonia, there are several examples, most noticeably the Russian Orthodox Cathedral of 1894–1900, as well as smaller buildings such as a bank, probably of 1918, in the lower town. In Copenhagen several examples have been noted around Dantasplas, both in red and yellow brick.

In Holland, Belgium and Northern France there is brickwork in abundance from various historical periods and especially from the late nineteenth and early twentieth centuries, but so wedded were the builders to English Cross Bond that no Header Bond brickwork has been noticed, apart from one example in Dunkirk, and the extensive nineteenth-century modification of earlier fortification to the Citadelle of Montreuil-sur-Mer nearby in small Header Bond cut bricks.

Central and eastern Europe has been more productive. Although many German cities suffered from bombing and post-war reconstruction, enough of the brick buildings of the late nineteenth and early twentieth centuries survive to indicate the popularity of the technique. There are examples in the former East Berlin, in both office and apartment buildings. The charming little town of Gera, near Weimar, retains a number of villas in leafy streets that employ the technique. A short stroll revealed 17 examples along one street, some in red brick others in yellow. One is dated 1887. A further example in red brick was noted on the outskirts of Rostock, another was noted in Poznan, two were seen in Koblenz. Even in the courtyard of the famous Colditz Castle one building has Header Bond in yellow brickwork.

In Warsaw most buildings are of post-war reconstruction, but several examples of Header Bond have been noted. Cracow is quite rich in buildings of this technique: 14 examples were noted in a stroll around the former Jewish quarter. Several buildings of the early twentieth century in yellow brick display Header Bond. In Wroclaw (the former German Breslau) several churches are built with large bricks in Header Bond. On the road to Auschwitz there are small houses in Header Bond, which seem to be of late eighteenth-century date.

In the glorious city of Budapest with so many buildings from the Art Nouveau period there is a substantial quota of Header Bond brickwork in public, office and apartment buildings. Some of the Header Bond may be tile cladding rather than brick.

Summary
In England the first phase of building in Header Bond brickwork began in the early eighteenth century and was abandoned about the turn of the nineteenth century.

The second phase began in the Manchester area about the middle of the nineteenth century and continued until 1914. Header Bond in this second phase was employed in many building types culminating in its use on small houses and terraced cottages in the Manchester suburbs and increasingly was used in cavity wall construction. The Header bond of the Georgian period was found among the colonies of Chesapeake Bay in what became the United States. The Header Bond of the Victorian period has its counterpart in many cities of northern and eastern Europe.

The reintroduction of Header Bond brickwork in England seems to be related to the antiquarian studies and the Gothic Revival inclinations of three Manchester architects: Henry Bowman, J. S. Crowther and Thomas Worthington. Header Bond brickwork sits well with Gothic Revival design; its emphasis on squarish exposed brick ends relates to the squared masonry blocks used in early medieval buildings (and is compatible in size and shape to the once popular knapped flint blocks); its suggestion of strength relates to the perceived quality of Gothic buildings. It plainly is not Flemish Bond and so owes nothing to the favourite bond of preceding architects and builders. Whether or not Crowther intended a revolution in bricklaying when he built St Philip's Church School or his own house in Alderley Edge, a minor revolution did occur. He can hardly have expected that building owners would have accepted the greater cost of the technique for the sake of neatness of appearance, but that is what came to pass.

Special Topic 4
Brickwork in Scotland and Ireland

Scotland
According to R. J. Naismith in his *Buildings of the Scottish Countryside*, 'Scotland is a stone country because that is what she chose to be.' Although suitable clay was quite widely available and although few areas of Scotland have not had brickwork or tiling at one time or another, brick-walled buildings, in the countryside at least, are rare. The Scottish Countryside Commission's survey of buildings in the countryside revealed only four parishes with as many as 30% of the buildings having brick walls, and all those were in the south-west of the country. In the Lothians and in the Central Lowlands there were other parishes with small, but still significant proportions of brick-walled houses, otherwise brickwork was confined to some nineteenth-century industrial buildings, to some buildings in the cities, and to brick dressings to stone-walled houses and farm buildings. The lack of brick buildings is surprising in view of the old-established

tradition of clay construction and in view of the widespread production of drainage and roofing tiles in the nineteenth century. It appears that the almost universal availability of building stone and the prestige of that material discouraged the widespread use of brickwork. Furthermore, the small local brickworks producing materials for partitions, chimney-stacks, etc., could not compete when good-quality bricks from large English manufacturers could be transported by rail or steamer.

Nevertheless, production of bricks was significant as evident from the tax returns. In 1802 tax was paid on over 15 million bricks and in 1840 on nearly 48 million bricks manufactured in Scotland. In 1835 the Commissioners of Excise noted that there were 128 brickmakers in Scotland (as against 5711 in England and Wales). They seemed to hope for greater brick production in Scotland, stating, 'Scotland, notwithstanding the great and increasing size and wealth of several of its cities and towns, contributed only about ¹⁄₅₀ the amount collected in England and Wales.' No doubt many of the bricks produced in the second half of the nineteenth century were used in railway bridges, though at 300,000 for a single-arched bridge even that use did not apparently foster a great deal of brick manufacture.

Brickmaking techniques were apparently similar in Scotland to those in England, the slop-moulding process predominating. An account of brickmaking by the Garnkirk Fireclay Company near Glasgow in 1869 recorded that an expert moulder would make between 4000 and 5000 bricks a day, a boy dipping the mould in water and placing it on the table, the moulder throwing in and striking the clay, the boy upending the mould to drop the brick onto the floor and replacing it by a new wetted mould on the table. The green bricks were dried in the open air, or under cover subjected to heat piped from steam engines, and dried in about twenty-four hours. Although clamp burning was known, most bricks at that time were burnt in rectangular downdraught kilns, three or four kilns being served by a single chimney. The kilns held 20,000 bricks and firing was usually completed in a week.

However important or otherwise the general brickmaking industry might have been in Scotland, its production of firebricks was large and of world importance. The fireclay deposits of the Glasgow area ranked with those of Stourbridge and Newcastle upon Tyne in British production of firebricks. Fireclay is associated with coal seams and was usually mined rather than extracted from the surface. The Garnkirk Fireclay Company, for instance, which operated from about 1843 to 1901 and was one of the largest manufacturers of firebricks, was originally formed to mine coal but found fireclay more profitable. The clay (or shale) was finely ground by means of iron rollers in a perforated trough then mixed with water before being moulded. In contrast to Stourbridge and Newcastle, where firebrick production originated with the needs of glass-making in mind, the Glasgow firebrick production was associated, from its origins in the 1820s, with iron- and steel-making. By the 1870s production of firebricks in Scotland exceeded 80 million annually.

Firebricks were exported in large and small quantities: one of the ships landing firebricks in San Francisco in 1883 unloaded 219,000, but another shipment from Glasgow in 1887 amounted to only 7000 firebricks. It was understood that firebricks were often taken to the west coast of North America in ships collecting wheat for export; it was also alleged that firebricks were sold at less than the cost of importing them once competition from local manufacturers began. Scottish firebricks were widely used in New Zealand, the products of the Glenboig Company which flourished from about 1867 to 1965 being the most popular, but in the Scottish settlement of Dunedin, the Garnkirk Patent Bricks of the Garnkirk Fireclay Company were imported.

Terracotta production was developed in parallel with firebricks. The Garnkirk Company produced terracotta

as well as firebricks, but as decorative rather than structural items. Alexander Wilson and Sons, firebrick manufacturers of Dunfermline, made a good deal of the terracotta used in the South Kensington museums.

A study by Bruce Walker of building construction in Angus, Fife and Perthshire indicated that brick on edge infill panels were used during the nineteenth century. Brick replaced clay as an external walling material, at first replicating the thick walls at 18- to 22½-in thickness but then reducing to 9-in thickness, with stud and plaster linings and with rendering outside. Larger bricks, 6 ins wide and 12 ins long, were produced for partition walls and for paving in farm buildings.

After 1918 brick construction largely superseded stone construction in most parts of Scotland, yet official bodies deplored the lack of a Scottish facing brick of good quality and attractive appearance. Readily available supplies from England seemed to have inhibited the development of local facing bricks. In the inter-war years almost all the brick-walled houses were finished and made weatherproof with the aid of rendering—rough cast or dry dash—with sadly drab effects in too many cases, especially when exposed to the dust and dirt of the towns. Walls one brick thick were still assumed to be weatherproof, if rendered, and only after 1945 did cavity-wall construction become normal in new houses in Scotland.

Ireland

The building materials used predominantly in Ireland in the past were stone and earth. In parts of the island building stone was plentiful and readily available; where it was expensive to quarry, transport and lay, then, as we have seen, earth as turf (clod) or clay (mud), or in other variations, was the predominant building material and continued in use for the smallest cottages almost to within living memory. Brick was not a material generally found within the builder's repertoire in Ireland, but it was introduced in the early seventeenth century and eventually became, as in Britain, the principal material for use in towns and, less predominantly so, in the countryside.

The techniques of brickmaking and bricklaying seem to have been imported from England at the time of the Plantations during the seventeenth century. Through the industry of Philip Robinson there is a detailed account of brickmaking, based on the observations of Gerard Boate in 1652. He described how a square pit was dug, one or two spits deep, to reveal the clay after the topsoil had been removed; the necessary amount of clay was dug up and divided with the spade; water was gradually poured onto the material and it was then a case of working it and labouring it together with the spade and their feet, until the whole mass became uniform, firm and tough like stiff dough. The mixture was then barrowed to the brickmaker's table, which was attended by a team of three: the brickmaker, a woman assistant, and a boy with a barrow. The boy had then to barrow clay to the vicinity of the bench, the woman to pass clods of clay to the brickmaker who would throw it to fill a sanded mould, and the boy would finally take away the 'green' bricks and lay them on an adjacent piece of ground. After a few days they were placed in small piles with spaces between the bricks for ventilation (or 'transparent', as Boate put it). After another few days the green bricks were placed in a long wall about 5 ft or 6 ft high and 2 ft broad, again 'transparent', in what in England would be called a 'hack'. The top of this assembly was covered with straw, which was covered in turn with broad grass turves to keep off the rain.

Having been judged sufficiently dry, the bricks were built into 'great ovens or kilns' which were filled with further loads of green bricks set to allow ventilation and strewn with 'sea-cole' broken small and called 'comb' or 'croome'. Next the top of the pile was covered with clay. Finally, the coal was lit and the kiln (or, strictly the clamp) and its contents burned.

It was important to ensure that all the load of bricks and all those making the wall were sufficiently burnt, the fire having been continued, 'until not only all the bricks piled within the kiln but all the walls quite through and at the outside as well as at the inside be perfectly burnt and turned into good brick'. Mr Oates regretted the wastage caused 'oftentimes through the unskilfulness or neglect of those who make and fill these kilns and of those that govern the fire'. Sometimes, it appears, a great part of the bricks are insufficiently burnt or a part may be overburnt, 'into great unshapely masses of lumps which are good for nothing'.

Notwithstanding the careful processes, which will be familiar to readers of this book, it seems that brickmaking in the seventeenth century in Ireland was a risky business commercially and although techniques no doubt improved over time it is not surprising that visitors from England condemned such brickwork as they saw in Ireland. Wakefield, for instance, in 1812, complained that, among other defects, bricks in Ireland were so badly burnt in the clamp that, 'half of them are scarcely good for anything'.

As one might expect, brickwork was used relatively early by those high in the social order but was still in competition with stone. Even so, it was not seen before about 1600 and was little used even by the landowning class. It came into use for farmhouses and estate cottages from the mid-eighteenth century onwards (perhaps aided by the absence of the Brick Tax in Ireland). The exceptions to the influence of status on building were those being erected during the waves of plantations during the seventeenth century. The settlers from England imported their familiar techniques of timber-frame construction and some of them used brick-nogging in place of wattle-and-daub infill. Some of them built houses of brick, but they were few—only nineteen were plotted on a map based on Plantation Surveys including that of 1611.

Generally, after this period, brickwork was found initially in towns, and the urban spread continued through the eighteenth and nineteenth centuries both for new construction and for replacement of earth-walled houses and cottages as they fell out of favour. In many towns, houses were built of stone, but the Georgian streets of other towns built in brick and slate eventually became as familiar in Ireland as in the rest of the British Isles, giving an appearance of comfort and plenty. This contrasted with the impression of poverty that tourists and observers carried away with their derogatory comments on houses and cottages of clay and thatch.

For good or ill these impressions reflected practically all there was to be seen in the countryside. In the stone-bearing areas builders had substantial material on hand. The main alternative, earth, in one form or another, gave the rural builder little by way of indigenous materials with which to work. Brick made from the widespread deposits of clay previously used for clay houses could have been a welcome alternative, but it was expensive. Even for transient buildings and using clamp firing, an appreciable capital investment was required even for the erection of a single house or cottage. Apart from the cost of fuel, transport and wages to the craftsmen and labourers had to be added. Nevertheless, until well into the nineteenth century the superior qualities of brick and slate could not compete with the economic advantages of self-build in clay and thatch. However, for details such as chimney-stacks, flues, chimney-hoods and, eventually, fireplaces and ovens, brick was very desirable.

Inevitably, as both clay and stone fell out of use, brick took their place at least until the mid-twentieth century when rendered breeze block proved to be even cheaper than brick. There was a period during the Industrial Revolution of c. 1750–1900 when brick was needed for engineering works, such as the bridges and tunnels on the railways, as well as for goods warehouses and station buildings. Brickwork was also in demand in the nineteenth century for workers' housing, such as the two-storey terraces that make some of the quarters of Dublin and Belfast look as if they had been transported from Wigan or South Wales.

Notes and references

References to the works listed in the bibliography are by the surname of the author and the date of publication.

Preface and Acknowledgments and Introduction

The origin and background of the present work relate to Brunskill, 1970–87, 2000, and Brunskill and Clifton-Taylor, 1977. General books on the history of bricks and brickwork include Lloyd, 1925, Woodforde, 1976 and Hammond, 1981. Progress in the study of the subject is discussed in Campbell, 2001 and 2003, and put into a world context in Campbell, 2004.

Part One: Clay, Brickmaking and the Use of Bricks

1. The raw material, labour and transport

Raw material: clay and brick earth: for these materials and their geological basis see Harley, 1974 and Firman and Firman, 1967; for the special meaning of 'brick earth' see Smalley, 1987 and Firman and Firman, 1989; for further connections between geology and distribution of the raw materials for brickmaking see Hammond, 1981, p. 4; for the Oxford clays and the Fletton industry see Cox, 1979.
Fuel: for the use of wood, turves (peat) and coal in firing medieval bricks see Smith, 1985, pp. 32, 52–4, 71; Lloyd, 1925, quotes Dr Plot that in 1679, in Staffordshire, about 7 tons of coal straight from the pit was needed to fire 16,000 bricks.
Labour: see Salzman, 1952, p. 142 and Lloyd, 1925, p. 13, for bricks made in 1416–17 by 'les Flemynges'; for the work of Baldwin Docheman at Tattershall, 1435–46, see Wight, 1972, p. 130; for the work of Anthony Docheman at Kirby Muxloe, 1480–84 see, e.g., Wight, 1972, p. 133; see also Smith, 1985, pp. 7–10. The term 'building owner' is used quite generally nowadays for the person or body commissioning the design and construction of a building.
Transport: for medieval transport see Smith, 1985, p. 58; for modern transport see Cox, 1979 and Woodforde, 1976, pp. 136–45; see Dobson, 1850 and 1971, Vol. I, pp. 9–10 for suggested use of 600 to 800 million bricks annually as early as 1850 on railway work and use of 300,000 bricks for a single bridge and 14 million bricks for a mile of railway tunnel.
Characteristics of bricks and brickwork: the relationship between early brickwork and prestigious building is made clear in Wight, 1972 and Smith, 1985.

2. Brickmaking

Generally: see Smith, 1985, for a thorough treatment of medieval brickmaking in all its manifestations, and Moore, 1991; see the Architectural Publication Society *Dictionary*, 1852–92, under BRICK AND BRICKMAKING, for a detailed and illustrated account of practices in the nineteenth century; see Dobson, 1850 and 1971 for an ambitious account of brickmaking in various parts of this country and abroad in the early nineteenth century; see Cox, 1979 for brickmaking generally and the Fletton industry in particular; see McKay, 1944 for early twentieth-century brickmaking; for the life of brickmakers see Woodforde, 1976, pp. 99–109 and Beswick, 1986 and Los, 1986; see also Drury, 1981.
Getting and preparing the material: interesting accounts of this part of the process appear in Dobson, 1850 and 1971, Vol. I, pp. 21–2, and for the process in the London area, Vol. II, pp. 1–4; he illustrates a pug mill on pp. 7, 14, 15 and a clay mill with rollers on pp. 62–6 of Vol. I; a reconstructed horse-operated pug mill may be seen at the Weald and Downland Museum, Sussex (the seventeenth-century origin for the pug mill has now been disproved; see Campbell, 2001); for the relationship between brickfields and brickyards at the present day see Hudson, 1984, pp. 10–12.
Moulding: for his codification see Harley, 1974; for the development of the frog see Harley, 1974, p. 80 and for the possible derivation of the term see Hines, BBS *Information*, No. 43, November 1987, p. 9; for the depressed rim indicating repair of the mould box see Firman, 1983; figures for the rate of production of moulded green bricks appear, for example, in Lloyd, 1925, pp. 17–21 and Dobson, 1850 and 1971, Vol. I, pp. 19–30, 84 and Vol. II, p. 98; changes of meaning of the terms 'place' and 'stock' bricks are discussed in Lloyd, 1925, pp. 37–8.
Drying: again, Dobson, 1850 and 1971 is a copious source of information on the techniques; Firman, 1986, points out the close connection between the local clays and drying techniques; for an illustration of a wood-covered drying hack see Cox, 1979, p. 25; for chamber and tunnel dryers see Hammond, 1981, p. 19 and McKay, Vol. II, 1944, p. 5. A rebuilt hack may be seen at the Weald and Downland Museum.
Firing: the subject is comprehensively covered in Dobson, 1850 and 1971, Mitchell, Part II, 1944, pp. 120–25 and McKay, Vol. II, 1944, pp. 6–12, all with illustrations of clamps and kilns; for details and survey drawings of surviving kilns see Hammond, 1977, 1984 (a) and (b), 1987, 1988; details of a kiln in the context of a complete brickworks are in Andrews, 1986.
Sand-lime Bricks and Concrete Bricks: see McKay, 1944, p. 17 and Ashurst, 1988, Vol. 2, p. 46.
Transport: for the relationship between cost of bricks at the kiln and at the site see Dobson, 1850 and 1971, Vol. I, p. 114. For Bedfordshire and Arlesey brickworks see Cox, 1979.
Sorting the bricks: this process entailed the invention of many names for bricks of different qualities, for one list see Mitchell, Part II, 1944, pp. 125–6; Smith, 1983, discusses the term 'samel brick'.
Size and shape: Reeder, 1983 (a) and (b), considers the factors which have determined brick sizes and discounts the importance of the size and shape of the bricklayer's hand as a determinant; Lloyd, 1925, gives tables of brick sizes from early days to the seventeenth century, pp. 10–16; eighteenth century, p. 49, and from eleventh century to c. 1790, on

pp. 89–100. He lists the various Acts which have attempted to determine the size of bricks; proportions determined by fitting bricks in the clamp appear under BRICK in the Architectural Publication Society *Dictionary*; for the Lutyens items see the article on Folly Farm, Sulhampstead, Berks. In *Supplement* to *Architect's Journal*, Dec. 1984, pp. 16–21; for discussion of Dudok's Hilversum Town Hall and other modern Dutch buildings see Smith, British Brick Society *Information* No. 34, Nov. 1984, pp. 5–9, and further discussion of thin bricks on modern buildings in Smith, 1986.

Moulded bricks: for discussion in relation to early brickwork see Smith, 1975 and 1985, p. 68.

Colour: see Clifton-Taylor, 1972, pp. 230–41 for a good summary of the factors involved; an article on the subject in relation to contemporary buildings appears on pp. 2–8 of the *Brick Bulletin*, Vol. 3, No. 3.

Special-purpose bricks: see McKay, Vol. II, 1944, pp. 16–17; for a thorough account of firebrick production in Britain see Gurcke, 1987, pp. 59–75.

3. The use of bricks

Structural matters: for a summary of what was understood in the mid-nineteenth century see BRICKWORK, BRICKS, STRENGTH OF, BRICK ARCH, BRICK BEAM, etc. in the Architectural Publication Society *Dictionary*, 1852–92; there was much concern about the crushing strength of bricks though brickwork rarely fails through crushing alone; the extreme case of the satisfactory design of a factory chimney 450 ft high is quoted; for so-called 'structural brickwork', which is medieval brickwork rendered to imitate stone, see Kennett, 1984(c), and Smith, 1988, commenting on the brick walls of the church of St Nicholas, King's Lynn; the absence of expansion joints in historic brickwork is puzzling, especially as boundary walls can be very long, but it is assumed that the slow-setting lime mortar in thick joints gave greater flexibility than the strong cement mortar of modern brickwork.

Bricklaying: for bricklayers' tools see Gwilt, 1867 and 1982, para. 1890 in which 27 tools are listed; see also Mitchell, Part I, 1946; in McKay, Vol. I, 1943, p. 29, 20 different tools are listed; the evils of facing walls with a skin of superior brickwork are condemned in Longman's, 1893, p. 56; for rates of work by bricklayers see Lloyd, 1925, p. 23 quoting Primatt of 1667, Leybourne of 1668 and Neve of 1703; the 1000-a-day rate seems surprisingly constant over several centuries.

Bonding: building construction textbooks of the late nineteenth and early to mid-twentieth centuries have elaborate descriptions and illustrations of bonding, e.g., McKay, 1943, 1944, 1968, Mitchell, 1944 and 1946, Longman's, 1893, Adams, 1905; see also Brian, 1972 and 1980, for chronology and distribution of brick bonding in England; Smith comments in BBS *Information*, No. 37, Nov. 1988 on the use of Flemish Bond in England and English (and English Cross) Bond in northern Europe, according to a letter from Dr Ellen van Olst of the Arnhem Museum, Holland, the Dutch term 'Vlaams Verband' is a literal translation for Flemish Bond which was in use in the Low Countries from the early thirteenth century, but started to become obsolete during the first half of the fourteenth century. The use of Header Bond in the eighteenth century in southern England may relate to the use of knapped flints for decorative façades in the same general areas; an example of Header Bond of the late nineteenth century is illustrated in A. Pass, 1988, pp. 135 and 137 at Altrincham New Chapel of 1872 by Thomas Worthington. See also Special Topic 3.

Bricknogging: use of the technique in outer walls is well covered in McCann, 1987; use in partitions is covered in the Architectural Publication Society *Dictionary*, 1852–92, under that heading.

Openings: Drury, 1983, gives an account of the early use of aspects of brick details of classical inspiration, including door and window openings.

Polychrome: for one aspect of brickwork painted to look like brickwork see Easton, 1986; Dixon and Muthesius, 1978, put brick polychrome work in its Victorian setting on pp. 201–71; the importance of Waterhouse is stressed in Maltby, Macdonald and Cunningham, 1983; in Chapter 17 of Muthesius, 1982, the social significance of ornamental brickwork, including polychromy, is discussed with reference to the terraced house; for Ruskin see p. 55 of the 1880 edition.

Mortar, jointing and pointing: the Architectural Publication Society *Dictionary*, 1852–92, under MORTAR and POINTING, deals with the mid-nineteenth-century concern about the qualities of lime mortar and the prospects for cement mortar; a note on use of such materials as moulding sand for black mortar reflects the Victorian interest in this odd variety; other colours are considered under POINTING MORTAR; under TUCK POINTING the technique is thoroughly described with quotations from Batty Langley's *London Prices* of 1750; tuck pointing on a chapel of 1720 at Capesthorne Hall, Cheshire seems to be an early example; other forms of jointing are illustrated in the nineteenth- and twentieth-century textbooks; the question of laying bricks 'frog up' or 'frog down' was faced in a note in the Spring 1989 issue of *Brick Bulletin*, the journal of the Brick Development Association; it appears that 'In practice, most bricklayers prefer to lay bricks frog down because they believe it to be faster and it will certainly use less mortar', though all technical advice seems to be to lay 'frog up'; the problems of repointing are covered in many technical notes, e.g., Carey, 1987, and in Ashurst, 1988. For galleting see Trotter, 1989.

Brick tiles (mathematical tiles): for a thorough reappraisal and much new information see Smith, 1979 and 1985 together with Exwood, 1981(b) and (c), 1985(b) and 1987; for a suggestion that use of brick tile cladding related to the desire to retain elevational proportions while refacing a building see Kennett, 1984; the tile dated 1724 at Westcott, Surrey was discovered by Miss Joan Harding of the Domestic Buildings Research Group (Surrey); in a curious reverse, Briklap tiles were recently available, which are bricks faced to give the appearance of tile hanging; quotation from Loudon is in Woodforde, 1976, p. 192.

Terracotta: see Ashurst, Vol. 2, 1988 for a succinct account of terracotta, Coade stone and faience; also Fidler, 1983, has much useful information; Howard, 1987, puts early terracotta into its sixteenth-century setting; Morris, 1988, gives recent information on terracotta work at Sutton Place and Hampton Court Palace; see Clifton-Taylor and Ireson, 1983, pp. 239–43, for Coade stone; for the 'pot churches' of Edmund Sharpe in the Manchester area see Stewart, 1956, pp. 58–60 and also under TERRACOTTA in the Architectural Publication Society *Dictionary*, 1852–92; Dixon and Muthesius, 1978, put terracotta into a Victorian setting; Maltby, Macdonald, Cunningham, 1983, give evidence for the contribution of Waterhouse; see generally Stratton, 1993.

Chimneys: for the basis of fireplace, flue and chimney design see building construction textbooks such as McKay, 1944, pp. 64–7; for tall chimney design see Mitchell, Part II, 1944, pp. 364–73; also W. Pickles, *Our Grimy Inheritance*, 1971, and J. Douet, *Going up in Smoke*, 1988.

Part Four: Building in Cob, Clay, Mud, Wychert, Turf, and Mud-and-Stud

Introduction: general introductions to the subject include those by McCann, 1983, 1995 and 2004, Harrison, 1984, and Hurd and Gourlay, 2000.

Cob: the account of cob construction by Rev. Coppinger Hill has been summarised from the full quotation in McCann, 2004. Supplementary information appears in, e.g., Beacham (ed.), 1990. The relationship of cob walling to cruck construction appears in illustration 181. Various experiments in reproducing the technique include that by Nash at the Museum of Welsh Life, St Fagans.

Shuttered earth and pisé-de-terre are also shown in illustration 181 and drawings of pisé construction appear in McCann, 2004; see also Johnson, 1806 and Rees, 1819.

Clay daubing: the technique has been further described and illustrated in Brunskill, 1962 and Harrison, 1989 and 1991; a series of articles by Nina Jennings culminated in her book published in 2003.

Clay lump: extensively and intensively studied by McCann, 1987 (a) and (b) and Bouwens, 1988. The 150-lbs weight sometimes quoted for a clay lump seems unrealistic; the 50–55 lbs quoted here seems more reasonable.

Wychert: the characteristic but restricted subject attracted Clifton-Taylor, 1972, and many writers since.

Turf: little has been reported of its use in England or Wales, but it has been extensively covered in Scotland, principally by Walker, 2006, and has formed part of the subject of earth construction in Ireland. The use of turf by the Roman army, e.g., in Hadrian's Wall and the Antonine Wall, has been widely published, e.g., by Blair, 1963 and by Historic Scotland in its bid for World Heritage status for the Antonine Wall.

Mud-and-Stud: the technique attracted the attention of two pioneers in the study of vernacular architecture in Britain: Addy, 1898 and Innocent, 1916.

Distribution: the compilation of distribution maps is complicated by the lack of consistent data and the difficulty in determining the date-range and status of buildings to be mapped. The survival of clay buildings does not necessarily indicate their former distribution. The diagrammatic map here is based on field work, and published illustrations and references. Other maps appear in Harrison, 1984 and 2000 and in Hurd and Gourlay (eds.), 2000. For Scotland see the works of Walker and for Ireland O'Danachair and Gailey. Otherwise, comprehensive surveys, such as the *Inventories* of the Royal Commissions on Historical Monuments, provide little information, not least because surviving examples are beyond the dates in their remit.

Regional variations: the Bibliography lists the appropriate publications, e.g., by Beecham (ed.), 1990, for Devon, Walker, 1977, 1996, 2006, for Scotland. Walker has traced the plan to improve earth building in Russia by employment of Scottish mudmasons. There are plentiful references to the use of the various techniques in Ireland in O'Danachair, 1957, etc., and the works of Evans, Gailey, and Robinson; some surprises include the use of clay lump in Northern Ireland.

The international context: the use of earth on a world scale is a massive subject and only brief and scattered references can be given here. The well-illustrated volumes by Oliver, 1969, 2003, have been particularly helpful. In detailed study the material published by Meirion-Jones, 1982, has a rare quality, even including a distribution map. The diagram 195 is based on illustrations from books listed in the Bibliography, e.g., Oliver, 2003.

Part Five: Special Topics

1. The Brick Tax

The Brick Tax: the true significance of the Brick Tax has been argued in Smith, 1979 and Exwood, 1981 (a); I am also indebted to essays by Alyson Cooper in 1979 and A. D. Bower in 1981, while graduate students; Shannon, 1934, pp. 188–201 demonstrated how the production of bricks increased during the period of the Tax and was related rather to the fluctuations of the building industry and economic activity generally; for the Brick Tax and large bricks see Exwood, 1981 (a) on Wilkes' Gobs.

2. Cavity walling and damp-proof courses

1. William Atkinson, *Views of Picturesque Cottages with Plans*, London, 1805 (reprint Gregg Press, 1971), pp. 15–16. I am grateful to Grant Muter for this reference.
2. Report in *Refurbishment Products* magazine, October/November 1987, p. 56.
3. Thomas Dearne, *Hints on an Improved Method of Building*, London, 1821.
4. Pasley, *Outline of a Course . . .*, Chatham, 1826, Quoted in *Dictionary* of the Architectural Publication Society 1852–92 (DAPS).
5. S. H. Brooks, *Designs for Cottage and Villa Architecture*, London, c. 1839, p. 59.
6. See also DAPS under 'Hollow Walls', p. 70; examples quoted at Chichester and Twickenham.
7. H. Roberts, *The Dwellings of the Labouring Classes*, London, 1850, pp. 24–5.
8. See T. Ritchie, 'Notes on the History of Hollow Masonry Walls', Bulletin of the Association for Preservation Technology, Vol. V, No. 4, 1973, pp. 40–49. The article is a most comprehensive review of cavity wall construction in the United States and Canada.
9. G. Vaux, *Villas and Cottages*, New York, 1867, pp. 76–7 and A. J. Downing, *Country Houses*, New York, 1850.
10. *The Builder*, 28 Jan., 1860, p. 64.
11. J. J. Stevenson, *House Architecture*, Vol. II, London, 1880, pp. 172–4.
12. J. Gwilt, *Encyclopaedia of Architecture* (Papworth edn), 1894, pp. 564–5 (paras. 1902c and 2293a) and p. 1210.
13. *The Builder*, 19 April, 1862, p. 283.
14. Wm. Peachey in *The Builder*, 3 March, 1860, p. 142.
15. Home Counties, *How to Build or Buy a Country Cottage*, London, 1905, pp. 88–93 and p. 164.
16. R. Williams and F. Knee, *The Labourer and his Cottage*, London, 1905, pp. 46–7 and p. 77.
17. See H. B. Philpott, *Modern Cottages and Villas*, London, c. 1905, designs for small houses costing £150–£1000, among others.
18. W. N. Twelvetrees, *Rivington's Notes on Building Construction*, London, 1915, pp. 112 and 114.
19. W. R. Jaggard and F. E. Drury, *Architectural Building Construction*, Vol. I, 1916, Vol. II, 1923.
20. E. Gunn, *Little Things that Matter for Those Who Build*, London, 1923, p. 9.
21. G. A. and A. M. Mitchell, *Building Construction and Drawing*, Vol. I, London, 1st edn, 1911, p. 62.
22. Bruce Castle, 'Interwar Vernacular', article on a house at Chigwell, Essex, by Sydney Castle, built 1923, in *Supplement* to *Architect's Journal*, December 1984.
23. P. Abercrombie (ed.), *The Book of the Modern House*, London, 1939, p. 156.
24. Department of Scientific and Industrial Research (Building Research Station), *Principles of Modern Building*, 1938.

25. Although W. B. McKay said of 'Cavity or Hollow Walls' that 'this type of construction is now very common and . . . is generally to be preferred to solid wall construction for many types of buildings, especially houses', he still felt it sufficiently advanced to be left to Volume II of his series *Building Construction*, London, 1944, pp. 40–44.

26. *The Architectural Use of Building Materials*, Post-War Building Study No. 18, by a committee convened by the RIBA, London, 1946, p. 28.

27. As noted in Brooks, 1839.

28. Gwilt, 1894, para. 617h on p. 564.

29. Illustrated in *Longman's Building Construction (Advanced)*, 1893, p. 62.

30. Various cavity ties are illustrated in the diagram from the Architectural Publication Society *Dictionary*. Others are known in lead as well as cast iron.

31. Letter to the editor on p. 283 of *The Builder*, 19 April, 1862.

32. Gwilt, 1894, paras. 1886 to 1886f.

33. John Brandon-Jones, 'Arts and Crafts' article on Philip Webb's house, Standen, East Grinstead, Sussex, pp. 14 and 15 in *Supplement to Architect's Journal*, December 1984.

3. Header Bond brickwork

Adapted from my contribution to *Making Manchester*, Transactions of the Lancashire and Cheshire Antiquarian Society, Vol. 102, 2006, pp. 202–16, Clare Hartwell and Terry Wyke (eds) and agreed by the society.

1. A. Brian, 'A regional survey of Brick Bonding in England and Wales', *Vernacular Architecture*, Vol. 3, 1972, pp. 12–15.

2. R. W. Brunskill, *Brick and Clay Building in Britain*, London, 2009, pp. 64–8.

3. See A. Arschavir, 'False Fronts in Minor Domestic Architecture', *Transactions of the Ancient Monuments Society*, Vol. 4, 1956, p. 114. 'In normal practice, Flemish bond is most common, with "heading" bond a fairly close second; black glazed titles are used only in "heading" bond.' An example is illustrated in A. Clifton-Taylor, *The Pattern of English Building*, London, 2nd edn, 1972, plate 267 d.

4. Material about J. S. Crowther and his buildings is based on M. Hyde, 'J. S. Crowther in Manchester', TAMS, Vol. 46, 2002, pp. 41–54.

5. Material about Worthington and his buildings is based on Pass, 1988. A. J. Pass suggested in conversation that Bowman may have introduced Worthington to Header Bond brickwork.

6. Attributions and many dates are taken from C. Hartwell, M. Hyde, N. Pevsner, *Lancashire: Manchester and the South-East*, Buildings of England, New Haven and London, 2004.

7. See Hartwell, Hyde, Pevsner, op. cit., p. 515.

8. Information from Ian Foster.

9. Batty Langley, *London Prices*, London, 1750, p. 93, mentioned in C. W. Pasley, *Practical Architecture*, 1826 and 1862 (reprinted by Donhead, 2001), together with general condemnation of false headers pp. 39–44.

10. *Dictionary of the Architectural Publication Society*, Vol. IV, London, 1852–92, p. 33.

11. See Longmans' *Advanced Building Construction*, London, 1893, p. 56.

12. Information from guides produced by M. M. Miller, O. Ridout V and others for the Spring 1998 meeting of the Vernacular Architecture Forum.

4. Brickwork in Scotland and Ireland

See Naismith, 1985, p. 86 for the quotation; Hammond, 1983, includes a list of 12 Scottish brickmaking companies; Hay and Stell, 1986, include a cutaway isometric drawing of a kiln and further details of Scottish brickworks; the export of Scottish firebricks to the west coast of the USA is covered in detail in Gurcke, 1987, and to New Zealand in W. J. Harris, BBS *Information*, No. 34, Nov. 1984, pp. 16–17.

See Robinson, 1979, p. 21 for the account of brickmaking in Ireland; O'Danachair, 1957, p. 68ff for Wakefield's comment; Robinson, 1979, p. 15 for the surveys.

Metric equivalents of imperial measures used in this book

⅜ inch = 9.5 mm	4 ½ ins = 114.3 mm	22 ½ ins = 571.5 mm
½ inch = 12.7 mm	4 ¹³⁄₁₆ ins = 114.3 mm	2 ft (24 ins) = 609.6 mm
¾ inch = 19.1 mm	5 ins = 127.0 mm	2 ft-6 ins (30 ins) = 762 mm
1 inch = 25.4 mm	6 ins = 152.4 mm	3 ft (36 ins) = 914.4 mm
1 ¼ inch = 31.7 mm	7 ins = 177.8 mm	4 ft (48 ins) = 1.219 m
1 ½ inch = 38.1 mm	8 ins = 203.3 mm	5 ft (60 ins) = 1.524 m
1 ⅞ inch = 47.6 mm	8 ¼ ins = 209.5 mm	6 ft (72 ins) = 1.829 m
2 ins = 50.8 mm	8 ⅝ ins = 219.1 mm	7 ft (84 ins) = 2.134 m
2 ⅛ ins = 54.0 mm	8 ¾ ins = 222.2 mm	8 ft (96 ins) = 2.438 m
2 ¼ ins = 57.1 mm	9 ins = 228.6 mm	10 ft = 3.048 m
2 ⅜ ins = 60.3 mm	9 ½ ins = 241.3 mm	14 ft = 4.267 m
2 ½ ins = 63.5 mm	10 ins = 254.0 mm	30 ft = 9.144 m
2 ⅞ ins = 73.0 mm	11 ins = 279.4 mm	40 ft = 12.192 m
3 ins = 76.2 mm	12 ins = 304.8 mm	100 ft = 30.48 m
3 ⅛ ins = 79.4 mm	14 ins = 355.6 mm	300 ft = 91.44 m
4 ins = 101.6 mm	16 ins = 406.4 mm	450 ft = 137.16 m
4 ⅛ ins = 104.8 mm	18 ins = 457.2 mm	

Bibliography

H. Adams, *Cassell's Building Construction*, n.d., probably 1905

S. O. Addy, *The Evolution of the English House*, 1898

A. and J. Andrews, 'Colwich Brickworks Survey', *Journal of the Staffordshire Industrial Archaeology Society*, No. 12, 1986

Architectural Publication Society, *Dictionary* (edited by W. Papworth), 1852–92

J. and N. Ashurst, *Practical Building Conservation*, Vols. 2 and 3, 1988

M. W. Barley, *The English Farmhouse and Cottage*, 1961

M. W. Barley, *Houses and History*, 1986

P. Beacham (ed.), *Devon Building*, 1990

M. Beswick, 'Dual occupations', BBS *Information*, No. 34, May 1986, pp. 14–15

M. Beswick, *Brickmaking in Sussex: a History and Gazetteer*, 1993

P. H. Blair, *Roman Britain and Early England 55 BC–871 AD*, 1963

G. Boate, *Ireland's Natural History*, 1652

D. Bouwens, 'Clay Lump in South Norfolk', *Vernacular Architecture*, Vol. 19, 1988, pp. 10–18

A. Brian, 'A regional survey of brick bonding in England and Wales', *Vernacular Architecture*, Vol. 3, 1972, pp. 11–15

A. Brian, 'The distribution of brick bonds in England up to 1800', *Vernacular Architecture*, Vol. II, 1980, pp. 3–10

Brick Development Association, *Bricks, Their Properties and Use*, 1974

S. B. Broeksmith and A. T. Sullivan, 'Dry-Press Brick: A Nineteenth-Century Innovation in Building Technology', *Bulletin of Association for Preservation Technology*, Vol. XXXVII, No. 1, 2006

R. W. Brunskill, 'The clay houses of Cumberland', *Transactions of the Ancient Monuments Society*, Vol. 10, 1962, pp. 57–80

R. W. Brunskill, *Illustrated Handbook of Vernacular Architecture*, 1970, 1978, 1987, 2000

R. W. Brunskill, 'Header Bond Brickwork', *Transactions of the Lancashire and Cheshire Antiquarian Society*, Vol. 102, 2006, pp. 202–16

R. W. Brunskill and A. Clifton-Taylor, *English Brickwork*, 1977

J. W. P. Campbell, 'The Myth of the Seventeenth-Century Pug Mill', BBS *Information*, No. 86, 2001, pp. 7–9

J. W. P. Campbell, 'The Study of Bricks and Brickwork since Nathaniel Lloyd', *Construction History Newsletter*, Vol. 66, 2003

J. W. P. Campbell, *Brick: a World History*, 2004

J. W. P. Campbell and Andrew Saint, 'A Bibliography of Works on Brick published in England before 1750', *Construction History*, Vol. 17, 2001

J. W. P. Campbell and Andrew Saint, 'The Manufacture and Dating of English Brickwork, 1600–1720', *Archaeological Journal*, Vol. 159, 2002

J. Carey, 'Tuck pointing in practice', *SPAB Information Sheet* 8, Autumn 1987

B. F. L. Clarke, *Church Builders of the Nineteenth Century*, 1938 (1969 edn)

A. Clifton-Taylor, *The Pattern of English Building*, 2nd edn, 1972

A. Clifton-Taylor and A. Ireson, *English Stone Building*, 1983

R. Cousins, *Lincolnshire Building in the Mud and Stud Tradition*, 2000

A. Cox, *Brickmaking: A History and Gazetteer*, 1979, pp. 9–17

A. Cox, 'The Pug Mill Reconsidered', BBS *Information*, No. 89, 2002

D. W. Crossley (ed.), CBA Report No. 40, *Medieval Industry*

N. Davey, *A History of Building Materials*, 1961

R. Dixon and S. Muthesius, *Victorian Architecture*, 1978

E. Dobson, *A Rudimentary Treatise on the Manufacture of Bricks and Tiles*, 1850, reprinted with an introduction by F. Celoria in *Journal of Ceramic History*, No. 5, 1971

G. Douglas and M. Oglethorpe, *Brick, Tile and Fireclay Industries in Scotland*, 1993

P. J. Drury, 'The production of brick and tile in medieval England', in D. W. Crossley (ed.), CBA Research Report No. 40, *Medieval Industry*, 1981, pp. 126–9

P. J. Drury, '"A Fayre House Buylt by Sir Thomas Smith", the development of Hill Hall, Essex, 1557–81', *Journal of the British Archaeological Association*, Vol. CXXXVI, 1983, pp. 98–123

C. P. Dwyer, *The Economic Cottage Builder*, 1856

T. Easton, 'The internal decorative treatment of sixteenth- and seventeenth-century brick in Suffolk', *Post-Medieval Archaeology*, Vol. 20, 1986, pp. 1–17

E. E. Evans, *Irish Folk Ways*, 1957

M. Exwood, 'The Brick Tax and Large Bricks', BBS *Information*, No. 24, May 1981, pp. 5–7

M. Exwood, *Mathematical Tiles: Notes of the Ewell Symposium*, 1981

M. Exwood, 'Mathematical Tiles', *Vernacular Architecture*, Vol. 12, 1981, pp. 48–53

M. Exwood, 'Wilkes' Gobs', BBS *Information*, No. 27, May 1982

M. Exwood, 'Early "Brikes" at Farnham Castle, Surrey', BBS *Information*, No. 37, Nov. 1985, pp. 12–13

M. Exwood, 'More on mathematical tiles', BBS *Information*, No. 37, Nov. 1985, pp. 16–18

M. Exwood, 'Mathematical tiles—the latest count', BBS *Information*, No. 41, Feb. 1987, pp. 11–13

M. Exwood, 'Mathematical Tiles and the Brick and Tile Taxes', BBS *Information*, No. 62, June 1994, pp. 12–14

A. Fenton, 'Stone and Turf Walling', *Folk Life*, Vol. 6, 1968, pp. 94–103

A. Fenton, 'Clay Building and Clay Thatch in Scotland', *Ulster Folk Life*, Vol. 16, 1970

J. Fidler, 'The manufacture of architectural terracotta and faience in the United Kingdom', *Journal of the Association for Preservation Technology* (Canada and USA), Vol. XV, No. 2, 1983, pp. 27–32

R. J. Firman, 'Techniques for drying bricks—a critical appraisal of the evidence', BBS *Information*, No. 39, May 1986, pp. 8–13

R. J. Firman, 'The colour of Brick in Historic Brick-work', BBS *Information*, No. 61, Feb. 1994, pp. 3–9

R. J. and P. E. Firman, 'A geological approach to the study of medieval bricks', *Mercian Geologist*, Vols. 2 and 3, 1967, pp. 299–318

R. J. and P. E. Firman, 'Bricks with sunken margins', BBS *Information*, No. 31, Nov. 1983

R. J. and P. E. Firman, 'Loessic brickearth and the location of early pre-Reformation brick buildings in England—an alternative interpretation', BBS *Information*, No. 47, Feb. 1989, pp. 4–14

A. Gailey, 'Vernacular Dwellings in Ireland', *Revue Roumaine d'Histoire de l'Art*, Tome XIII, 1975

A. Gailey, 'The Housing of the Rural Poor in Nineteenth-Century Ulster', *Ulster Folklife*, Vol. 22, 1976, pp. 137–155

A. Gailey, 'Vernacular Dwellings of Clogher Diocese', *Clogher Record*, Vol. IX, No. 2, 1977, pp. 187–231

A. Gailey, 'Bricks and Brickmaking in Ulster in the 1830s', *Ulster Folklife*, Vol. 28, 1982, pp. 61–4

A. Gailey, *Rural Houses of the North of Ireland*, 1984

R. T. Gunther (ed.), *The Architecture of Sir Roger Pratt*, 1928

K. Gurcke, *Bricks and Brickmaking*, 1987 (Moscow, Idaho, USA)

J. Gwilt, (revised by W. Papworth), *The Encyclopaedia of Architecture*, 1867 edition, reissued 1982

M. Hammond, 'Brick kilns: an illustrated survey', *Industrial Archaeology Review*, Nos. 1 and 2, Spring 1977, pp. 171–92

M. Hammond, *Bricks and Brickmaking*, 1981

M. Hammond, 'Scottish bricks', BBS *Information*, No. 31, Nov. 1983, pp. 16–18

M. Hammond, 'Brick kilns: an illustrated survey—II; Clamps', BBS *Information*, No. 33, May 1984, pp. 3–6

M. Hammond, 'Brick and tile kiln, Stanmore, Middlesex', BBS *Information*, No. 33, May 1984, pp. 13–14

M. Hammond, 'Beech Hirst, Poole', BBS *Information*, No. 42, May 1987, p. 4

M. Hammond, 'More about kilns', BBS *Information*, No. 44, March 1988, pp. 13–16

C. C. Handisyde and B. Haseltine, *Bricks and Brickwork*, 1975

L. S. Harley, 'A typology of brick with numerical coding brick characteristics', *Journal of the British Archaeological Association*, Vol. 38, 1974, pp. 63–87

L. S. Harley 'Bricks of eastern England to the end of the Middle Ages', *Essex Journal*, Vol. 10, No. 4, Winter 1975/76, pp. 131–41

J. R. Harrison, 'The Mud Wall in England at the Close of the Vernacular Era', *Transactions of the Ancient Monuments Society*, Vol. 28, 1984

J. R. Harrison, 'Some Clay Dabbins in Cumberland: their construction and form', *Transactions of the Ancient Monuments Society*, Part I, 1989; Part II, 1991, Vols. 33 and 35, pp. 97–152 and 29–88

J. R. Harrison, *Earth, The Conservation and Repair of Bowhill*, Exeter, 2000

G. D. Hay and G. P. Stell for the Royal Commission on the Ancient and Historical Monuments of Scotland, *Monuments of Industry*, 1986

M. Howard, *The Early Tudor Country House*, 1987

K. Hudson, *Industrial History from the Air*, 1984

J. Hurd and B. Gourlay (eds.), *Terra Britannica: A Celebration of Earthen Structures in Great Britain*, 2000

B. Hutton, 'Rebuilding in Yorkshire: the evidence of inscribed dates', *Vernacular Architecture*, Vol. 8, 1977, pp. 819–24

C. F. Innocent, *The Development of English Building Construction*, 1916

Jörn Janssen, 'The Transformation of Brickmaking in 17th Century London', *Construction History Society Newsletter*, No. 71, May 2005

N. Jennings, *Clay Dabbins: Vernacular Buildings of the Solway Plain*, 2003

D. Johnson, 'Friedrich Edouard Hoffman and the Invention of the Continuous Kiln Technology',

Industrial Archaeology Review, Vol. XXIV, 2, 2002

S. W. Johnson, *Rural Economy, containing a Treatise on Pisé Building etc.*, New York, 1806, p. 41

N. Jones, 'Brickworks', *Building Refurbishment*, Jan. 1988, pp. 38–9

A. Kelly, *Mrs. Coade's Stone*, 1990

F. Kelsall, 'A brick-making agreement of 1693', *Vernacular Architecture*, Vol. 14, 1983, pp. 48–9

D. H. Kennett, 'Taxes and bricks: wealthy men and their buildings in early Tudor Norfolk', BBS *Information*, No. 32, Feb. 1984, pp. 5–12

D. H. Kennett, 'Early brick buildings: a question of size', BBS *Information*, No. 33, May 1984, pp. 7–12

D. H. Kennett, 'Decorative brickwork in High St., Winslow, Buckinghamshire: a preliminary survey', BBS *Information*, No. 33, May 1984, pp. 15–17

D. H. Kennett, 'Mathematical tiles and the Great House: height and proportion', BBS *Information*, No. 34, Nov. 1984, pp. 12–13

D. H. Kennett, 'Structural brick', BBS *Information*, No. 34, Nov. 1984, pp. 13–14 (followed by an appendix by T. P. Smith)

D. H. Kennett, 'Rat-trap bond and Flemish bond', BBS *Information*, No. 34, Nov. 1984, p. 18

D. H. Kennett, 'Church towers of brick', BBS *Information*, No. 35, Feb. 1985, pp. 4–8

D. H. Kennett, 'Brick piers', BBS *Information*, No. 41, Feb. 1987, pp. 15–16

D. H. Kennett, 'Blythburgh Church, Suffolk', BBS *Information*, No. 41, Feb. 1987, pp. 20–21

D. H. Kennett, 'Some early brick houses', BBS *Information*, No. 45, July 1988, pp. 4–5

D. H. Kennett, 'Polstead Church, Suffolk', BBS *Information*, No. 50, Oct. 1990, pp. 9–16

D. H. Kennett, 'Bridges: the Material Consideration', BBS *Information*, No. 53, July 1991, pp. 16–22

D. H. Kennett, 'Brick and its uses in the Twentieth Century', BBS *Information*, No. 83, 2001; No. 84, 2001; No. 88, 2002

J. E. Klee, 'The Vernacular Architecture Forum 2005 Meeting, Arizona and North Mexico', *Vernacular Architecture*, Vol. 37, 2006, pp. 75, 76

N. Lloyd, *A History of English Brickwork . . . from Medieval Times to the end of the Georgian Period*, 1925 (reissued 1983)

A. Longcroft, 'Medieval Clay Houses: A Case Study from Norfolk', *Vernacular Architecture*, Vol. 37, 2005/6, pp. 61–74

Longman's Building Construction (*Advanced*) (no author named) 1893

W. A. Los, 'Accounts from archives: East Yorkshire', BBS *Information*, No. 31, Nov. 1983, pp. 21–4

W. A. Los, 'Brickmaking—a seasonal and dual occupation', BBS *Information*, No. 40, Nov. 1986, pp. 4–10

G. Lynch, *Gauged Brickwork*, 1990

G. Lynch, *Brickwork History, Technology and Practice*, Vols. 1 and 2, 1994

J. McCann, *Clay and Cob Building*, 1983, 1995, 2004

J. McCann, 'Bricknogging in the fifteenth and sixteenth centuries with examples drawn mainly from Essex', *Transactions of the Ancient Monuments Society*, Vol. 31, 1987, pp. 107–33

J. McCann, 'Is clay lump a traditional building material?', *Vernacular Architecture*, Vol. 18, 1987, pp. 1–18

J. McCann, 'The first cottage of clay bats?', *Proceedings of the Cambridge Antiquarian Society*, Vol. LXXVI, 1987

J. McCann, 'The origin of clay lump in England', *Vernacular Architecture*, Vol. 28, 1997, pp. 57–67, pp. 58–60

J. McCann, 'Clay-walled houses in Norfolk: some comments', *Vernacular Architecture*, Vol. 38, 2007

W. B. McKay, *Building Construction*, Vol. 1, 2nd edn, 1943, Vol. II, 1944

W. B. McKay, *Brickwork*, 2nd edn, 1968

Maltby, Macdonald and Cunningham, *Alfred Waterhouse, 1830–1905, an exhibition catalogue*, 1983

G. Meirion-Jones, *The Vernacular Architecture of Brittany*, 1982

E. Mercer, *English Vernacular Houses*, 1975

P. Minter, 'Traditional Brick-Making at Bulmer, Suffolk', *Transactions of ASCHB*, Vol. 26, 2001

G. A. Mitchell, *Building Construction*, Part 1, 18th edn, 1946; Part II, 14th edn, 1944

N. J. Moore, 'Brick' in J. Blair and N. Ramsey (eds.), *English Medieval Industries*, 1991

R. K. Morris, 'Architectural Terracottas at Sutton Place and Hampton Court Palace', BBS *Information*, No. 44, March 1988, pp. 3–8

J. Moxon, *Mechanick Exercises*, edition of 1700

J. Musgrove (ed.), *Sir Banister Fletcher's A History of Architecture*, 19th edn, 1987

J. Musty, 'Brick Kilns and Brick and Tile Supplies', *Archaeological Journal*, Vol. 147 (for 1990), 1991, pp. 411–19

S. Muthesius, *The English Terraced House*, 1982

N. Nail, 'The Ewell Symposium on Mathematical Tiles of November 1981 Revisited' and 'The Ewell Symposium Paper', BBS *Information*, No. 67, March 1996, pp. 3–14

R. J. Naismith, *Buildings of the Scottish Countryside*, 1985

G. Neilson, 'Peel, its meaning and derivation', *Transactions of the Dumfries and Galloway Antiquarian Society*, 1894

R. R. Noble, 'Turf-walled houses of the Central Highlands', *Folk Life*, Vol. 22, 1983–4

J. Norton, *Building with Earth*, 1986

C. O'Danachair (Kevin Danaher), 'Materials and Methods in Irish Traditional Building', *Journal of the Royal Society of Antiquaries of Ireland*, Vol. 87, 1957, pp. 61–74

P. Oliver, *Shelter and Society*, 1969

P. Oliver, *Dwellings*, 2003

F. L. Olmsted, *Walks and Talks of an American Farmer in England*, 1852, 1859, 1967

C. W. Pasley, *Practical Architecture*, 1826, 1862, re-issued 2001

A. J. Pass, *Thomas Worthington, Victorian Architecture and Social Purpose*, 1988

G. Pearson, *Conservation of Clay and Chalk Buildings*, 1992

J. & J. Penoyre, *Houses in the Landscape*, 1978

A. Percival, 'Netherlandish Influence on English Vernacular Architecture—Some Considerations', BBS *Information*, No. 47, Feb. 1989, pp. 15–20

A. Plumridge and W. Merlenkamp, *Brickwork: Architecture and Design*, 1993

B. C. Pratt and C. Wilson (eds.), *The Architecture and Cultural Landscape of North Central New Mexico*, 1991

P. Rahtz, 'Buildings and Rural Settlement' in D. M. Wilson (ed.), *The Archaeology of Anglo-Saxon England*, 1976, pp. 49–98

M. G. Reeder, 'Bricks and the frog question in Suffolk', BBS *Information*, No. 22, Nov. 1980, pp. 4–6

M. G. Reeder, 'The size of a brick', BBS *Information*, No. 29, Feb. 1983, pp. 1–4 and No. 30, May 1983, pp. 1–3

M. G. Reeder, 'The quality of bricks', BBS *Information*, No. 40, Nov. 1986, pp. 13–15

Refurbishment Products, Oct./Nov. 1987, p. 56 (illustrates Brereton Lodge, Bitterne, Southampton with wall ties 'dating back to the construction of the house in 1804')

A. Rees, *Cyclopedia or Universal Dictionary of Arts, Science and Literature*, 1819

D. L. Roberts, 'The Persistence of Archaic Framing Techniques in Lincolnshire', *Vernacular Architecture*, Vol. 5, 1974; Vol. 6, 1975, pp. 19–20

P. Robinson, 'Urban Vernacular Housing in Newtownards', *Folk Life*, Vol. 17, 1978

P. Robinson, 'Vernacular Housing in Ulster', *Ulster Folklife*, Vol. 25, 1979, pp. 1–28

P. Ryan, *Brick in Essex*, 1996

P. Salway (ed.), *Roman Archaeology and Art*, 1969

M. Seaborne, 'Cob Cottages in Northamptonshire', *Northamptonshire Past and Present*, Vol. 3, No. 5, 1964

H. A. Shannon, 'Bricks—A Trade Index 1785–1849', *Economica*, Vol. I, 1934

I. Smalley, 'The nature of "brick earth" and the location of early brick buildings in Britain', BBS *Information*, No. 41, Feb. 1987, pp. 4–11

T. P. Smith, 'Rye House, Hertfordshire and aspects of early brickwork in England', *Archaeological Journal*, Vol. 132, 1975, pp. 111–50

T. P. Smith, 'Refacing with Brick-Tiles', *Vernacular Architecture*, Vol. 10, 1979, pp. 33–6

T. P. Smith, 'A note on "Samel Bricks"', BBS *Information*, No. 31, Nov. 1983, pp. 5–7

T. P. Smith, 'Brick prices and the cost of living 1700–1828', BBS *Information*, No. 32, Feb. 1984, pp. 3–4

T. P. Smith, *The Medieval Brick-making Industry in England*, BAR British Series 138, 1985

T. P. Smith, 'Brick-tiles (Mathematical tiles) in eighteenth- and nineteenth-century England', *Journal of the British Archaeological Association*, Vol. 138, 1985, pp. 132–64

T. P. Smith, 'Two-way influence between England and the Netherlands in the fifteenth century', BBS *Information*, No. 37, Nov. 1985, pp. 13–16

T. P. Smith, 'Three brick churches by Sir Giles Gilbert Scott', BBS *Information*, No. 38, Feb. 1986, pp. 9–13

T. P. Smith, 'Early Bond', BBS *Information*, No. 42, May 1987, pp. 1–3

T. P. Smith, 'Rendered details to brick buildings—some Kent examples', BBS *Information*, No. 42, May 1987, pp. 5–10

T. P. Smith, 'Medieval bricks in St Nicholas' Chapel, King's Lynn', BBS *Information*, No. 44, March 1988, pp. 17–18

T. P. Smith, 'The Diaper Work at Queen's College, Cambridge', BBS *Information*, No. 55, March 1992, p. 24

T. P. Smith, 'The Brick Tax and its effects', BBS *Information*, No. 57, Nov. 1992, pp. 4–11; No. 58, Feb. 1993, pp. 14–19; No. 63, Oct. 1994, pp. 4–13

T. P. Smith, 'What's in a Name', BBS *Information*, No. 60, Oct. 1993, p. 10

T. P. Smith, 'Bricks, Tiles and Ballast: a sceptical view', BBS *Information*, No. 85, 2001, pp. 5–9

T. P. Smith, 'An early eighteenth-century Dutch tile painting of a Pug Mill', BBS *Information*, No. 89, 2002

Society for Protection of Ancient Buildings, *Cornerstone*, Vol. 25/2, 2004

G. Stamp and C. Amery, *Victorian Buildings of London, 1837–1887*, 1980

C. Stewart, *The Stones of Manchester*, 1956

R. A. Storey, 'Hitch Patent Bricks', *Industrial Archaeology*, Vol. 1, No. 4 and Vol. 7, No. 3, Aug. 1970, pp. 319–24

M. Stratton, *The Terracotta Revival*, 1993

T. Tatton-Brown, 'Hampton Court Palace', BBS *Information*, No. 39, May 1986, pp. 2–5

M. Taylor-Soubeyran, *Architecture vernaculaire au Sultanat d'Oman*, n.d.

S. Thurley, 'Henry VIII and the Building of Hampton Court: a Reconstruction of the Tudor Palace', *Architectural History*, Vol. 31, 1988, pp. 1–57

W. R. Trotter, 'Galleting', *Transactions of the Ancient Monuments Society*, Vol. 33, 1989, pp. 153–68

B. Walker, *Clay Buildings in North-East Scotland*, 1977

B. Walker, *Scottish Turf Construction*, 2006

B. Walker et al., *Earth Structures and Construction in Scotland*, 1996

O. Ward and W. Harris, 'Charfield block, tile and brickworks', BBS *Information*, Nos. 25, 26, 27; Nov. 1981, Jan. 1982, May 1982

J. Warren, *Conservation of Earth Structures*, 1999

R. C. Watson and M. E. McClintock, *Traditional Houses of the Fylde*, 1979

D. Whitehead, 'Brick and tile making in the woodlands of the West Midlands in the sixteenth and seventeenth centuries', *Vernacular Architecture*, Vol. 12, 1981, pp. 42–7

J. Wight, *Brick Building in England and Wales from the Middle Ages to 1550*, 1972

E. Wiliam, *Home-Made Homes: Dwellings of the Rural Poor in Wales*, 1988

E. H. D. Williams and R. C. Gilson, 'Brick buildings in Somerset', *Vernacular Architecture*, Vol. 13, 1982, pp. 31–4

C. Williams-Ellis, *Cottage Building in Cob Pisé, Chalk and Clay*, 1919 (revised and enlarged edition of 1947)

J. Woodforde, *Bricks to Build a House*, 1976

R. B. Wood-Jones, 'The architectural history of Peover Hall, Cheshire', *Transactions of the Lancashire and Cheshire Antiquarian Society*, Vol. 72, 1962, pp. 151–66

A. Wright, *Craft Techniques for Traditional Buildings*, 1999, pp. 40–8

D. Yeomans, 'The quality of London Bricks in the early eighteenth century', BBS *Information*, No. 42, May 1987, pp. 13–15

G. Young, 'Charlestown, South Australia', *Vernacular Architecture*, Vol. 14, 1983, pp. 36–44

G. Young, 'Colonial Building Techniques in South Australia', *Vernacular Architecture*, Vol. 17, 1986, pp. 1–20

G. Young (ed.), *Onkaparinga Heritage*, Adelaide, 1988

Note: BBS *Information* refers to the bulletin of the British Brick Society published for members from April 1973 to the present day.

Index

The figures printed in bold type refer to illustration numbers, not page numbers

Accrington bricks, 86, 172
Achill Island, 229
Addy, S. O., 214–16
Adobe, 202, 233
Africa, 233
Agricultural Revolution, 223
Air bricks, 86
Alderley Edge, Cheshire, 241, 245
Algeria, 233
All Saints, Manchester, glazed bricks, **83**
Althorp, Northants., 65, 67
Alton, Hants.,
    Dearne's Bond, **50**
    Rat-Trap Bond, **25**
Altrincham/Hale area, Cheshire, 242–3
America (North and South), 233
American Bond, 86
Anglesey, 220
Annapolis, Maryland, USA, 244
Antonine Wall, 206, 222
Apron, **47**, 86
Arabia, 233
Arch bricks, 86
Architectural Publication Society, *Dictionary*, 248–9, 251
Arlesey, Beds., brickworks, 35, 248
Armagh, 228
Arris, 86
Arundel, West Sussex, 241
Ashurst, J. & N., 11, 248–9
Asia, 233
Atkinson, W., 193–4
Atlas Mountains, Morocco, 231

Aylsham, Norfolk, Old Hall, **134**, **135**

Bachegraig, Flint, N. Wales, 50, 130–1
Bags, bag wall, 29–30
Bailey Hall, Hertford, Herts., **149**
Ballingdon, Sudbury, Suffolk, chimney, **71**
Balls Park, Herts., **91**, **92**, **130**, **131**
Bally, 226
Barlwood, Surrey, Sussex Bond, **55**
Barry, C., 71
Bastard tuck pointing, 62
Bat, brickbat, 86
Beccles, Suffolk,
    Monk Bond, **58**
    Roos Hall, **120**
    Sir John Leman's School, **151**
Bedford Square, London WC1, **31**
Bed joint, 86
Beehive kiln, 30, 86
Bekesbourne, Kent, St Peter, 66
Belfast, 247
Belgian kiln, 32, 86
Bengeo, Herts., cottages, **28**
Bengeo Hall, Herts., Hitch bricks, 86
Bentley, J. F., 179
Berkshire, 219, 241
Berlin, 244
Berwickshire, 228
Beverley, Yorks., ER,
    North Bar, **104**, 116
    Tie plate, **98**
Bideford, Devon, Bridgeland St., 141
Birmingham, Victoria Law Courts, 72

'Black houses', 224, 229
Black mortar, 60, 86, 171
Blackwell and Booth, 242
Blanchard, H. N., 70
Blind window, 87
Block bonding, 87
Blue bricks, 16–17, 40, 87 (*and see* Staffordshire Blue bricks)
Blyth, Notts., English Garden-Wall Bond, **53**
Boate, Gerard, 246–7
Bodwrdda, Caernarvonshire, N. Wales, 140
Bonding, 49–56, 87
Bonding bricks, 92
Bonding timbers, 92
Booley, 206, 226, 230
Booths, 225
Border counties, 220
Boston, Lincs.,
    Dutch Gable, **79**
    South St., detail, **144**
    Spains's Court, cottages, **152**
Boswell, James, 223
Bowhill, Exeter, Devon, 212
Bow St., Manchester, offices, **178**
Bramhall, Cheshire, brick tile, **33**
Bramshill House, Hants., **127**
Breast plough, 206
Breconshire, 220
Breeze, 18, 27–8, 92
Bretherton, Lancs., Carr House, **128**
Brian, Anthea, 241
Brick earth, 17, 92, 248
Bricklayers' tools, **15**, 46–9
Bricklaying, 46–9
Brickmaker's table, 24, 92
Brickmaking, 21–42

Brickmaking machines, 25
Bricknogging, **64**, 62–3, 92
Brick on edge, **65**, 93
Brick on end, 93
Brick slips, 93
Brick Tax, 14, 38, 64, 67–8, 93, 115, 156, 171, 204, 219, 236–7, 247, 250
Brick tiles (mathematical tiles), **66–70**, 64–8, 93, 156
Brickwork in Ireland, 247, 251
Brickwork in Scotland, 245–6, 251
Brightley, Devon, cob wall detail, **182**, 199
Brighton, Sussex, 64–5, 67, 241
Bristol Channel, 220
British Isles, 233
British Standards Institution, 38–9
Brittany, 233
Brocklesby, Lincs., **23**
Brooks, S. H., 238, 240–50
Bruton Place, London W1, **18**
Buckinghamshire, 219–20, 241
Budapest, 245
Bullnose bricks, 94
Burnage, Manchester, St Nicholas, **171**
Burnet, Tait & Lorne, 38
Burnham Overy, Norfolk, **77**
Burns, Robert, 215
Burrs, 36, 94
Burscough, Lancs., 214
Burton Agnes Hall, Yorks., ER, **20**, **125**

Burton Constable Hall, Yorks., ER, **124, 148,** 130

Bury, Lancs., 242

Butterfield, W., 58, 72, 161, 172, 174, 176

Butts, 18

Caber and daub, 208

Cabin, 225, 229–30

Calcium silicate bricks, 33–4, 94

California, 233

Callow, 21, 94

Cambered arch, 94

Cambridge, 241

Cambridge, Girton College, 72

Cannon St., London EC4, Bracken House, **176**

Canonbie, 224

Cant brick, 94

Canterbury, Kent, 241

Capesthorne Hall, Cheshire, 249

Capping brick, 94

Cardigan, Cardiganshire, 220, 222

Carisbrooke, Isle of Wight, 241

Carlisle, 215, 224

Carmarthenshire, 220

Carved brickwork, 95

Casings, 95

Castle Acre Priory, Norfolk, fireplace, **37**

Cat and clay, 209, 223, 228

Catters and daubers, 216

Cavity walls, 14, 95, 171, 193–6

Cement mortar, 95

Chalk, 219

Chamberlin, H., 31

Charlestown, Maryland, USA, 244

Cheadle, Cheshire, 242

Chequered brickwork, 95

Chesapeake Bay, Maryland, USA, 244–5

Chesham, Bucks., brick and flint, **26**

Chester, terracotta, **96**

Chevening, Kent, 66

Chicheley Hall, Bucks., **81, 142,** 140

Chichester, Sussex, Pallant House, **140**

Chiddingfold, Surrey, bricknogging, **85** segmental arch, **93**

Chignal Smealey, Essex, St Nicholas, **11**

Chimney-pot, 76, 96

Chimneys, **38–9, 41, 43–4, 71,** 75–7, 95, 141

Chinese Bond, 54, 87

Chuffs, 96

Clam, staff and daub, 207, 214

Clamp, clamp firing, **3,** 19, 27–8, 36–7, 41, 57, 96, 115, 130, 140, 247

Clare, Co. Ireland, 226

Clay, 16–18, 20–24, 35, 96, 208, 219–26

Clay bat, 226

Clay dabbin, 214–15

Clay daubing, Cumbria, **184,** 201, 250

Clay house, Great Orton, Cumbria, **192**

Clay lump, **185,** 202–3, 218–19, 228, 233, 250

Clay mortar, 227

Clearance Movement, 223

Clerk, Sir John, 224

Clifton-Taylor, A., 11, 58, 214, 219, 248–9

Clinker, 96

Clom, 220

Closer, 96

Closure, 96, 238

Coade, Miss, 70

Coade Stone, 68, 70

Coal fuel, 18–19, 140

Cob, cob construction, 202, 211–12, 221, 223, 226–8, 231, 233

Cobbett, William, 217

Cob cottages, **189**

Coddenham, Suffolk, Shrubland Old Hall, 68

Colchester, Essex, St Botolph's Priory, **102**

Cold Ashby, Northants., 218

Collingham, Notts., 218

Colney Heath, Herts., Rat-Trap Bond, **61**

Colour in brickwork, 40–1

Common Bond, 96

Common bricks, 35–6, 96

Compass bricks, 96

Compo mortar, 96

Concrete bricks, 33–4, 41, 96

Continuous kilns, 31–3, 96, 172

Conwy, Wales, 222

Copdock, Suffolk, diaper, **75**

Copenhagen, Denmark, 245

Coping bricks, 96

Corbelling, **72,** 96

Cork, Ireland, 226

Cornwall, 211–12, 233–4

Cossey whites, 96

Courses, 96

Cownose bricks, 96

Cox, A., 199

Cracow, Poland, 245

Crawley, P., 12

'Creats', 226, 230

Crinkle-crankle wall, **14, 73,** 97

Crossland, W. H., 179

Crow-step gable, **74,** 97

Crowther, J. S., 242, 245

Cruck truss, **181, 191,** 214, 216–17, 223, 226, 228

Cubitt, W. J., 79

Cumbria, 202

Curf, 97

Cut and rubbed bricks, 97

Cutters, 97

Cuxham, Oxon., cottages, **19**

Damp-proof course, 97, 240–1

Dartmoor, 211

Daub and stower, 207, 208

Deal, Kent, St Leonard, 66

Dearne, T., 238, 250

Dearne's Bond, **50,** 54, 87, 238

Denbigh, Wales, 222

Dendrochronology, 215, 218

Dentilation, 97

Derbyshire, 208, 216

Devon, 211–12, 227, 233–4

Diaper, **75,** 57–9, 97, 115, 140

Dickson, R. W., 208

Dobson, E., 25, 35–6, 248

Dog-leg bricks, 98

Dog-tooth brickwork, **76,** 98

Donegal, Ireland, 226

Dornock, Scotland, 200

Dorset, 211, 219, 241

Double Flemish Bond, 91

Downdraught kiln, **5–7, 78,** 27–30, 41–2, 71, 98

Downing, A. J., 238, 250

Dressings, **77,** 98

Drury, P. J., 11, 249

Drying, 26–7

Dublin, 247

Dudok, W. M., 38, 182, 249

Dumfriesshire, 200

Dunkirk, France, 245

Dutch Bond, 87

Dutch clinkers, 99

Dutch Gable, **79,** 99

East Anglia, 202, 218

East Budleigh, Devon, **189,** 211

Easter Ross, Scotland, 223

East Midlands, 216, 218

Easton Park, Suffolk, crinkle-crankle wall, **14, 73**

Eden Valley, Cumbria, 214

Efflorescence, 99

Egan, J., 161, 168

Egham, Surrey, Royal Holloway College, **165**

Egypt, 231, 233

Engineering bricks, 99, 172

English Bond, **51,** 50–4, 65, 87, 115, 140, 171, 241

English Cross Bond, **52,** 50, 88

English Garden-Wall Bond, **53,** 50–1, 88, 241

'English' houses, 228–9

Erwarton Hall, Suffolk, **121**

Essex, 218

Eton College, Bucks., 116

Exmoor, 211

Exwood, M., 200

Fabbroni, G., 42
Face, 99
Facing bricks, 38, 99
Faience, 74, 99
Farnham, Surrey,
    Castle St., **145**
    Rat-Trap Bond, **27**
    Willmer House, **88**
Farthinghoe, Northants.,
    peach wall, **90**
Fermtouns, 223
Firebricks, 17, 41–2, 76,
    99, 246, 251
Fireclay, 17, 42, 99, 246
Fireholes, 99
Fireplaces, **37**, 75
Firing, 19, 27–33
Firman, R. J. & P. E., 248
Flared bricks, 99 (and see
    Vitrified Bricks)
Flat arch, 99
Flaughter spade, 206
Flemish Bond, **54**, 51–2,
    54–5, 65, 88, 140, 156,
    171, 241
Flemish bricks, 100
Flemish Cross Bond, 88
Flemish Garden-Wall
    Bond, **55**, 89
Flemish Stretcher Bond,
    56, 52, 89
Fletton, Beds., 18
Flettons, 17, 21, 23, 100,
    172
Flint, 220
Flint-lime bricks, 34
Flush joint, 100
Flush pointing, **91**, 100,
    105
Flying bond, 100
Fossil bricks, 42, 100
Fowke, Capt., 71
France, 233
Frog, 24–5, 100, 140,
    182
Fuel, 18–19, 27, 33, 199
Furze fuel, 18, 34
Fylde, Lancs., 209

Gailey, Alan, 250
Gainsborough Old Hall,
    Lincs., 30, **109**
Galleting, **80**, 60, 100
Galloway, 200
Galway, 226
Gauged brickwork, **81–2**,
    38, 100, 140

Gault bricks, 101
Gault clay, 16, 40
Gera, Germany, 245
Germany, 234
Gibson, A. C., 201
Gill, E., 172
Gillespie, Kidd & Coia,
    190
Gimson, Ernest, 212
Glazed bricks, **83**, 41–2,
    101
Glebe terriers, 217
Glenboig, Strathclyde,
    Scotland, 42
Gloucestershire, 211
Great bricks, **84**, 37, 101
Great Cressingham
    Priory, Norfolk, 68
Great Ormond St.,
    London WC1, **147**
Great Orton, Cumbria,
    192
Great Wall of China, 233
Green bricks, 23–8, 101
Greetham, Lincs., 218
Gretna, Scotland, 224
Grizzles, 36, 101
Grog, 42, 71
Grosvenor St., Chester,
    Stack Bond, **62**
Guildford Cathedral,
    Surrey, **173**
Gurcke, K., 251
Gwilt, J., 250–1

Hack, 26, 101
Hack barrow, 101
Haddenham, Bucks., **186**,
    194, 204, 220–1
Hadrian's Wall, 206
Hafod-y-Bwlch,
    Denbighs., **43**
Hafoty, 222
Hailsham, Sussex,
    Wickstreet, **141**
Hammond, M., 11, 248
Hampshire, 211, 219, 241
Handforth, Cheshire, 242
Hampton Court Palace,
    Middx., 69, 130–1
Hand-made bricks, 23–5,
    101
Harding, J., 200
Harley, L. J., 23, 248
Harrison, Ray, 212, 250
Hartley, J., 38
Harwich, Essex, High

Lighthouse, **157**
Header Bond, **57**, 52–3,
    65, 89, 156, 171, 241–5,
    251
Headers, 101
Heald Green, Cheshire,
    242
Heaton House,
    Manchester, 70
Hebrides, 223
Hemel Hempstead,
    Herts., High St., **47**
Hendre, 222
Henley-on-Thames,
    Oxfords., 241
Hereford, Herefordshire,
    201, 213, 220, 226
Herringbone brickwork,
    85, 101
Heslington, Yorks., ER,
    49, **65**
Heytesbury, Wilts.,
    maltings, **159**
Hill Hall, Essex, 130
Hilversum Town Hall,
    Netherlands, 38, 182,
    249
Hinckley, Leics., Gt.
    Meeting House, **29**
Hitch bricks, **86**, 102, 156
Hoddesdon, Herts., Rye
    House, **105–6**
Hodnet, Salop.,
    chimneys, **41**
Hoffmann, F., 31
Hoffmann kiln, **8**, 31–3,
    102
Holborn, London EC1,
    Holborn Union
    Offices, **46**
Holkham Hall, Norfolk,
    146, 80
Holland, H., 65, 67
Hollow bricks, 102
Hollow wall see Cavity
    wall
Holy Trinity, Sloane St.,
    London SW1, 243
Honeycomb brickwork,
    87, 102
Hoop-iron Bond, 103
Hope St., Liverpool,
    Philharmonic Hall, **175**
Horizontal draught kilns,
    29
Housman, J., 201
Hovel, 27

Hughenden, Bucks., **197**,
    243
Hull, Yorks., ER,
    Holy Trinity, **51**, 115
    Wilberforce House, **129**
Hungerford, Berks., 241
Hurd and Gourlay, 250
Hutchinson, W., 201
Hyde, Mathew, 242

Inca civilisation, 233
Industrial Revolution,
    247
'Infield', 226
Innocent, C. F., 216
Inskip, Lancs., 207, 214
Intermittent kiln, 27–30,
    71, 103, 172
Ipswich, Suffolk,
    Christchurch Mansion,
    122
    Pykenhams's gateway,
    110
Iran, 233
Iraq, 233
Ireland, 205–8, 225–30,
    246
Ireland, brickwork in, 247
'Irish' houses, 229
Ironbridge, Salop., brick
    paving, **89**
Irregular bonding, 89, 115
Isle of Wight, 211, 219
Isles of Scilly, 231

Jack arch, 103
Jennings, Nina, 214–15
Jennings Patent bricks,
    240
Jesus College,
    Cambridge, 115, 131
Jointing, 59–62, 103, 156,
    171

Keay, L. H., 239
Kebber and mott, 208
Keble College, Oxford,
    162
Kennett, D. H., 11, 249
Kent, W., 79
Kent, 219, 241
Kentwell Hall, Suffolk,
    130
Kerry, Ireland, 226
Keuper Marl, 17–18
Kew, Surrey, Dutch
    House, 52, 140

Keyed brick, 103
Keyed joint, 103
Kick, 103
Kilburn, London NW6,
    St Augustine, 58
Kiln, 27–33, 57, 103, 140,
    247
King closer, 103
King's Lynn, Norfolk,
    St Nicholas, **16**, 249
Kingussie, Scotland, 207
Kinnersley Castle,
    Herefordshire, **74**
Kirby Muxloe Castle,
    Leics., **111–12**, 115, 116
Kiss marks, 28, 103
Kneesall, Notts., Old
    Hall, 69, 130
Koblenz, Germany, 245

Labour, 19
Lacing courses, 103, 156
Lack, 24
Lamb, E. B., 243
Lambeth Palace, London
    SE1, 130–1
Lancashire, 208, 212, 214
Langley, Batty, 48, 237,
    244, 249
Lap, 103
Larrying, 104
Laughton, Leics., mud
    wall, **193**
Layer Marney Tower,
    Essex, **117**, 68, 130
Leaf, 104
Leez Priory, Essex, **119**
Leicestershire, 216
Lemsford, Herts.,
    chimney, **38**
Lever Bridge, Bolton,
    Lancs., St Stephen, 70
Lewes, Sussex, 64, 67,
    241
    Jireh Chapel, 65
Leyland, Lancashire, 208,
    212, 214
Lime mortar, 59–62, 104
Lime putty, 62, 104
Lincolnshire, 208, 216,
    218
Little Coggeshall, Essex,
    St Nicholas, **101**
Little Wenham Hall,
    Suffolk, **1**, 37, 115
Liverpool, Albert Docks,
    38

Philharmonic Hall, **175**
    University, 72
Liverpool Bond, 104
Lloyd, N., 13, 24, 68, 248
Llŷn, Wales, 220–1
Loam, 16
London, 219
Long Melford Hall,
    Suffolk, 130
Long Street Wesleyan
    Church, Middleton,
    Manchester, 242
Loudon, J., 64
Loudon's Hollow Wall,
    104
Louth, Lincs., Westgate,
    Header Bond, **57**
Lutyens, Sir E., 38, 72,
    185, 248
Lynch, G., 11, 254

McCann, J., 11, 63, 219,
    250
McKay, W. B., 248–51
Madeley, Salop., Quarter
    bonding, **59**
Malm, malming, malms,
    16, 36, 104
Mappleton, East Yorks.,
    215–16
Margaret St., London
    W1, All Saints, **160**, 58,
    72
Marlborough, Wilts.,
    241–5
Marlow, Bucks., 241
Maryland, USA, 244
Mastaba tombs, Egypt,
    231
Mathematical tiles see
    Brick tiles
Mathew, Johnson-
    Marshall Partners, 191
Maufe, Sir E., 186
Mayo, Ireland, 226
Mercer, E., 214
Metric bricks, 39, 104, 182
Metric equivalents, 251
Midland Hotel,
    Manchester, 74
Mitchell, G. A., 239, 240,
    250
Mixed Garden Bond, **57**,
    90
Mixing pan, 22
Mond Laboratory,
    Cambridge, **172**

Monk Bond, **58**, 52, 54,
    90
Monmouthshire, 220
Monterey, California,
    USA, 233
Montgomeryshire, 220
Montreuil-sur-Mer,
    France, 244
Moran, M., 214
Morocco, 231–3
Mortar and jointing, 59–
    62, 104, 171, 183
Motor transport, 35
Mould, mould box, 23–4,
    104
Moulded brickwork, **88**,
    39–40, 104, 171, 182
Moulding, 23
Mud-and-stud, **181**, **187**,
    190, **195**, 207–8, 214,
    218, 223–6, 233, 250
Mud brick, 202, 233
Mud (cob) walls, **193**,
    216, 219, 226, 246
Mudmason, 223
Mud-wall, 219, 223
Museum of Welsh Life, St
    Ffagans, Cardiff, 250
Mwd, 220

Naismith, R. J., 197, 201
Nantwich, Cheshire,
    Welsh Row, **47**
Natural History Museum,
    South Kensington,
    London SW7, 72
Nebraska, USA, 233
Neilson, G. A., 222
Newbury, Berks., 241
Newcastle kiln, **4**, 29, 104
Newcastle-on-Tyne, 216
Newcastle-under-Lyme,
    Staffs., Holy Trinity,
    156, **158**
New Knebworth, Herts.,
    St Martin, **170**
New Mexico, USA, 233
Newport, Essex,
    House of Correction,
    153
    Tudor House, **44**
New Quay, Ceredigion,
    Wales, 222
Nigeria, 233
Nile Valley, Egypt, 233
Nonsuch Palace, Surrey,
    69

Norfolk, 202, 218, 231
Northamptonshire, 218
North and South Dakota,
    USA, 233
North-East of England,
    215
Northenden, Cheshire,
    242
North Meols, Lancashire,
    214
North-West England,
    212, 214
North Wheatley, Notts.,
    12, **56**, **100**
Norwich, Norfolk, Old
    Meeting House, **136–7**
Nun Monckton, Yorks.,
    ER, **94**

Oakley, Suffolk, **185**
Odeon Cinema, York, **174**
Oliver, Paul, 250
Olmsted, Frederick Law,
    213–14
Ordnance Survey Memoirs,
    225
Orford, Suffolk,
    brick wall, **13**
    dog-tooth ornament, **76**
Ormskirk, Lancs., **190**,
    191, 213–14
Orton, Cumbria, 201
'Outfield', 226, 230
Oxford clays, 17–18, 23,
    171
Oxford Rd., Manchester,
    Refuge Building, **36**
Oxfordshire, 219, 241

Pallet, Pallet boards, 23,
    26, 104
Pallet moulding, 23–4,
    104
Pamments, 105
Parker's Cement, 60
Parsonages, 217
Paviour (Paving) bricks,
    36, 105, 182
Peach wall, **90**, 105
Pearson, J. L., 58
Peat, 205–7, 214, 230
Peat fuel, 18
Pembrokeshire, 220
Pennant, William, 224
Penrhyn Castle,
    Caernarvonshire,
    N. Wales, 65, 156

Peover Hall, Cheshire, 131

Perforated bricks, 25, 105, 182

Pershore, Worcs., Georgian houses, **42**
Perrott House, **150**

Pimlico, London SW1, St James the Less, 58

Pisé-de-terre, **181**, 198–200, 223, 227, 233, 250

Pitt, William, 216

Place bricks, 36, 105

Plantations in Ireland, 246

Plantation surveys, 247

Plat Band, 105

Platt Lane, Manchester, Holy Trinity, 70–1

Pleshey, Essex, 37

Plinth bricks, 105

Plot, Dr (*Natural History of Staffordshire*), 214, 248

Poole, Dorset, 241

Plymouth Grove, Manchester, Raking Stretcher Bond, **60**

Pointing, 59–62, 105, 183

Polish Bond, 52

Polstead, Suffolk, St Mary, **114**

Polychrome brickwork, 57–9, 72, 77, 106

Porth-wen, Anglesey, Wales, kiln, **5**, **7**, **78**

Portland Cement, 60, 172, 231

Poznan, Poland, 245

Pressed bricks, 25, 106, 182

Preston, R. B., 242

Prestwich, Manchester, 242

Projecting headers, 106

Prudential Assurance Company, 72

Puddled clay, 228

Pug mill, 22, 106

Purpose-made bricks, 106

Putlog holes, 106

Quarter bonding, **59**, 90

Queen Anne's Gate, London SW1, **139**

Queen closer, 106

Quetta bond, 91

Quoins, **131**, 106

Racking, 106

Rad and dab, 207

Raddle and daub, 207

Radial bricks, 106

Radnorshire, 220

Rail transport, 35, 59

Raked-out joint, 103

Raking Stretcher Bond, **60**, 90

Rat-Trap Bond, **61**, 54, 91, 156, 237–40

Recessed joint, 106

Redmayne, 242

Regional variations, **188**

Reinforced clay, 228

Relieving arch, **92**, 106

Rendered brickwork, 106

Richardson, A. E., 186

Road transport, 20, 182

Roberts, H., 238, 250

Robinson, Philip, 246

Robinson College, Cambridge, **177**

Rochester, Kent, 241

Roman bricks, **102**, 107

Rostock, Germany, 245

Rough brick arch, **93**, 107

Rowlock Bond, 107

Rowse, H. J., 186

Royal Albert Hall, London SW7, 71

Ruabon, Denbighshire, N. Wales, 72, 172

Rubbed joint, 103

Rubber bricks, 56, 107, 140

Rundale, 226

Ruskin, J., 58, 72

Rustication, **94**, 107

Ruthin, 222

Rutland, 216

Rye, Sussex, brick tiles, 67

Rye House, Herts., **105**

St Anne's Church School, Wilmslow, Cheshire, 242

St Benedict's Church, Ardwick, Manchester, 242

St John's College, Cambridge, **116**, 130–1

St Pancras Station, London NW1, Hotel, **164**, 35, 172

St Paul's Church School, Withington, Manchester, 242

St Philip's Church School, Alderley Edge, Cheshire, **196**

Salford, Lancs., 243

Salisbury, Wilts., 241

Salzmann, L., 75, 248

Sammel bricks, 28, 41, 107

Sana'a, Yemen, 233

Sand-faced bricks, 107

Sand-lime bricks, 33–4, 41, 107

Sandon, Essex, St Andrew, **118**

Scored joint, 103

Scotch kiln, **4**, 28–9, 108

Scotland, brickwork in, 14, 251
earth/clay/turf, 206–8, 222–4, 245–6, 251

Scott, E., 183

Scott, Sir G. G., 178

Seaborne, Malcolm, 218

Second Statistical Account of Scotland, 200

Sedding, J. D., 243

Segmental arch, **48**, 103

Seighford, Staffs., **87**, **154**, **166**

Semi-dry process, 26

Shales, Coal Measure Shales, 16–18

Sharpe, E., 70–1, 250

Shaw, R. N., 172

Shere, Surrey,
Galleting, **80**
House at, **21**
Tie plate, **99**

Shropshire, 214, 220

Shuffs, 36, 108

Shuttered clay/earth, 198, 223, 227, 231, 233, 250

Silbury, Wilts., 231

Silloth, Cumbria, 214

Silverlock's Bond, 54

Single Flemish bond, 91

Sizes of bricks, 36–9

Skewback, 108

Skintle (Skintling), 26, 108

Slater, H. F., 242

Slop moulding, 23–4, 26, 108

Smallhythe, Kent, English Cross Bond, **52**

Smith, T. P., 11, 248–9

Snap headers, 108, 183, 244

Sod *see* turf

Sod House Frontier, USA, 196, 233

Soft-mud process, 26, 108

Soil, soiling, 27, 35, 108

Soldier arch, 108

Soldier course, 108

Solway Firth, 200–1, 212, 222, 224

Solway Plain, 200–1, 212–15, 222

Somerset, 211

Sonning, Berks., Deanery, 38

South-East England, 219

Southport, Lancs., 214

South-West England, 211–12, 222

Spain, Spaniards, 233

Spanish *see* soiling

Specials, 39–40, 108, 182

Springer, 108

Square stop end, 108

Squatters' cottages, 200, 230

Squint brick, 108

Stack Bond, **62**, 53, 91

Staff, staves, 208, 212, 218, 222, 228

Staffordshire Blue bricks, 41, 59, 108, 182

Staffordshire kiln, 30, 33, 108

Stake and rice, 207–8, 224

Standard specials, 39–40

Statute bricks, 37

Stevenson, J. J., 194, 201

Stiff plastic process, 26, 108

Stock (Stock board), 24, 108

Stock brick, 36, 108

Stockholm, Sweden, 244

Stockton, Wilts., brick and chalk, **24**

Stoke St Gregory, Somerset, **182**

Stone and cob walls, 216

Stone-faced earth, 226, 229
Stopped end, 108
Stourbridge, Staffs., 214
Straight joints, 109
Stratford-upon-Avon, Warwicks., Theatre, **169**, 183
Street, G. E., 58, 72, 172
Stretcher, 109
Stretcher Bond, **63**, 53, 65, 92, 171, 183, 195, 241
Strike, 23–4
String course, **76**, 109
Struck joint, 103
'Structural brickwork', **16**, 11, 200
Structural matters, 43–6
Studs, studwork, 208
'Stumpies', 34–5
Stupids, 25, 109
Sudbury Hall, Derbys., **126**, 140
Suffolk, 202, 218
Suffolk kiln, **4**, 29, 109
Sulhamstead, Berks., Folly Farm, 38
Summerscales, Cumbria, 214
Sundried (Adobe), brick, 233
Surrey, 219
Sussex, 219
Sussex Bond, **55**, 52, 54, 89, 241
Sutton Place, Surrey, **35**, **95**, **115**, 69, 130

Tattershall Castle, Lincs., **107**, 116
  Guardhouse, 108
  Stable block, **71**
Tempered earth, 223–4, 226–7
Tempering, 22, 109
Tenterden, Kent, brick tiles, **34**, **70**
Terracotta, **35–6**, 68–74, 109, 171, 182
Thame, Oxon., Flemish Bond, **54**
Thornton Abbey, Lincs., **48**, **103**
Thornton Curtis, Lincs., Hall, **138**
Three-quarter bat, 86
Tie plates, **97–9**, 109

Tie rods, 110
Tile, 109
Tile-creasing, 109
Timber reinforcement, 216
Toothing, 110
Torchis, 233
Towcester, Northants., 241
Tower houses, 222, 233
Town, I., 194
Transhumance, 225
Transport, 29, 34–6
Trent Valley, 216
Tuck pointing, 60–2, 105, 110, 156
Tumbling-in, **100**, 111
Tunnel drying, 27, 33
Tunnel kiln, 33, 42, 111
Turf (sod), 205–7, 214, 219–20, 222–6, 229–30, 234, 237, 250
Tyttenhanger, Herts., window, **17**
'Ty-unnos', 220

Unfired brick, 228
Updraught kiln, 27–9, 41, 110, 140
Uxbridge, Middx., Hillingdon Civic Centre, **179**, **180**

Vaux, G., 194, 250
Visby, Sweden, 244
Vitrified Headers, 41, 57–8, 111, 115, 140
Voussoirs, 111

Wainfleet, Lincs., School, **113**
Wakefield, 247
Wales, 202, 207, 212, 220, 222
Walker, B., 197, 250
Wall-tiles see Brick tiles
Waltham Abbey, Essex, Great bricks, **84**
Ware, Herts, pumping station, **39**
Warp, 111
Warren's Patent Kiln, 32
Washback, 111
Waterhouse, Sir A., 58, 72, 172
Wattled stud work, 209
Weathered joint, 103

Webb, P., 196, 251
Weedon, H., 38, 186
Weep Hole, 111
Welch, Cachemaille-Day & Lander, 185
Welsh Back, Bristol, granary, **163**
Welwyn, Herts., Digswell Viaduct, **40**, 161
Westcott, Surrey, brick tiles, **32**, 65
Westfield, Sussex, Spraysbridge, **133**
West Lancashire, 208
West Malling, Kent, gauged brickwork, **82**
West Midlands, 212
Westminster Cathedral, London SW1, **167–8**
White bricks, 16, 40, 111, 156–72
Wicket, 111
Wight, J., 248
Wilmslow, Cheshire, Header Bond, 242
  Stretcher Bond, **63**
Wiltshire, 211
Winchester, Hants., bricknogging, **64**
  Header Bond, 241
Winster, Derbys., Market Hall, 132, 141
Wire-cut bricks, 25–6, 33, 111, 182
Wisbech, Cambs., Peckover House, **143**
  Union Place, **155**
Witchert, Witchit, see Wychert, 205, 219
Wolds, 216
Wood, Edgar, 242
Woodbridge, Suffolk, Shire Hall, 45
Woodforde, J., 35, 199–200
Wood fuel, 18, 27, 34, 41
Woodham Walter, Essex, St Michael, **22**
Worcestershire, 201, 220, 226
Worthington, Thomas, 242, 245
Wyatt, J., 66, 70
Wyatt, S., 67
Wychert, Haddenham, Bucks., **186**, 205, 219, 250

Yarmouth, Isle of Wight, 241
Yemen, 233
York, **37**, 65
Yorkshire and Humberside, 215–16
Yorkshire Bond, 111
Young, Arthur, 227